THE DEFEAT OF A RENAISSANCE INTELLECTUAL

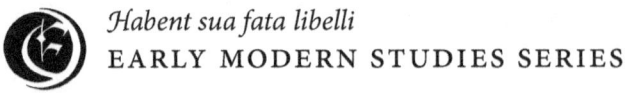

Habent sua fata libelli
EARLY MODERN STUDIES SERIES

GENERAL EDITOR
Michael Wolfe
Queens College, CUNY

EDITORIAL BOARD OF EARLY MODERN STUDIES

Elaine Beilin
Framingham State University

Raymond A. Mentzer
University of Iowa

Christopher Celenza
Johns Hopkins University

Robert V. Schnucker
Truman State University (Emeritus)

Barbara B. Diefendorf
Boston University

Nicholas Terpstra
University of Toronto

Paula Findlen
Stanford University

Margo Todd
University of Pennsylvania

Scott H. Hendrix
Princeton Theological Seminary

James Tracy
University of Minnesota

Jane Campbell Hutchison
University of Wisconsin–Madison

Merry Wiesner-Hanks
University of Wisconsin–Milwaukee

Mary B. McKinley
University of Virginia

THE DEFEAT OF A RENAISSANCE INTELLECTUAL

Selected Writings of Francesco Guicciardini

BY FRANCESCO GUICCIARDINI
Edited and translated by Carlo Celli

The Pennsylvania State University Press
University Park, Pennsylvania

Library of Congress Cataloging-in-Publication Data

Names: Guicciardini, Francesco, 1483–1540, author. | Celli, Carlo, 1963– editor, translator.
Title: The defeat of a Renaissance intellectual : selected writings of Francesco Guicciardini / by Francesco Guicciardini ; edited and translated by Carlo Celli.
Other titles: Early modern studies series.
Description: University Park, Pennsylvania : The Pennsylvania State University Press, [2019] | Series: Early modern studies series | Includes bibliographical references and index.
Summary: "A collection of writings by papal advisor and historian Francesco Guicciardini (1483–1540), including letters, treatises, reports, and orations spanning his long career in service to the Medici"—Provided by publisher.
Identifiers: LCCN 2019004846 | ISBN 9780271083483 (cloth : alk. paper)
Subjects: LCSH: Italy—History—1492–1559. | Italy—Politics and government—1268–1559. | Florence (Italy)—History—1421–1737. | Florence (Italy)—Politics and government—1421–1737. | Papal States—History—1417–1605. | Medici, House of. | Guicciardini, Francesco, 1483–1540.
Classification: LCC DG738.14.G9 A25 2019 | DDC 945/.06—dc23
LC record available at https://lccn.loc.gov/2019004846

Copyright © 2019 Carlo Celli
All rights reserved
Printed in the United States of America
Published by The Pennsylvania State University Press,
University Park, PA 16802-1003

The Pennsylvania State University Press is a member of the Association of University Presses.

It is the policy of The Pennsylvania State University Press to use acid-free paper. Publications on uncoated stock satisfy the minimum requirements of American National Standard for Information Sciences—Permanence of Paper for Printed Library Material, ANSI Z39.48–1992.

CONTENTS

List of Illustrations vi

Acknowledgments vii

Introduction: The Limits of Self-Interest 1

To Himself 33

Report on Spain 34

How to Ensure the State for the House of the Medici 51

On the Use of Force 64

On Suicide for Political Reasons 67

On Progressive Taxation: The Scaled Tenth 72

Report on the Defense of Parma 89

Letter to Francesco Maria della Rovere 100

Consolation 104

Accusation 124

Defense Against the Preceding 166

Savonarolian Excerpts (Selections) 192

Response on Behalf of the Duke to the Complaints of the Exiles 211

Index 225

ILLUSTRATIONS

1. Portraits of Girolamo Savonarola; Pope Julius II; Charles VIII, king of France; and Giulio di Giuliano de' Medici   8
2. Giuliano Bugiardini, portrait of Francesco Guicciardini, ca. 1538–40   9
3. Giorgio Vasari and Marco Marchetti, mural in Palazzo Vecchio, ca. 1556–58   35
4. Tintoretto, *The Capture of Parma*, ca. 1580   90
5. Maarten van Heemskerck, *Sack of Rome*, ca. 1555–56   101
6. Filippo Dolciati, *Execution of Savonarola*, 1498   193
7. Agnolo Bronzino, *Portrait of Duke Alessandro*, ca. 1555–65   212
8. Juan Pantoja de la Cruz, portrait of Charles V, after Titian, ca. 1605   213

ACKNOWLEDGMENTS

For generous and kind assistance with the present volume, I thank the following from Bowling Green State University: the interlibrary loan office, Sherri Long, Linda Brown, the staff at the Office of Sponsored Research, the staff at the Department of World Languages and Cultures; the editors and staff at Truman State University Press and Penn State University Press; Sara Piccolo, and Marga Cottino-Jones.

INTRODUCTION

The Limits of Self-Interest

The Italian Renaissance was a period of cultural and artistic rebirth, a rediscovery of classical culture that brought epochal creativity to science, commerce, and the arts, with the city of Florence as a cradle of achievement. However, between the fourteenth and sixteenth centuries, Italy and Europe suffered periods of economic depression and societal chaos stemming not solely from cataclysms like the 1348 Black Death but also from continuous wars, religious turmoil, famine, and increasing authoritarian interference into political and economic life.[1] In this climate, the ascendant national monarchies in France, Spain, and England, and regional corollaries such as the Medici family of Florence, affirmed dominance over oligarchical and republican civic institutions.

Renowned intellectuals of the period wrote treatises, histories, letters, and poems rationalizing authoritarian rule and the consequent suppression of economic and political liberty. In political and social terms, these writers behaved as *establishment intellectuals*, harnessing their talents to further the power of hegemony, in this case of monarchical rule. Dante Alighieri (1265–1321) brilliantly decried the moral failings of his generation and resulting political strife in the *Divine Comedy*. However, Dante also championed the political cause of Holy Roman Emperor Henry VII of Luxemburg (1269/74–1313), penning *De monarchia* (*On Monarchy*), a treatise

---

1. Murray N. Rothbard, *An Austrian Perspective on the History of Economic Thought*, vol. 1, *Economic Thought Before Adam Smith* (Camberley, UK: Edward Elgar Publishing, 1995), 177–210.

providing intellectual cover for temporal rule over Italian communes and cities by a German Holy Roman emperor. Dante's political stance would have meant the descent of German troops into Italy, a contingency inhabitants of the peninsula have historically sought to avoid. Francesco Petrarca (1304–1374) penned a famous poem inciting Italian princes and republics to renew ancient Roman military policy, *My Italy* (*Canzoniere*, CXXVIII). However, he also wrote a fawning letter (*Senili*, XIV, 1) to Francesco da Carrara, overlord of Padua, on the duties of a prince in the tradition of humanists seeking patronage from local despots. Niccolò Machiavelli (1469–1527) may have had a firm foundation in republican ideology and practice. However, once the Florentine Republic where he worked fell to a Medici coup supported by Spanish troops in 1512, he penned *The Prince* (1513), promoting himself to Florence's Medici rulers, advising them to mask ruthless extremism with piety to maintain power. Similarly, Baldassare Castiglione's (1478–1529) *The Book of the Courtier* (1528) advises individuals to strive for personal promotion as nonchalant gentlemen adept at currying favor with a ruling lord. These writers adapted to and wrote for the power establishment of their day, which was increasingly autocratic.

During the lifetime of Francesco Guicciardini (1483–1540), Florentine politics were dominated by the struggle of republican leaders to retain civic political autonomy against the ambitions of the Medici family. Competition for power between popular, aristocratic, and monarchical factions had characterized Florentine politics since the late Middle Ages but took an authoritarian turn with the rise of the Medici family from a financial to a political power. The Florentine Republic became a de facto Medici principality during and following the rule of the Medici clan patriarch, Cosimo de' Medici (1389–1464). The geopolitical context during Guicciardini's lifetime was the Italian Wars (1494–1559), when Italy was a battlefield in the contest for continental hegemony between the Habsburg monarchs of Spain and Austria and the Valois of France, beginning with the invasion by the French king Charles VIII (1470–1498) in 1494 and ending with the Peace of Cateau-Cambrésis in 1559, when the French relinquished claims in Italy.

Guicciardini spent his professional life as representative, functionary, and apologist for the Medici clan, serving a long list of Medici lords over his career. He advised Lorenzo di Piero de' Medici (1492–1519) and Giuliano di Lorenzo de' Medici (1479–1516), the first Medici lords of Florence following the 1512 fall of the Florentine Republic and the subject of

Guicciardini's treatise "How to Ensure the State for the House of Medici." He was counsel to Giovanni di Lorenzo de' Medici (1475–1521), who ruled as Pope Leo X from 1513 to his death in 1521 and appointed Guicciardini governor of Romagna. Guicciardini was lieutenant general and advisor to Giulio di Giuliano de' Medici (1478–1534), who ruled as Pope Clement VII from 1523 to his death in 1534. Guicciardini aided the accession to the duchy of Alessandro de' Medici (1510–1537), the alleged illegitimate son of Lorenzo di Piero de' Medici (1492–1519) or the future Clement VII. Guicciardini encountered other Medici who opposed Alessandro's ascension to the duchy of Florence, such as Ippolito de' Medici (1509–1535) and Alessandro's eventual murderer, Lorenzino de' Medici (1514–1548), also known as Lorenzaccio. Guicciardini was eventually removed from the Medici administration by Cosimo I (1519–1574), who succeeded Alessandro.

Guicciardini's service to the Medici did not result in personal defeat, at least in venal terms. During and after Francesco Guicciardini's life, the Guicciardini family maintained and consolidated a position among Florence's elite. However, ultimately, Guicciardini put his considerable talents and energy to the service of a cause—the consolidation of Medici power—which served their interests more completely than his own. Guicciardini's efforts on behalf of the Medici clan resulted in the thwarting of the political aspirations both of his class and that of his fellow citizens, who lost their proud republican heritage and definitively succumbed to Medici rule.

After retiring from political office in 1537, Guicciardini tried to make sense of his experiences in the Italian Wars by composing the *History of Italy* (1538–40), recounting events from the death of Lorenzo de' Medici (the Magnificent) in 1492 to the death of Pope Clement VII in 1534, when Guicciardini's participation in papal administration and for the Medici attenuated. The compelling aspect of Guicciardini's *History of Italy* is that he lived and was intricately involved in the political and military decisions and events he recounts. Yet, Guicciardini's reputation in posterity remains as the main historian of early sixteenth-century Italy rather than as a participant. The documents herein present Guicciardini as a protagonist rather than as an historian.[2] Guicciardini opens his prolix *History of Italy*

---

2. The sources for the documents in the present collection are the following: Francesco Guicciardini, *Scritti autobiografici e rari*, ed. Roberto Palmarocchi (Bari: Laterza, 1936); Guicciardini, *Opere inedite di Francesco Guicciardini illustrate da Giuseppe Canestrini e pubblicate per cura dei conti Piero e Luigi Guicciardini: Del reggimento di Firenze libri due.*

with a rare metaphor describing the political affairs of Italy between 1492 (the death of Lorenzo de' Medici) and 1534 (the death of Clement VII) as a vessel tossed about the waters under uncontrollable winds. Guicciardini was describing Italy; however, considering his involvement in events and the results of his efforts, he may well have been describing himself.

In such an unpredictable and chaotic milieu, Guicciardini's approach was to anticipate contingencies and to act prudently, and the meter he chose to predict events was self-interest, with assessment contingent upon results. As he states in "On the Use of Force," "All the actions of men may be defined as good or bad according to their outcomes." In this vein, Guicciardini was not solely an historian but also a precursor of the dismal social science of economics, which attempts to reduce all human endeavors to quantifiable data. Included herein is Guicciardini's contribution to economic theory, namely, his analysis in "On Progressive Taxation" of the "scaled tenth" taxation policy of the Florentine Republic, which analyzes the effects of progressive tax rates on individual behavior.

In the C28 redaction of the *Ricordi/Maxims*, Guicciardini confesses with a sense of shame that his personal self-interest, his *particulare*, drove him to serve the Medici popes, Leo X and Clement VII, despite misgivings about the corruption of the papacy.[3] A reading of this *ricordo* by literary historian and educational reformer Francesco De Sanctis established the *particulare* as the epithet determining Guicciardini's critical reputation in the modern period. De Sanctis wrote during the nationalist moment of the Italian national unification of the *Risorgimento* (Resurgence) during

---

Discorsi intorno alle mutazioni e riforme del governo fiorentino (Florence: Barbèra, Bianchi, 1858); Guicciardini, *Dialogo e discorsi del reggimento di Firenze*, ed. Roberto Palmarocchi (Bari: Laterza, 1932); Guicciardini, *Scritti politici e ricordi*, ed. Roberto Palmarocchi (Bari: Laterza, 1933); Guicciardini, *Carteggi di Francesco Guicciardini*, ed. Pier Giorgio Ricci and Roberto Palmarocchi (Milan: Istituto per gli studi di politica internazionale; Istituto storico italiano per l'età moderna e contemporanea, 1943–).

3. *Ricordo* C28. "I know of no one who loathes the ambition, the avarice, and the sensuality of the clergy more than I—both because each of these vices is hateful in itself and because each and all are hardly suited to those who profess to live a life dependent upon God. Furthermore, they are such contradictory vices that they cannot coexist in a subject unless he be very unusual indeed.

"In spite of all this, the positions I have held under several popes have forced me, for my own good, to further their interests. Were it not for that, I should have loved Martin Luther as much as myself—not so that I might be free of the laws based on Christian religion as it is generally interpreted and understood; but to see this bunch of rascals get their just deserts, that is, to be either without vices or without authority." Francesco Guicciardini, *Maxims and Reflections of a Renaissance Stateman (Ricordi)*, trans. Mario Domandi (New York: Harper Torchbooks, 1965), 48.

the nineteenth century. For De Sanctis, Guicciardini's *particulare*, his personal self-interest, explained why Italy came to suffer and even deserve foreign domination in the sixteenth century, and why Guicciardini's legacy posed a threat to the ethical fiber of a newly united Italy in the 1860s.[4] For De Sanctis, the lesson from Guicciardini is how working for a corrupt system may benefit personal short-term interest but have long-term consequences negative to oneself and society.

Guicciardini's service to an undeniably corrupt papacy and the personal advantages he gained from service to the Medici clan, which ruled both Florence and the Papal States under Leo X and Clement VII, would seem to confirm De Sanctis's negative characterization. A lesson from Guicciardini's life and writings is the realization that working within a corrupt system does not lead to solutions. Guicciardini's personal philosophy was not limited to the evaluation of his own self-interest alone but also applied the self-interests of others as a meter to judge people and events and to forge a prudent course of action. The advantage to Guicciardini's approach championing individual self-interest above other considerations, whether ideological, religious, or emotional, is the lure of simplification of analysis and the pretense of purporting to provide advice for the anticipation of future events. If all factors may be reduced to self-interest, then other factors are either superfluous or contingent and therefore do not require consideration. The disadvantage, and the cause for frustration and personal defeat for Guicciardini, is that such rationality may be logically coherent but does not account for the frailty, capriciousness, and emotional charge in human behavior, as the course of Guicciardini's own life attests. Guicciardini did attempt to include extra-rational influences in his histories and in some of the writings included herein, such as the "Accusation," "Consolation," and "Defense" orations,

---

4. See Francesco De Sanctis, "L'uomo del Guicciardini," *Nuova antologia* (Oct. 1869), in L. Russo, *Saggi critici* (Bari: Laterza, 1952). For details regarding the influence of De Sanctis's reading, see Vincent Luciani, *Francesco Guicciardini and His European Reputation* (New York: Karl Otto, 1936); Mark Phillips, "Reappraising 'Guicciardinian Man': Changing Contexts of Judgment on Guicciardini Since De Sanctis," *Rivista di studi Italiani* 1, no. 2 (1983): 1329; Roberto Ridolfi, "Su un famoso saggio di DeSanctis: 'L'uomo del Guicciardini,'" *Nuova antologia* 86 (1961): 3544; Gennaro Sasso, "Guicciardini e Machiavelli," in *Francesco Guicciardini, 1483–1983: Nel V centenario della nascita* (Florence: Olschki, 1984); Sasso, "I volti del particulare," in *Francesco Guicciardini: Giornata lincea indetta in occasione del V centenario della nascita* (Rome: Academia Nazionale dei Lincei, 1985); Sasso, *Per Francesco Guicciardini: Quattro studi* (Roma: Gestisa, 1984); Sasso, "Postilla guicciardiniana: I problemi del particulare," in *Studi in onore di Pietro Silva* (Florence: LeMonnier, 1957), 284–303.

the note "To Himself," and the "Savonarolian Excerpts." However, Guicciardini never fully incorporated these extrarational considerations into his conduct, nor into the advice he offered his Medici masters. Guicciardini spent his career calculating, but also miscalculating, his self-interest, as well as the self-interests of the Medici overlords he served, the leaders of Italian city-states, the republican populists and frustrated aristocracy in Florence, and the kings of the consolidated European monarchies whose armies rampaged across the peninsula during the Italian Wars.

The lesson from Guicciardini's experiences is not just a De Sanctian disdain for self-serving ambition, but also the realization that reason and rationality are not the ruling factors deciding and predicting human behavior. Guicciardini reminds one of contemporary economists whose record of predicting changes in economic conditions is far from reliable and whose reduction of behavior to quantifiable data may provide not so much a guide for deciding a course of action as much as a manner to justify faulty decisions after the fact. In short, economic analysis as a tool in policy decision may be more useful for a posteriori justification than future planning. Guicciardini was therefore arguably one of the first political counselors who was also an economist. If there is a Guicciardinian moment, it is the transition in public-policy analysis in line with the expansion of knowledge during the Renaissance, when economists and economic analysis replaced astrology and traditional soothsayers.

Guicciardini displayed an ambitious character precociously. In his "Accusation," he reveals how his schoolmates nicknamed him Alcibiades, after the notorious Athenian general, betrayer of his country.[5] When his uncle Rinieri, archdeacon of Florence and bishop of Cortona, died, Guicciardini considered pursuing an ecclesiastical career but was dissuaded by his father, who had been sympathetic to Savonarolian invective against the corruption of the church. Had Guicciardini undertaken an ecclesiastical career, one can almost envision him as a predecessor of éminences grises like Cardinals Richelieu or Mazarin, who were key figures in the regimes of French kings Louis XIII and XIV.

Instead, Francesco decided to become a lawyer, attending university in Florence, Ferrara, and Padua.[6] He gained an education in the humanist

---

5. Alcibiades (450–404 BC).
6. See Paul Grendler, *The Universities of the Italian Renaissance* (Baltimore: Johns Hopkins University Press, 2002).

manner, with study of classical rhetoric and a solid command of Latin, although not Greek. He earned a degree in civil law in 1505 and established a practice in Florence. He married Maria di Alamanno di Averardo Salviati, despite the reservations of his father, who had hoped for a marriage into a less politically exposed family. Guicciardini's future father-in-law, Alamanno Salviati, was an influential figure with family ties to the Medici clan, an indication of Guicciardini's future political leanings.[7]

Guicciardini's career enjoyed auspicious beginnings, aided by the influence of his father-in-law. Despite his youth, Guicciardini received prestigious offers to serve the Florentine Republic, including a diplomatic charge at the reacquisition of Lucca. In 1511, he accepted the ambassadorship to the court of King Ferdinand II (1452–1516) of Aragon-Castile after initial reservations about leaving his legal practice. His father insisted that he could not decline such an honor, and Guicciardini left for Spain early in 1512, beginning a brilliant and lucrative career in government service, first for the Florentine Republic and subsequently for the Medici in Florence and the two Medici popes, Leo X and Clement VII, in the Papal States.

During his ambassadorship to the court of Aragon-Castile, Guicciardini penned a terse note entitled "To Himself," which has a self-loathing tone about his unworthiness to be the recipient of honors at such an early age. At thirty, Guicciardini had yet to reach the influence that would make him one of the top power brokers in early sixteenth-century Italy. In "To Himself," Guicciardini laments the flaws in his character with a tone of religious shame about his willingness to work for a corrupt system for personal gain. Guicciardini's concern about worldly ambition echoes the current of millenarian religious fundamentalism prevalent in Europe during the early modern period. Political suppression under authoritarianism provoked popular reactions in the form of religiously inspired revolts, some including elements of communistic messianism, with a history of murderous consequences in crusades against the Dolcinites and Walensians, the Cathars, the Anabaptists, and civil strife between Catholics and Lutherans. Yet, this self-awareness would not suffice to drive Guicciardini to become a beacon of one of the religious, political, or ideological currents that were alternatives to the increasingly autocratic political and social climate of the period.

7. Roberto Ridolfi, *Life of Francesco Guicciardini* (New York: Alfred A. Knopf, 1968).

FIG. 1 | Portraits (clockwise) of Girolamo Savonarola; Pope Julius II; Charles VIII, king of France; and Giulio di Giuliano de' Medici, who ruled as Pope Clement VII. Photo: Wikimedia Commons / The Illusional Ministry.

In 1490s Florence, a populist, millennialist wave brought the Dominican friar Girolamo Savonarola (1452–1498) to the center of city affairs. Savonarola's fundamentalist message, delivered in fiery sermons, with processions for mass penance and the burning of artwork and books at "bonfires of the vanities," dominated Florentine political life from 1494 until the friar's excommunication, trial, and execution in 1498. When Savonarola rose to influence, Florence was one of the richest cities in the world, enjoying a wave of artistic, scientific, economic, and cultural awakening. The Medici astutely channeled wealth into works to elevate their prestige by inspiring public awe and consolidating power in accordance with subsequent political theory from Machiavelli's *The Prince*. However, Savonarola rejected the fruits of Florence's burgeoning economy and materialist culture for a fundamentalist recursion to austerity, fasting, and disdain for luxury and art. His sermons and acts, such as his reticence to grant Lorenzo de' Medici deathbed absolution in 1492, influenced and even determined Florentine governmental policy, leading to the expulsion of Piero de' Medici in 1494. Savonarola's political prestige was enhanced when he reportedly dissuaded the French king,

FIG. 2 | Giuliano Bugiardini, portrait of Francesco Guicciardini, ca. 1538–40. Yale University Art Gallery. Gift of Hannah D. and Louis M. Rabinowitz, accepted by deed of gift, April 29, 1959. Photo: Yale University Art Gallery.

Charles VIII, encamped outside Florence with his invading army, from sacking Florence.

Guicciardini grew up under the shadow of Savonarolian fundamentalism and prophecy that a divine scourge would punish Italy and her corrupt rulers. In 1498, the year of Savonarola's excommunication, trial, and execution, Guicciardini would turn fifteen years of age and must have felt the reverberations of the political turmoil Savonarolian fundamentalism inspired in Florence's citizenry. Savonarolian religious fundamentalism would remain as an influence for Guicciardini, who at the end of "How to Ensure the State to the House of the Medici" admonishes citizens for their lavish lifestyles and dress in accordance with Savonarola's call for sobriety and austerity. Yet, Savonarolian fundamentalism and prophecy would be precisely the sort of unworldly impulse that found little space in Guicciardini's philosophy, which perceived material self-interest as the definitive key to reality. However, at a personal level Guicciardini did retain a fascination for otherworldly predictions. The publication of Guicciardini's horoscope reveals how, perhaps in his closet council,

Guicciardini was very much prone to the superstitions of his day.[8] He subsequently collected excerpts from the sermons of Savonarola, the "Savonarolian Excerpts," which he scoured for evidence that the Italian Wars beginning in the late fifteenth century had been the fulfillment of the friar's prediction of a divine scourge punishing the immorality of Italy's people and her rulers.

As ambassador to the court of King Ferdinand II in 1512, Guicciardini observed the intrigues of a Castilian-Aragonese court that had consolidated power by expelling the Moors from the Iberian Peninsula in 1492, was pursuing interests across Europe, and was receiving fresh dispatches from conquests in the Americas. The astute machinations of King Ferdinand II provided Guicciardini with a political schooling comparable with Machiavelli's experience with Cesare Borgia as recounted in *The Prince*.

The Piero Soderini–led Florentine Republic fell in 1512 to a Medici coup when Spanish troops savagely sacked Prato and routed the republican militia purportedly organized by Machiavelli. Guicciardini's ambassadorship to the court of Spain just before Spanish troops reinstalled the Medici regime raised suspicions among republicans, particularly after Guicciardini received posts in the postrepublican Medici regime. When Medici fortunes fell following the 1527 Sack of Rome, Florentine republicans would bitterly recall the coincidence, with repercussions for Guicciardini. To date, there is no absolute confirmation that Guicciardini was privy to information regarding Ferdinand's plans to support a Medici coup. However, if Guicciardini had been unable to discover and warn the Florentine Republic that Ferdinand had planned to supply the troops for a Medici coup, then he failed his mission as ambassador, which was to gather information and apprise his superiors in Florence of Ferdinand's intentions. Perhaps Guicciardini's seeming unawareness of Spanish plans to support a Medici coup is proof of Ferdinand's ability and guile rather than collusion on Guicciardini's part. Or perhaps Guicciardini's failure to provide a warning of a Medici coup could be an early indication of the flaws in his philosophy, whereby he was unable to calculate the self-interest and motivations of all players including himself, a failing that would repeat in subsequent episodes of Guicciardini's career.

---

8. Raffaella Castagnola, *Guicciardini e le scienze occulte: L'oroscopo di Francesco Guicciardini: Lettere di alchimia, astrologia e cabala a Luigi Guicciardini* (Florence: L. S. Olschki, 1990).

During his Spanish ambassadorship, Guicciardini composed a "Report on Spain" that offers acute analyses of Spanish history, culture, and the court politics of King Ferdinand II. After opening with an unflattering characterization of the Hispanic character, Guicciardini's "Report on Spain" delves into explanations of the Hispanic attitudes regarding commerce and industry that would eventually mark the nation's economic decline. Guicciardini also offers insights on Spanish military strategy, religious practice, history, geography, law, architecture, court politics, and social structure. Guicciardini wrote his "Report on Spain" when Ferdinand II's Castilian-Aragonese regime was on the cusp of global empire and the Spanish court was a flurry of intrigue and expansion. He offers a picture of a country and a wily ruler, Ferdinand II, a master of discretion who was to be respected and feared.

The breadth of Guicciardini's report raises suspicions that he would have been unable to learn of the plans of the monarch to support a Medici restoration in 1512. The concluding section of the report is a detailed analysis of Ferdinand's finances, with the insight that without papal concessions, the Spanish regime would risk insolvency and become unable to project power beyond its borders. Guicciardini's detailed analysis supported by precise projections of the Spanish regime's budget indicates a capacity to gather information about Ferdinand's regime at a very high level. Guicciardini's seeming competence to complete the charge expected of an ambassador raises doubts that he would be unaware of the Spanish court's plans to support a Medici coup in Florence. Guicciardini's "Report on Spain" and the expertise and experience he gained therefrom made him an attractive candidate for subsequent papal administrations, for whom Spain was a continuing concern. Spanish intervention in Italian affairs escalated after the restoration of the Medici regime in 1512 with the support of Spanish troops. Spain would claim hegemony in Italian affairs after the Sack of Rome in 1527 and the ensuing Siege of Florence, when most of Italy came under Spanish domination as proxy states to a global Spanish empire ruled by Ferdinand II's successor, Charles V (1500–1558). The thrust of Spanish imperialism into Italian affairs and the eventual defeat of France had been the continuing challenge for the principal Italian city-states of Milan, Venice, Florence, the Papal States, and Naples, offering a geopolitical parallel to the declining political influence of Guicciardini's peers in the optimate class in Florentine civic politics.

In 1513, Cardinal Giovanni de' Medici became Pope Leo X, succeeding Julius II and expanding Medici power in central Italy from dominion over Tuscany to include the Papal States' control of Romagna and Lazio. Upon returning to Florence from Spain, Guicciardini penned "How to Ensure the State to the House of the Medici." The treatise is an analysis of the factional interests in Florentine politics after the Medici restoration. Guicciardini discusses the interests of the vestiges of the overthrown republic and Guicciardini's own class, the optimate nobility, which aspired to retain at least a semblance of republican institutions under the authoritarian tendencies of the Medici overlords Lorenzo di Piero de' Medici (1492–1519) and Giuliano di Lorenzo de' Medici (1479–1516), de facto rulers of postrepublican Florence. As always, Guicciardini hoped his optimate class would enjoy an advisory role to temper both the popular and the monarchical factions in city politics.

In the treatise, Guicciardini ably analyzes the self-interests of all parties. He does so with a cynical and world-weary realization of the contingencies and caprices of each, pointing out how all are "influenced above all by their personal interest, as the guide that drives all men." Guicciardini reveals how the Medici partisans who had remained loyal during the Medici exile of 1494–1512 were initially unenthusiastic at the prospects of the return of the Medici. After their reduced fortunes during the Medici exile, these Medici supporters would have to put extra effort and resources to support a Medici restoration. Guicciardini offers another insight whereby those who initially supported the return of the Medici were the least reliable of Florence's citizens. After having been at odds with the republic, they were soon to be at odds with the Medici.

These subtle analyses of self-interests characterize Guicciardini's worldview and personal philosophy, which concentrates on material self-interest but devalues unpredictable impulses in human behavior. Guicciardini admits that irrational factors may also have an influence, writing, "I do not deny that certain natural inclinations toward hatred or love may prevail." However, his inability or unwillingness to accept or to discern these unpredictable factors in human nature would be the Achilles' heel in both his professional life and philosophy. Guicciardini concludes the treatise with a stern warning against the Medici assuming authoritarian rule and not properly recognizing Florence's republican traditions, a position he would abandon at the end of his career.

In 1516, the leader of the Medici clan, Pope Leo X, appointed Guicciardini papal governor of Modena, with responsibilities eventually extending to Parma and Reggio and the entire Romagna region under papal control. Guicciardini reportedly handled his appointment as governor with competence in a time of general ineptitude and corruption among rulers and governors, leading to an extended career in papal service until 1534. Guicciardini composed treatises on government in this period, promoting the Venetian model of an oligarchical republic, always searching for a solution to the dilemma of how to reconcile the tradition of republican rule and oligarchical reticence to the reality of Medici authoritarianism.[9]

"On Force" is a pro-and-contra study on the moral implications of state-sanctioned violence enforcing policy goals. The piece examines the reasons for and against government recursion to violence, with the added relevance that Guicciardini would have the political means and influence as governor of the Papal States to consider such topics not as mere intellectual exercises. Playing devil's advocate, Guicciardini cites Lycurgus, the founding father of Spartan totalitarianism and one of Guicciardini's favorite historical examples, as a model for how severity applied and accepted may achieve authoritarian goals. Yet, Guicciardini warns against allowing a single individual to monopolize public force. This conclusion contrasts with the course of Guicciardini's later career as an adviser, governor, and advocate for the Medici clan in Florence and the Papal States.

In "On Suicide," the conclusion regarding the propriety of committing suicide devolves to a question not so much of otherworldly consequences according to Christian teaching but of character and class in a classical vein. Guicciardini identifies with classical examples of suicides for political reasons out of an understanding of the affront to station and living standards that can result from political defeat to a populist faction. "On Force" had revealed aspects of Guicciardini's mindset as a decision maker forced to resort to public violence to obtain policy goals. "On Suicide" examines the question of oppression from the point of view of defeated aristocrats forced to submit to popular uprisings, revealing prejudices against representative republican government as a window

---

9. Francesco Guicciardini, *Dialogue on the Government of Florence*, ed. and trans. Alison Brown (Cambridge: Cambridge University Press, 1994).

into Guicciardini's mindset, where dignity, pride, and class identity have greater value than life itself. "On Suicide" also serves as a materialist response to the self-loathing tone expressed in "To Himself," where Guicciardini considered the toll of personal ambition on one's soul. The underlying question in "On Suicide" is whether self-interest is served by spiritual or class values. In his career, Guicciardini would opt for the latter, although his more personal writings and even his *History of Italy* would list doubts about the consequences of the former.

Guicciardini's "On Progressive Taxation: The Scaled Tenth" is one of the first treatises to discuss the advantages and disadvantages of progressive taxation.[10] Guicciardini ably delineates the primary and most forceful arguments supporting each opposing position. He offers the principal point in favor of progressive taxation: that the percentage of income spent on inelastic goods, the necessities of life without which one cannot survive, is greater for those with lower incomes. Therefore, to tax the poor at the same rate as the wealthy is unjust. However, Guicciardini also offers the main argument against a scaled tenth, progressive tax. If a government representing a constituent majority realizes that the law may be a tool to redistribute wealth, then the consequences may hamper economic activity and encourage the flight or rebellion of capable or wealthy citizens, in effect impoverishing the collectivity and harming everyone.

In 1521, Guicciardini served as commissioner general in Leo X's papal army allied with Charles V of Spain against Francis I of France. Just as papal fortunes improved in the war against the French, Leo X died suddenly, leaving Guicciardini commander of the besieged city of Parma and unable to receive orders until the election of a new pontiff. Despite this predicament, Guicciardini saved Parma from a French siege as described in the "Report on the Defense of Parma." The episode reveals the tenuous reality of events in the Italian Wars, where alliances were constantly shifting and rumor or ill humor among a citizenry or mercenaries could determine the outcome of a military clash. Many of Guicciardini's adversaries in the Parma defense would become allies in the later war against Charles V. Guicciardini's analysis of the perception and misperception of the self-interests of all the players in the events at Parma demonstrates

---

10. The work has received attention in the field of economics. See Nikola Regent, "Guicciardini's *La Decima scalata*: The First Treatise, The Scaled Tenth," *History of Political Economy* 46, no. 2 (2014): 307–31.

his political acumen, but also the level of confusion and chaos that was a staple in Guicciardini's professional life.

At Parma, Guicciardini turned the expectation of a quick rout of a defenseless city by the French into a victory for papal forces. He adeptly discerned and channeled the moods of the pusillanimous citizens and reticent mercenary troops within the city walls and correctly interpreted the hasty moves of his adversaries in the French camp with a cunning breadth of guile for negotiation and action. Guicciardini understood that he had no firm allies or support on either side and that his only possibility for success was to act according to his anticipation of the self-interests of both the French at the gates and the vacillating citizens and mercenaries within the walls of Parma. Guicciardini's defeat of the French assailants ensured his personal goal, which was to avoid his own capture and ransom. The success of his experience at Parma would seem to offer an example confirming Guicciardini's personal philosophy of the primacy of self-interest as the guide to interpret reality and set a course for action. In the defense of Parma, he had apparently correctly read and analyzed the motives of all parties for a favorable result. However, a reading of his account of events reveals that the determining factors in his victory were the unpredictable emotional reactions of all the parties rather than rational calculations of self-interest. Each faction miscalculated their self-interests and thereby allowed Guicciardini to direct events to his own advantage owing to a combination of guile and good fortune. Guicciardini recounts how a Parma town council meeting on the verge of voting to surrender was interrupted by a French artillery barrage that sent all hands rushing to man the city walls.

In 1523, Cardinal Giulio di Giuliano de' Medici assumed the pontificate as Clement VII, succeeding Leo X's short-lived, Dutch successor, Hadrian VI. The newly elected pontiff renewed Guicciardini's appointment as president of the Romagna region. A turning point of the Italian Wars between the French and Spanish came with the Spanish victory at the Battle of Pavia in 1525, which resulted in the imprisonment of the French king, Francis I, in the remote tower at Pizzighettone in the Po Valley.

Political alliances in this period of Italian political alliances were frustratingly variable, recalling the opening metaphor of Guicciardini's *History of Italy* of the nation as a ship driven by unpredictable winds. Guicciardini would later regret not advising Clement VII to turn to the French side sooner, realizing that the victory of Charles V's Hispanic imperial troops at the Battle of Pavia posed the greater threat to Medici interests. Guicciardini subsequently advised Clement VII to form an anti-imperial Holy League in an alliance with Spain's potential rivals Venice, France, and England. As the Holy League army's lieutenant general, Guicciardini advocated attack on Milan in order to drive imperial forces from Italy.

Guicciardini levels much of the blame for the Holy League's defeat in the *History of Italy* (1540) on Francesco Maria della Rovere (1490–1538), commander of Venetian forces. In 1516, della Rovere had been displaced as lord of Pesaro by the Medici pope, Leo X. Della Rovere fought an unsuccessful war against the Medici to regain Urbino the following year, as Guicciardini recounts in chapter 13 of the *History of Italy*. Della Rovere would regain a duchy in the Marche in Urbino only after the death of Clement VII. Thus, della Rovere's inaction against forces threatening Clement VII is understandable, as his interests were in direct contrast to those of the Medici clan.

Della Rovere's Venetian troops finally attacked Milan, however, without blocking the troops of Charles V from descending into Italy. The mercenary soldiers at the service of the Spanish Empire included the infamous *Landsknechts* (soldiers of the land), fresh from the murderous Peasant Wars of 1525 between Catholic and Protestant principalities in Germany. The *Landsknechts* descended on the Italian peninsula with the fervor of religious conviction as if in fulfillment of Savonarola's dire prophecies about divine retribution for the corruption of the church and Italy's rulers.

In November 1526, the papal army's most feared and capable military leader, Ludovico de' Medici (1498–1526), also known as Giovanni dalle Bande Nere (John of the Black Bands), fell to one of the new firearms changing battlefield tactics. After his death, the mercenary troops he commanded, the Black Bands, became almost ungovernable. As lieutenant general of the Holy League army, Guicciardini faced a situation where the unpredictable influence of an individual personality had determined events, negating any further possibility for redress by calculation of the interests of the players involved.

On May 6, Charles V's imperial army invaded Rome, sacking the city with a fury beyond expectation. Again, the commander of the Venetian army, Francesco Maria della Rovere, perhaps a bit unnerved by the lesson in modern warfare and the power of firearms the French suffered at the Battle of Pavia, did not actively engage his forces. However, Della Rovere was also careful to cure his own personal interests, which as above did not necessarily align with those of the Medici pope, Clement VII. A decline in Medici fortunes could allow an opportunity for the della Rovere clan to reassume control of cities in central Italy such as Urbino and Pesaro.

Guicciardini wrote a stiff letter to della Rovere on May 10, 1527, a few days after Spanish imperial troops breached Rome's defenses and Clement VIII took refuge in the Castel Sant'Angelo on the banks of the Tiber. In the letter, della Rovere's actions, or inactions, are described in the third person; perhaps Guicciardini penned the letter to explain and document his own actions rather than out of any hope to spur della Rovere and his troops into battle. The letter describes the predicament of papal forces and essentially accuses della Rovere of indifference to the plight of the besieged pontiff. Guicciardini could offer no argument to spur della Rovere beyond a perfunctory exhortation to remain loyal to the leader of Christendom. Again, the terse realization that della Rovere's personal interests would not be served by defending the pope offers the best explanation for his inaction.

Contemporaries referred to the military, political, cultural, and psychological blow felt in the Italian Peninsula after the 1527 Sack of Rome. Serving the authoritarian lords who had suppressed Italy's tradition of republican rule, many notable figures of the time were directly involved in the tragedy: Baldassare Castiglione was the papal ambassador to Charles V's court in Madrid; Benvenuto Cellini was among those besieged with Clement VII in Castel Sant'Angelo; Machiavelli was in Rome as advisor to the pope; and Guicciardini was the lieutenant general of the Holy League's routed, mercenary troops.

Following the Sack of Rome in 1527, Guicciardini fled to his villa near Florence at Finocchietto while a plague raged in the region, possibly spread by the retreating Holy League troops Guicciardini had hoped to lead as lieutenant general of the Holy League against Charles V. In their retreat from Lazio, these marauding mercenaries would also be accused of pillaging the Florentine countryside and holding inhabitants for ransom.

Reliance on mercenary troops, heavily criticized by Machiavelli in *The Prince*, is tangential to Guicciardini's philosophy of adopting self-interest rather than emotional and irrational motives as a meter to interpret reality. The papal troops who had fought for pay, or had been loyal to a fallen leader (Giovanni dalle Bande Nere), or had found themselves under a reticent commander such as Francesco Maria della Rovere, proved to be useless. In comparison, elements of the imperial

Landsknechts were motivated by their interest to collect booty as well as Lutheran propaganda, precisely the sort of irrational and unpredictable factor not a party to Guicciardini's philosophy.

With the pope negotiating a ransom with the Spanish imperials, the Medici regime in Florence fell, and republicans installed a final Florentine republic expelling Medici supporters. The republican government in Florence felt the ideological influence of the Savonarolian-influenced republic of 1494–98. The Sack of Rome and the pestilence raging in the Florentine countryside seemed to be a fulfillment of threats of divine retribution from Savonarolian prophecy.

Safe in his villa in the Florentine countryside in 1527, Guicciardini composed the orations "Consolation," "Accusation," and "Defense."[11] These orations treat Guicciardini's personal drama in the classical *in utramque partem* (in both directions) format, with declarations of opposing points of view. An examination of events from opposite points of view forces consideration not only from a perspective one may prefer, but also from an opposite vantage point. Guicciardini approaches the exercise by framing the topic according to the imagined authors' first-person perceptions. In the "Consolation," Guicciardini assumes the voice of a friend who tries to convince the disgraced former lieutenant general of papal forces to accept the changes in his position and reputation after the Sack of Rome. In the "Accusation," Guicciardini assumes the voice of a vengeful prosecutor trying Guicciardini before the *Quarantia* (Forty), a judicial body that during the last Florentine republic purged the city of Medici supporters. In the final oration, the "Defense," Guicciardini completes the rhetorical exercise by defending himself from the prosecutor's charges in the "Accusation." As Guicciardini had anticipated, the Florentine Republic did level charges against him when he was advising Clement VII and Charles V in their siege of the city, the last stand of Florentine republican government before the establishment of a Medici duchy.

The *in utramque partem* format is common in the histories of classical authors, such as Thucydides's *History of the Peloponnesian War* or Livy's *History of Rome*, and it is a feature of Guicciardini's *History of Italy* (1540), which recounts events of the Italian Wars from multiple perspectives. There is the viewpoint of factions within Italian city-states split

---

11. Roberto Ridolfi has definitively corrected the idea that Guicciardini wrote the orations in 1530. See Ridolfi, *Life of Francesco Guicciardini*.

between those favoring wide participation in government and those, like Guicciardini, who favored oligarchical restriction by wealth or lineage according to the Venetian republican model. There are the Italian elite like the Medici seeking to establish hereditary duchies in these same city-states. There is also the wider continental perspective of the consolidated monarchies of France and Spain competing for hegemony in the Italian Peninsula and continental Europe. Guicciardini's history also has an eschatological undercurrent whereby the wars and pestilence that scourged Italy were divine retribution for the corruption of Italian princes. In this view, events unfolded in fulfillment of the prophecies of fundamentalist friar Girolamo Savonarola, who briefly influenced a theocratically conditioned Florentine Republic after the expulsion of the Medici in 1494 until his excommunication by the Borgia pope, Alexander VI (1431–1503), and trial and execution in Florence in 1498. Through the "Consolation," "Accusation," and "Defense," Guicciardini began to reconsider the events that had led to the Sack of Rome as part of a larger process of the Italian Wars that began in 1494 with the invasion of the French king Charles VIII.

The opening paragraph of the "Consolation" reveals just what is bothering Guicciardini. Because of the failure of the Holy League against Charles V and the Sack of Rome, he lost his position as the president of the Romagna region in the Papal States, which gave him "considerable benefits and prestige that would have honored any great man born to a station above that of a commoner." Guicciardini vaunts that he enjoyed so much authority that the pope "reserved nothing higher even for himself." Guicciardini's fall from grace was not just economic, but social. As the father of several daughters, he would have to provide dowries for their marriages or annuities for them to enter nunneries in accordance with their station. Without the prestige of his position as governor of Romagna, Guicciardini's offspring would have to marry within the Florentine or Tuscan nobility rather than aspire to higher positions among the Italian and even European elite.

The friend Guicciardini imagines as the author of the "Consolation" reminds him that the reason for the fall of Clement VII was the advice to pursue a war against the Spaniards. To counter the gloomy realization of the consequences of this advice, Guicciardini's imaginary friend offers philosophical and religious arguments that encourage a look beyond the vanities of the world to the eternal good of the soul, themes Guicciardini treated in his early note, "To Himself." However, Guicciardini's friend quickly abandons this approach as appropriate only for the innocent at heart and not for someone as worldly as Guicciardini. If Guicciardini is to be consoled, the friend realizes that arguments must be "in accordance with the nature of men and the ways of the world." Guicciardini's meter remains worldly and materialistic, even in a defeat as massive as the aftermath of the Sack of Rome. To this end, the friend reminds Guicciardini that the favors he enjoyed at the papal court were temporary and unstable, dependent on the whims of a prince rather than anything lasting. Guicciardini should feel some shame and discomfort at the reduced station of the pope, but not more than normal "compassion for someone else's suffering."

With the loss of position in the papal administration, the friend insists that what afflicts Guicciardini is the damage to his reputation and the specter of a dishonorable, forced retirement. Guicciardini's friend assures him that his honor is intact since he was one of the few members of the papal court to behave competently in the war against the Spanish imperials. Honor in Renaissance society was not just a relic of chivalric culture but also a public good whose value could lead to political advantage and favorable marriages for offspring.

The friend compares Guicciardini's predicament to those of august figures of the past, affording an idea of the level of Guicciardini's aspirations. Guicciardini is compared to the Roman emperor Diocletian, who retired to a life of leisure after the trials of service. For Guicciardini, damnation is not spiritual but public and material. The apex for a reputation—"to be godly," in Guicciardini's words—is public admiration in the manner of the ancient Athenian statesman Pericles. The importance of honor, of recovering a good name, takes precedence over questions of guilt, innocence, even life and death. To be godly means to be revered by your fellow men.[12]

Guicciardini's imagined friend describes the state of his reputation with meteorological metaphors: "it is normal for rare and excellent men

---

12. *Ricordo* C16. "Power and position are generally sought, because everything that is beautiful and good about them appears externally, emblazoned on their superficies. But the bother, the toil, the troubles, and the dangers lie hidden and unseen. If these were as obvious as the good things, there would be no reason to seek power and position, except one: the more men are honored, revered, and adored, the more they seem to approach and become similar to God. And what man would not want to resemble Him?" (Guicciardini, *Maxims and Reflections*, 44).

to be beaten by the winds of envy." He reaches for another metaphor of a rain-dampened coat that has kept inner garments and person still dry and unaffected by the weather. If Guicciardini is innocent, then his spirit is like the inner garments unaffected by the rain. Therefore, he should accept his fate and continue to have confidence in himself. The friend encourages Guicciardini to recall the enormous fortune that characterized his rise. Any complaint during a perhaps temporary reversal would be unseemly. He reminds Guicciardini that fortune is capricious, never stable for anyone. Guicciardini should realize that things could be much worse, and his reputation could improve if he successfully faces and overcomes adversity.

The friend then turns to the political situation that led to Guicciardini's fall. The advice given to Pope Clement VII about establishing a league with the Venetian Republic, the French, and the English against Charles V of Spain seemed valid when presented and given the calculation of the interests of the parties at the time. What Guicciardini's imaginary friend does not mention is that Guicciardini's focus on the short-term evaluation of self-interest is precisely what led to his predicament. The perpetually shifting alliances and need to rely on former enemies, such as Francesco Maria della Rovere, whose allegiance was suspect, led to the defeat of the Sack of Rome.

In the "Consolation," Guicciardini refers to Savonarola's prophecies about the divine wrath to befall Italy's rulers for their ungodly behavior, precisely the sort of unpredictable element that would throw Guicciardini's calculations about short-term self-interest into disarray. Guicciardini's friend asks, "How can a prince's counselor be expected to advise not only on human affairs but also astrologer's readings, spirit conjuring, and the prophecies of friars?" He advises acceptance of events with a sense of fatalism about powers greater than oneself.

The next oration, the "Accusation," is a courtroom harangue that refers to throngs of accusing witnesses and severe judges in the voice of an impassioned republican prosecutor who depicts Guicciardini's decision to serve the Medici popes as a betrayal of both the Florentine aristocracy and the republic. The "Accusation" recalls the self-loathing, crypto-Savonarolian tone in Guicciardini's C28 *ricordo* noted by De Sanctis. This longest and most impassioned of the three orations reveals the self-recriminations and remorse gnawing at Guicciardini's conscience. Guicciardini's accuser introduces themes of guilt, second-guessing, and hindsighted rationalization of defeat. The prosecutor accuses Guicciardini of abandoning classical virtues and Christian ethics for the short-term benefits of a career serving the Medici clan. The lesson that the prosecutor seeks to communicate, which is a valid description of Guicciardini's entire career, is that working for one's self-interest within and for the benefit of a corrupt system results in both personal and societal defeat.

In the "Accusation," the prosecutor charges that Guicciardini had been conspiring with the Medici clan since marrying into the Salviati family in 1508. Second, Guicciardini betrayed the republican cause as Florentine ambassador to the court of Ferdinand II when the Spanish monarch aided the Medici coup in 1512. Third, the prosecutor accuses Guicciardini of having prevented a popular uprising that would have led to a reinstallation of a republican government in 1527, when a group of citizens tried to take the Florentine city hall but were convinced by Guicciardini to desist. The final accusation, and perhaps the most pernicious given the enflamed tones from the prosecutor, is that Guicciardini knowingly diverted funds destined for payment to the mercenary troops hired to join the papal Holy League. These unpaid troops then pillaged and ransacked the Florentine hinterland.

A repeated theme in the prosecutor's speech is the difference in levels of civility between republican Florence and the corrupt, theocratically ruled Papal States. In Florence, statues of biblical figures Judith and David, representing courage, stood in front of the Palazzo della Signoria as emblems of republican and civic pride and in contrast to the corruption and tyranny of the Papal States governed by the Medici popes and Guicciardini. The prosecutor depicts Guicciardini as the representative of a den of tyrants who betrayed Florence for personal gain. The prosecutor's listing of the towns sacked by ravaging troops adds authenticity to the oration. The miscalculations so eloquently rationalized in the "Consolation" resulted in epochal havoc and suffering, which should have weighed on Guicciardini's conscience.

Above all, the prosecutor offers unflattering insights into Guicciardini's character, which, given that the author of the piece is Guicciardini himself, recalls the self-loathing tone of Guicciardini's earlier self-confession "To Himself," where Guicciardini with a sense of self-loathing laments his inability to consider nonmaterialistic goals.[13] Guicciardini admittedly

---

13. See Mark Phillips, *Francesco Guicciardini: The Historian's Craft* (Toronto: University of Toronto Press, 1977).

enjoyed the trappings and the aura of power as president of the papal territories in the Romagna. The prosecutor offers an image of Guicciardini as a lord of rich regions and in contrast to the suffering in the Florentine provinces at the hands of the pope's unpaid, marauding mercenaries.

For a republican, the idea of a Florentine citizen posing as a duke or lord, particularly one as talented as Guicciardini, was a betrayal. The prosecutor compares Guicciardini to mythical monsters like the Hydra and Cerberus and recalls how Guicciardini's schoolmates teased him with the nickname Alcibiades after the ambitious and traitorous Athenian general. The implication is that Guicciardini's lust for power and position was evident from his earliest days and conditioned every decision in his life.

When a citizen born into a republic betrays his country in this manner, the punishment must be severe to serve as a warning for future malefactors. The prosecutor offers precedents from classical times, repeating the name of Alcibiades, pointing to the Athenian practice of ostracism, and indicating the fate of Lucius Tarquinius, who was overthrown by the ancient Romans as the seventh and final king of Rome. The prosecutor's most impassioned examples are Florentine citizens who betrayed the republic and were exiled and even executed, such as Filippo Strozzi, Bernardo Rucellai, Donato Barbadori, Bernardo del Nero, and Corso Donati. With these examples, the prosecutor makes the argument that republican liberty requires the decisive punishment of corrupt citizens. By preventing a popular uprising in 1527 that could have restored the in 1512 republican constitution, Guicciardini joined the company of the worst figures in Florentine history.

The prosecutor suggests how the pope's affairs could have been handled. A leader like the pope, or even the head of a city-state like Florence, must risk involvement only when not to do so might provoke the ultimate victor. The prosecutor argues that the failure to follow this commonsense policy of approaching the eventual victor in a conflict to offer help against the loser brought ruin not just to the papacy and Florence but to all Italy. Here, Guicciardini's prosecutor presciently described the stereotypical duplicity that would condition subsequent Italian foreign policy under the practice of determining which side is stronger in a conflict and then offering aid to the winner. Ironically, Guicciardini imagines his prosecutor speaking in terms evoking the philosophy of the *particulare*, the idea of self-interest, where the only real sin is to miscalculate self-interest and thereby to suffer damage or defeat.

The prosecutor's speech seems too vibrant, damning, and brimming with Savonarolian invective to be a mere rhetorical exercise. Guicciardini must have felt the weight of his role in the political and military defeat of the papacy and, by extension, of Florence. After the soothing tones of the "Consolation," in which Guicciardini's imaginary friend advised him to take comfort in the lessons of religion and philosophy and to retire with honor, the strident attack in the "Accusation" forces the reader to reconsider the hardship and suffering of events in which Guicciardini played a pivotal role. Guicciardini's decisions had vast repercussions. He was tormented by the idea that his miscalculations of self-interest and decision to follow the path of personal profit, position, and class status by following the Medici were beyond the capacity of his free will to discern, an effective criticism of his philosophy.

The final and third oration, the "Defense," lacks the passion of the "Accusation" and the philosophical tones of the "Consolation." Guicciardini writes in his own voice in a concluding segment of the classical *in utramque partem*, pro-and-contra exercise he would adopt in the *History of Italy*, echoing the structure of Thucydides's *History of the Peloponnesian Wars*. In the "Defense," Guicciardini cites examples from classical and Florentine history of false accusations against virtuous men, in particular, Francesco's forbearer, Giovanni Guicciardini, who fended off accusations of malfeasance in a fourteenth-century siege of Lucca before eventual exoneration. Guicciardini also cites Roman general Fabius Maximus, who faced indictment in Rome before any victory over Hannibal became definitive.

Throughout this final oration, Guicciardini adopts rhetorical strategies revealing the brilliance of his legal abilities. He dismisses the charges as hearsay unconfirmed by reliable witnesses. He questions the credibility of the few available witnesses as driven by hopes for pecuniary gain rather than a desire to reveal the truth. Guicciardini cleverly focuses on the reliability of testimony from marauding soldiers caught in the act of stealing. Since such witnesses had no direct contact with Guicciardini, they cannot establish a direct link to him. His repeated call for an audit of papal treasurer Alessandro del Caccia further deflects blame.[14] By casting

---

14. Alessandro del Caccia was in the papal treasury and was eventually summoned by the last Florentine Republic to account for his handling of Florence's monetary contribution to the war effort. Melissa Meriam Bullard, *Filippo Strozzi and the Medici: Favor and Finance in Sixteenth-Century Florence and Rome* (Cambridge: Cambridge University Press,

doubt on a direct connection between himself and actual payments made to soldiers, Guicciardini ably diffuses the prosecutor's charge of corruption from the "Accusation."

Guicciardini questions the prosecutor's ability to establish motive and eloquently affirms his desire to retain a good name and reputation. Guicciardini admits a certain embarrassment at having to praise himself at this point, and he astutely portrays himself as a victim. He depicts his career for the Papal States not as an ambitious move to enhance his station in life but as a mission to bring good government to populations accustomed to the corruption of ecclesiastical rule. Guicciardini relates how he became the governor of Modena at the pivotal age of thirty-three and would have been able to steal and commit whatever crimes he may have desired. He claims to have refused gold weighing as much as the giant—a reference to the statue of David by Michelangelo outside the Palazzo della Signoria and commissioned as a symbol of Florentine republican ardor. Since Guicciardini ruled honestly, he gained the gratitude of the citizenry who, according to his version of events, petitioned Leo X's successor, Hadrian VI, to reappoint him as governor. As a Florentine appointed by another Florentine, the Medici pope Leo X, Guicciardini expected the short-lived Dutch pope to relieve him of his duties. However, Guicciardini gained reappointment because of his reputation as an able administrator. As in the "Consolation," Guicciardini convincingly concludes that he had no motive to steal from the pope, to risk the ruin of the Holy League, or to earn the wrath of the Florentines by not paying the soldiers.

After Guicciardini successfully rebuts the charges against him, the "Defense" affords insights into the inner workings of the papal Holy League against Charles V and the chaos that reigned in the papal military administration. These brief descriptions reveal reasons for the collapse of papal forces. Guicciardini allows himself recriminations against former colleagues in the Holy League, repeating allusions about the potential malfeasance of the papal treasurer, Alessandro del Caccia. He decries the conduct of Francesco Maria della Rovere, commander of the Venetian contingent of the Holy League, who never brought his troops into action to Guicciardini's satisfaction and who in Guicciardini's final version of events in the *History of Italy* receives much blame for the Sack of Rome.

2008); John N. Stephens. *The Fall of the Florentine Republic, 1512–1530* (Oxford: Oxford University Press, 1983).

Guicciardini gives a chilling description of the difficulty controlling the unruly mercenaries, the Black Bands, and the importance in the defeat of the Holy League of the death in a skirmish of their leader, Giovanni dalle Bande Nere, in 1526, which Guicciardini cites as a turning point in the war. Guicciardini's short and cutting descriptions of the havoc and danger caused by these ungovernable troops allows an insight into the disorder of the Holy League's armies. Finally, he paints a damning picture of the pettiness and incompetence of the pope's other military commanders, such as Guido Rangoni and Count Caiazzo, who according to Guicciardini's account stopped him on the road one morning with murderous intentions after the Holy League's defeat had become evident.[15]

Once the "Defense" arrives at this recriminatory level, the oration breaks off in midparagraph, interrupted as if Guicciardini felt no need to pursue the topic further. What remains is an impression of the chaotic drama of the events and the confusion reigning in papal forces in the preparation and aftermath of the Sack of Rome. Guicciardini vents his frustration that as a purported master in the art of calculation of self-interest, he found himself in a situation where events beyond his control or influence resulted in disaster. In the defense of Parma, Guicciardini, aided by fortune, had been able to appraise the situation by the quick determination of the self-interests of all parties for a successful outcome. In the events leading to the Sack of Rome, this ability failed him.

On the surface, Guicciardini ably examines different viewpoints in these orations. However, the goal of the *in utramque partem* exercise is to make capital of opposing points to arrive at a fuller understanding of a subject. Guicciardini's orations do not adequately delve into the flaws in his personal philosophy of the primacy of self-interest by resolving his inability or unwillingness to consider the emotional, the irrational, and the unpredictable. The "Consolation" does not reach the discomfort in Guicciardini's earlier note "To Himself." Guicciardini ably refutes the charges from the "Accusation" with almost too much ease in the "Defense." Despite undergoing the *in utramque partem* exercise, Guicciardini does not arrive at a synthesis for a true self-examination, even after a defeat as absolute and embarrassing as the Sack of Rome, which negated the reputation he had earned for competence via exploits such as the defense of Parma. After the

---

15. Guido Rangoni (1485–1539) and Roberto da Sanseverino, Count Caiazzo (1500–1532) were Italian *condottieri* (military leaders).

Sack of Rome, Guicciardini continued in his former ways, with further miscalculations of self-interests, serving not necessarily his interests or those of his class or compatriots, but of the Medici goal of a hereditary duchy.

In the same period as the composition of the orations, Guicciardini penned the "Savonarolian Excerpts" (1528). These summaries cover the time from Savonarola's sermons from January 1495 to the period following the expulsion of Lorenzo de' Medici's successor Piero (the Unfortunate) and entry of the troops of French king Charles VIII into Tuscany to the period preceding Savonarola's execution in 1498. For the "Savonarolian Excerpts," Guicciardini scoured Savonarola's fiery sermons with a mind that the 1527 Sack of Rome may have been the divine retribution of Savonarola's predictions rather than the 1494 French invasion of Charles VIII. A possible conclusion for Guicciardini in his review of Savonarola's sermons was that the players in the Italian Wars were merely pawns in the larger scope of events that included not just peninsular or continental politics but divine intervention, a fatalistic conclusion that would render moot Guicciardini's philosophy of the primacy of the interpretation of self-interest.

Attraction to the writings and sermons of the doomed friar was somewhat of a tradition in the Guicciardini family. Francesco's father, Piero, had been sympathetic to the Savonarolian faction in Florentine politics and discouraged Francesco from a career in the church.[16] Francesco's brother, Luigi, composed a dialogue on Savonarola, *About Savonarola*, as well as an account of the Sack of Rome, *The Sack of Rome*.[17] Francesco's contribution to Savonarolian literature pivoting off Guicciardini's reexamination of Savonarola's sermons included herein would reappear as a narrative thread in the *History of Italy* (1540). When Guicciardini finally rewrote his history of Italy for the third time—after his earlier attempts in

---

16. Ridolfi, *Life of Francesco Guicciardini*, 8.

17. Luigi di Piero Guicciardini, *Del Savonarola: Ovvero dialogo tra Francesco Zati e Pieradovardo Giachinotti il giorno dopo la battaglia di Gavinara*, ed. Bono Simonetta (Florence: L. S. Olschki, 1959). His *Historia del sacco di Roma* has been translated into English: Luigi Guicciardini, *The Sack of Rome*, trans. J. H. McGregor (New York: Italica, 1993). For a discussion of this "Savonarolian" genre, see Ginori Conti, *Bibliografia delle opere del Savonarola*, ed. Piero Ginori Conti (Florence: Fondazione Ginori Conti, 1939). See also Mario Ferrara, *Nuova bibliografia savonaroliana* (Vadus: Topos, 1981), and Armando Verde and Donald Weinstein, *Savonarola: La vita, le opere* (Venice: Marsilio, 1998). Ridolfi and Palmarocchi have identified the composition date of the "Estratti savonaroliani" as 1528 owing to an oversight in the manuscript in which Guicciardini dated one of Savonarola's sermons 1528 instead of 1498. See Guicciardini, *Scritti autobiografici e rari*, ed. Palmarocchi, 373; Ridolfi, *Life of Francesco Guicciardini*, 310.

the *Florentine History* (1508) and *Florentine Matters* (1527)—Savonarola's celestial view of Italian affairs and the apocalyptic consequences thereof would reappear in the *History of Italy*, with Guicciardini introducing Savonarola's prediction of dire events.[18]

By excerpting Savonarola's sermons, Guicciardini would seem to be revisiting themes from the early note "To Himself" penned when he was thirty and at the beginning of his political career. In "To Himself," Guicciardini had bemoaned the flaws in his character that did not allow for conduct that could lead to spiritual salvation. The question alluded to in "To Himself" is whether self-interest is better served by a worldly or spiritual meter. However, neither the "Consolation," "Accusation," "Defense," nor the "Savonarolian Excerpts" resulted in a transformation of Guicciardini's subsequent conduct. In the aftermath of the Sack of Rome, Guicciardini continued to serve as an intermediary between the republican government in Florence and the Medici pope in Rome, Clement VII, a role he reprised from his early career following the Medici coup of 1512. Again, in the last years of Guicciardini's life and career, unpredictable and irrational events would resurface, frustrating his approach to base action on interpretations of the self-interests of parties involved.

Guicciardini had successfully dissuaded radical republicans from restoring the republic in the immediate aftermath of the 1527 Sack of Rome. However, the more radical faction assumed power in Florence in 1529. In June of 1529, Pope Clement VII and Charles V came to terms in the Treaty of Barcelona. Clement VII crowned Charles V as Holy Roman Emperor in February 1530 after a procession to the Cathedral of San Petronio in Bologna. Part of the deal brokered by Clement VII was a return of the Medici to Florence under a Medici duchy ruled by Alessandro de' Medici (1510–1537), with Guicciardini serving as Alessandro's chief advocate.

In October 1529, imperial forces began a brutal siege of Florence. The republican government reacted with justifiable rage, summoning Guicciardini to answer charges before a republican court as anticipated in the "Accusation." The Florentine Republic fell to Spanish imperial forces in August 1530, despite Francesco Ferruccio's (1489–1530) heroic resistance and defeat by betrayal. After the fall of Florence, Clement VII sent

---

18. Francesco Guicciardini, *History of Italy*, book 2, chapter 2 (Milan: Garzanti, 1988), 165. See also Enrico Gusberti, "Il Savonarola del Guicciardini," *Nuova Rivista Storica* 55 (1971): 21–89; Francesco Guicciardini, *Guicciardini: History of Italy and History of Florence*, trans. Cecil Grayson (New York: Washington Square Press, 1964).

Guicciardini back to the city to organize a hereditary Medici duchy under Alessandro de' Medici.

In this period, Guicciardini composed treatises on Florence's political future. "Response on Behalf of the Duke to the Complaints to the Exiles" (1531) has a different tone from "How to Ensure the State to the House of the Medici" (1513) penned nearly twenty years earlier. The earlier contained little mention of extrapeninsular powers and retains hints of republican pride and dignity as Guicciardini adopts his meter of a somewhat cynical discernment of the self-interest of mainly civic factions. In the earlier treatise, Guicciardini had affirmed his long-held hopes regarding the participation of his optimate class for a Florentine oligarchical government. However, by the time of the ascension of Alessandro de' Medici as the latest in a long line of Medici rulers, the decline of the political position of Guicciardini's optimates who had sought to temper Medici rule since the rise of Cosimo de' Medici (1389–1464) was irreversible. Nevertheless, Guicciardini still promoted the idea of a government structure with a monarch guided and advised by citizens of his optimate class.

In the later treatise, "Response on Behalf of the Duke to Complaints of the Exiles" (1531), Guicciardini's arguments are no longer grounded on interpretation of good government or civic polity but on survival and acquiescence to the will of Charles V. Like all Guicciardini's work, the later treatise focuses on the calculation of the self-interest of the parties involved. Guicciardini recognizes the impracticality of a blanket expulsion of all Florentines who supported a restoration of the republic. To expel all such citizens would cripple the city's economy. Guicciardini seeks to guide affairs according to the need of participants to save face, including Cardinal Ippolito de' Medici, who wished to rule as regent instead of Alessandro. Guicciardini dismisses objections that the construction of a fortress, the still extant Fortezza da Basso, was a symbol of oppression in confirmation of Machiavelli's theory in *The Prince* of fortresses as bulwarks against popular rebellion rather than foreign invasion. Guicciardini disregards concerns from disgruntled republicans when, in fact, a sizeable exile community would attempt a revolt against the Medici after the assassination of Alessandro in January 1537.

"Response on Behalf of the Duke to the Complaints of the Exiles" (1531) evidences a fatal acceptance that the irrevocable authoritarian wave had reached fruition in Florence. Under the secular trend toward political authoritarianism, previously nominally republican governments, including Florence, were reduced to subservience to hereditary lords. The city's government did not derive from the competition between civic factions as much as from the whims and humor of external lords, whose personal ambitions and prejudices would have more say in determining the Florentine government than popular will or optimate counsel. Guicciardini's political prejudices, his desire to limit popular participation by oligarchical government, are evident in the piece, as is his mistrust of the motives and ability of hereditary rule under a regal house. To this end, Guicciardini saw himself, and those of his class, as the ideal councilors and participants in a government where participation was restricted to a ruling elite. However, that influence was to be marginalized under a Medici duchy, which in turn was subservient to the global empire of Charles V. When Clement died in 1534, Paul III succeeded him as pope. Guicciardini refused an offer from the new papal administration, ending a long career as a papal adviser and governor.

Guicciardini's next act on behalf of the Medici was to defend Duke Alessandro from the charges of Florentine exiles. The siege of Florence had produced a sizable and well-heeled exile community. Alessandro's reputation for lasciviousness further enraged the vestiges of republican sentiment in the city.[19] The Florentine exiles somewhat naively sought redress for damages suffered following the siege and fall of Florence before Charles V, now absolute arbiter of Italian affairs. Guicciardini penned speeches, including the "Response on Behalf of the Duke to the Complaints of the Exiles," defending Alessandro and a hereditary Medici duchy after Alessandro's consolidation of his position through marriage to Margaret of Parma (1522–1586), the illegitimate daughter of Charles V.

Despite his loyalty to the Medici, Guicciardini did not serve in the Florentine government after Alexander's assassination by his cousin Lorenzacccio in 1537. The next Medici Guicciardini advised, Cosimo I de' Medici (1519–1574), was the son of Giovanni dalle Bande Nere, the charismatic military leader whose death on the battlefield by newly introduced firearms in 1526 had compromised the military organization of papal forces before the Sack of Rome. Cosimo I hailed from a branch of the Medici clan previously marginalized from accession to power. He even had family ties with Guicciardini's wife, Maria Salviati. Cosimo I was

---

19. Catherine Fletcher, *The Black Prince of Florence: The Spectacular Life and Treacherous World of Alessandro de' Medici* (London: Bodley Head, 2016).

only seventeen at the time of Alessandro's murder. Guicciardini, this time miscalculating his own self-interest as well as that of the future duke, purportedly considered Cosimo I as the perfect vehicle for an optimate-moderated duchy. However, Cosimo I proved to be more politically astute than Guicciardini and perhaps did not want to arouse more anti-Medici sentiment by retaining Guicciardini, who was openly despised by remnants of the city's republican faction as a Medici lackey. Cosimo I quickly moved to establish himself as duke of Florence, dispatching Guicciardini from service in Florentine politics and paying lip service to Guicciardini's hopes for a duchy tempered by counsel from an optimate oligarchy.

When Guicciardini took forced retirement from political life, the Medici held Florence as hereditary dukes without any pretense of representative, constitutional rule. Guicciardini's hopes for a political future of Florence where a semblance of representative government might temper the authoritarianism of a Medici duchy were dashed. The Florentine exiles attempted to retake Florence militarily, but Cosimo I defeated them at the Battle of Montemurlo in 1537 with Spanish military support. Guicciardini later declined further papal appointment in Romagna to work on his *History of Italy*, allowing him a forum to explain and understand his actions and the fate of Italy in a wider global and even divine context.[20]

Guicciardini's abilities, the acumen and the grit he displayed at the siege of Parma as described in the "Report of the Defense of Parma," had served the Medici clan rather than his optimate peers and ultimately Guicciardini himself. Guicciardini had worked for authoritarianism with all of its abuses, wastes, and prejudices. He actively opposed the more heroic if irrational currents of his time: whether Savonarola's pre-Protestant religious fundamentalism or the desperate, heroic republicanism of Francesco Ferruccio and the doomed exiles who fought the Medici duchy for which Guicciardini was chief advocate.

The flaw in Guicciardini's mindset and approach was to focus on self-interest without accounting for irrational and unpredictable aspects in human behavior. Guicciardini seemingly miscalculated the intentions of the wily Spanish king Ferdinand II, whose military aid brought a Medici coup in 1512. His counsel and conduct of papal forces led to the

20. Emanuela Lugnani Scarano, "Le redazioni dei *Ricordi* e la storia del pensiero guicciardiniano al 1512 al 1530," *Giornale storico della letteratura italiana* 147 (1970): 183–259. See also Emanuela Lugnani Scarano, *La ragione e le cose: Tre studi su Guicciardini* (Pisa: ETS, 1980).

defeat and disgrace in 1527 of his benefactor, the Medici pope Clement VII. Guicciardini did reconsider the specter of Savonarolian prophecy in the aftermath of the Sack of Rome. However, he continued to focus on material self-interest rather than on impulses he could not calculate or understand: Savonarolian religious fundamentalism, the fervent anti-Medici sentiment of Florentine republicans or oligarchs, the gritty lust for violence and pillage of religiously inspired troops, or even the petty jealousies among the European elite, which led to events like the murder of Duke Alessandro. Guicciardini's method of calculating the self-interests of participants and planning for action therefrom was unreliable because it did not allow for the irrational, the unpredictable, and factors of greater breadth than Guicciardini's ability for foresight and adaptation. Guicciardini's advocacy and defense of a hereditary Medici duchy under Alessandro de' Medici became just another step toward the foundation of the Medici duchy. When the next Medici duke, Cosimo I, removed Guicciardini from any position in his regime after Alessandro's murder, Guicciardini's marginalization was complete and the flaw in his philosophy evident. Guicciardini's ultimate contribution may be as a precursor of the social science of economics. Guicciardini's concentration on self-interest presages the reduction by modern economists of human activity to quantifiable data. However, the results in terms of accuracy of prediction are not markedly more reliable than the celestial calculations of the astrologers or the divinations of the soothsayers who were replaced as the principal counselors for government policy.

TO HIMSELF

Spain, 1513

Francesco, you find yourself having surpassed thirty years of age. You recognize the grandeur of many and countless benefits received from God. You also have the intelligence to understand the vanity of this life. For if the just may lay their hopes in the future, the wicked must fear it. Accordingly, the reasons mentioned above should lead you to decide to behave more like an older rather than a younger man. God has endowed you with so many things of this world. Your country and its citizens freely and authoritatively assigned you to rank and responsibility beyond your age and years. Up to this day, divine grace has afforded you more reputation and glory than you perhaps deserve. Therefore, you must conduct yourself in spiritual and divine matters by undertaking works so God in His benevolence may grant you the same role in paradise that you desire in this world. Certainly, your life and behavior until today have not been worthy of a man who is noble, the son of a good father, raised in a holy manner. Nor have you kept to that standard of prudence by which you must judge yourself, nor can you continue to act thus without absolute shame.

REPORT ON SPAIN

In Spain while I was ambassador there in the year 1512–1513

The ancients gave the name Spain to the entire province between the Pyrenees Mountains and the Mediterranean and the ocean as demonstrated by sources that divided it into three sections encompassing the entire area: Tarraconense, Lusitanica, and Betica. Some ancient writers erroneously called the territory Iberia after the Ibero River, commonly known as the Ebro, extending the term to the entire region. The Ibero's source is near the Pyrenees Mountains and afterward reaches the border of Castile running through Aragon and Catalonia. Therefore, to give this name to all of Spain is unreasonable since the Ibero River passes through only a small part and is not even the main river. There are rivers of similar portage, such as the Beti, from which comes the name Betica, called Guadalquivir in the Moorish tongue; the Anna, today called the Guadiana; the Tago; and the Duero.

The Romans divided Spain by nearer and farther sections, with the nearer section from the Ibero to the Pyrenees and the farther from the Ibero to the sea. The division was not intended to be equal, like dividing a rich patrimony between a legitimate brother and a bastard. Rather, it was because they learned of the nearer part first. For a period, the Ibero was at the end of their empire, as demonstrated by the first confederation with the Carthaginians following the first Punic War.

Today, Spain is divided into three main kingdoms, not according to size but because there are different kings. Aragon, which includes Catalonia and Valencia, is ruled by Don Ferdinand of Aragon. Castile, which contains the rest of Spain to the sea to the border with Portugal as well as Galicia, Biscay, Andalusia, and Granada, is today ruled by Queen Joanna,

FIG. 3 | Giorgio Vasari and Marco Marchetti, mural in Palazzo Vecchio, ca. 1556–58. Lorenzo de' Medici kneeling and kissing the hand of Ferdinand II of Aragon. Below in an oval is Piero di Lorenzo de' Medici. Photo: Wikimedia Commons / Petar Milošević.

daughter of the aforementioned Don Ferdinand and the queen, Lady Isabel.[1] There remains a small portion across the Pyrenees Mountains and the Ibero River called Navarra, which has its own king. Despite there nominally being many other kingdoms, because of former rule by different princes, the two main ones are those described above. The third section, Portugal, borders the kingdoms of Castile and the ocean and is ruled by King Don Manuel. It is a small province known more for the great commerce conducted by merchants from Lisbon and for having discovered Calcutta and other new places than for any other reason.

The dimensions from the highest sections toward the Pyrenees is about seven hundred miles, which is the number of miles from Barcelona to Santa Maria at Lands End. From the other side, top to bottom, it is about five hundred miles, which is how many miles there must be from the Pyrenees to the Straits of Gibraltar and the ocean.

The province is sparsely populated, with little cultivation and few castles. Between one large urban area and another, one rarely even sees a

1. Queen Isabel of Castile (1451–1504).

house, and there are effectively few inhabitants. There are lovely cities like Barcelona, Saragossa, Valencia, Granada, and Seville. However, the cities are few for such a large kingdom, and the rest is wasteland. There are few forts. They have ugly buildings full of mud and garbage, most of which are in the countryside. The province is fertile and abundant, harvesting more grain than needed for its own use. The same goes for wine, which they send to Flanders and England. There are great quantities of oil, which is produced each year in the kingdom by the aforementioned places and Alexandria amount to more than sixty thousand ducats. The most fertile parts are the lower regions of Andalusia and Granada and would be even more fertile if everything were cultivated. However, apart from the land that has been worked, and not well cultivated, the rest is hard. The kingdom produces much wool, said to amount to two hundred and fifty thousand ducats, as well as fine silks produced in the lower regions. At Biscay, there is iron and steel in good quantity, as well as grain, leather, alum, and much merchandise. The nation would be wealthy if it were industrious and enterprising. The country is cold toward the Pyrenees Mountains and very hot toward Andalusia and Granada, and more temperate in the area along the Mediterranean.

The men of this nation are saturnine, dark in color, small in stature, prideful by nature, and have a fiery temper. In their opinion, no nation compares to theirs. In conversation, they exalt their own qualities and they seek to boast when they can. They do not like foreigners and are quite rude to them. They are inclined and quite adept at arms, perhaps more so than any other Christian nation. They hold honor in great esteem and, in order not to besot it, are universally untroubled by the idea of death. That they do not have able men-at-arms is true. However, they make much use of lancers. For the service of the country, many fine horses are raised to support these tactics rather than for men-at-arms owing to the constant wars with the Moors, who also used this military tactic. Their light cavalry and their lancers do not use crossbows, which are therefore of little consequence in battle. They are more adept at chasing down and disturbing rear encampments than engaging in the open. The infantry, especially in the kingdoms of Castile, has a powerful reputation, is well maintained, and is considered superior to all others in the defense and conquest of lands where physical ability and agility are valuable, which is also useful in battle. I leave to others the debate of whether the Swiss or the Spanish are better in the open field.

They begin by organizing themselves in the Swiss manner, which I am not sure is consistent with their nature because by maintaining such formations, they do not take advantage of their abilities, the aspect in which they are superior to others. They all go about armed. In former times, besides foreign wars, they were trained owing to experience in internal disputes, with every faction under arms every day. Spain previously had more mounted soldiers and more trained soldiers than today because in the time of peace and justice under Queen Isabel they were not developed. For this reason, it is my opinion that Spanish arms are less worthy than they ever have been.

They are considered subtle and astute, even if they have no ability in any art, whether mechanical or liberal. Almost all the artistry at the court of the king is from France or other nations. They also are not given to commerce, which they consider shameful. All of them have the notion of being a *hidalgo*, a nobleman, in their heads.[2] They would rather take up arms with little remuneration, or serve a lord incurring a thousand petty struggles, or become highwaymen before the reign of the current king than submit to any form of commerce or business. Although today, in some parts of Spain, they have started to work in textiles, as in the gold embroidering in Valencia, Toledo, and Seville. However, most of the nation is hostile to this sort of activity. Therefore, they take up the arts and work when necessity calls, and then they repose until they have spent everything they have earned. Therefore, manufactured goods here are quite expensive. The same may be said of the peasants working the fields, who do not want to exert themselves unless there is extreme need. Thus, the country is less cultivated than it could be, and the portion that is worked is poorly maintained.

There is much poverty, which I believe is due not so much to the quality of the land as to their lack of desire to work it. Nor do they leave Spain but prefer to send the resources of their kingdom to other nations for manufacture by others, as is done with wool and silk, which they sell to others. Then they buy the finished clothes and clothing. They are miserly, which must be a consequence of their poverty and the great luxury in which the few great lords of the kingdom live, from which one can infer

---

2. A *hidalgo* was a Spanish nobleman without a secure claim on the family patrimony; therefore, he often had to find placement in other venues such as the military. Here Guicciardini refers to the attitude of the nobility, which disdained manual labor or commerce because of their status.

that the rest live with great parsimony. When they do have something to spend, they find a way to keep it on their person or packed away, so that it does not remain at home, where they live in extreme pettiness and amazing squalor. Even though they know how to live with little, they are not without greed when earning. They are quite avaricious and, since they have few skills, are prone to thievery. In former times, when there was less law and order in the kingdom, there were assassins everywhere, aided by a landscape with many mountainous areas and few inhabitants. Since they are clever, they make good thieves. The French are said to make better lords than the Spanish, because even though both steal from their subjects, the French spend everything immediately, whereas the Spaniard accumulates. Since the Spaniard is subtler, he must be better at stealing.

They are not given to learning, and one cannot find in the nobility or in others any hint or, quite rarely, any knowledge of the Latin tongue. They are very religious in outwardly superficial display, but not in practice. They conduct countless ceremonies with great reverence and grand humility in word and address and kissing of hands. Everyone is a lord. Everyone commands. However, they are to be kept at arm's length and trusted little.

The nation is one of dissemblers, which all ranks of men master. Their reputation for cunning and intelligence lies herein rather than elsewhere. It is a Punic intelligence with Andalusians being the ablest, from which it is said their sense of ceremony and hypocrisy derives. Among the Andalusians, the ablest are from Cordoba, a city famous as the homeland of the Great Captain.[3]

Their women are well treated while husbands are alive and even afterward. Not only are their dowries reimbursed, but there is also an account of everything the husband possessed upon receipt. Any earnings or profits are divided in half and freely allotted to the woman, who may remarry and do with it as she pleases, even if they produced children in common. Not only is what was possessed prior divided, but also anything purchased after the marriage contract. Thus, if the husband came into property after having received from the woman, and then reinvested in something durable, then everything would be split in half even if the heirs could demonstrate that those properties had been acquired prior to the marriage. Also, if the husband's holdings decrease, the woman does not suffer. Despite such indulgence, they still lack a reputation for

---

3. Gonzalo Fernández de Córdoba (1453–1515), Spanish military leader.

faithfulness, despite severe punishments for adultery. A man may without penalty kill a woman and her lover caught in the act or after proving they committed the act.

Until our time, this nation has been more oppressed and had less glory and empire than any nation in Europe. In ancient times, the Gauls occupied and subjugated many provinces, holding them long enough for the provinces to take their names, a demonstration that they were perpetual inhabitants and owners. What they called Celtiberia is today Aragon and was conquered and inhabited by those French peoples, the Celts—as the poet writes, *Gallorum Celte miscentes nomen Hiberis*[4]—and called by them Gallecia, which today is Galicia. Afterward, the Carthaginians occupied a large part, before the Romans subsequently conquered everything. Then the Vandals took over, from whence came the name Andalusia. Finally, the African Moors took not only southern regions but had dominion up to Aragon and Castile bordering in some sections on the Pyrenees Mountains. Up to our day, they still held Granada. Therefore, Spain has long been under servitude, without empire over others, which cannot be said of Italy, France, Germany, or of any other region of Christendom. This is certainly notable, since the region is so warlike, and was thus even in ancient times. Sources, especially Livy, confirm that Spain was the first Roman conquest outside Italy on the continent, and the last they were to relinquish. To understand why such a warlike nation was defeated by so many different nations, of different religions, and held so long under servitude, would be useful.

One explanation could be that it had better soldiers than leaders. That its men were abler in combat than in governing and commanding. While I was discussing this question one day with King Ferdinand, he said to me that this nation has a capacity in war but is disorganized, and that positive results would come only under someone able to organize. In fact, the ancient sources have more praise for their ferocity in taking up arms and starting wars than for anything else. Livy calls them people born to make war and at another point says that they wage war with more temerity than consistency. I am not sure if this is the true explanation. It seems noteworthy that such a large province with so many men ready at arms has always lost so many wars to other nations over so many periods, only because there was no one able to rule them. Nor am I sure

---

4. Lucan, *Civil War* 4.9.1.

that a sufficient explanation is to ascribe their condition to being open to foreign nations, to France by land, and to Africa and Italy by sea, because other provinces are similarly exposed by land and sea to many enemies. This may provide an explanation for their infighting in accordance with their nature as a nation of restless intelligence. Thus, because of a tradition lacking in the basics of civilized living, the poor turn to banditry. The kingdom was not unified but divided among many kingdoms and lords, from which today the names remain: Aragon, Valencia, Castile, Toledo, Leon, Cordoba, Seville, Jaen, Portugal, Granada, and Gibraltar. Invaders never had to fight a unified Spain, but one part after another, which is an underlying characteristic continuing to the present. Today, we see the nation not only no longer under servitude but beginning to exert dominion over others, which is a result of the prudence of its rulers, and the joining into one kingdom and government of Aragon and Castile, as will be discussed further.

The two kingdoms of Aragon and Castile were ruled at length by different kings until the marriage between Don Ferdinand, only son of King Don John of Aragon, and Lady Isabel, daughter of King Don John of Castile. After the death of her brother King Don Enrico, she inherited the kingdom of Castile. The marriage was very fortunate, for besides joining many other kingdoms, it joined a remarkable woman with a very prudent prince. As was customary, the kingdoms of Castile came as dowry to King Don Ferdinand to form a single lineage and bloodline. As is the custom with many other kingdoms, males have the right to succession before females; thereby everything became his hereditary kingdom. Nor was the acquisition without difficulty as King Don Henry was reputed to be impotent in sexual relations, yet his wife had a daughter recognized by many to be by King Don Enrico. Thus, King Don Afonso of Portugal came forward planning to take the daughter as his wife with the support of many of the grandees of Castile. The opposing faction consisted of many lords and most of the people. Both kings participated personally in the Battle of Toro, with the war ending after King Don Ferdinand's victory.[5]

Having thus acquired the government of the kingdom, the king and queen found themselves in great difficulty owing to the chaos reigning over much of Castile. King Don Henry had been a man of limited ability who had distributed much of his possessions and ceded all the cities and

---

5. Battle of Toro (1475), for Spanish succession.

their incomes to the nobility, which reduced him to extreme poverty and impotence. Since the grandees had prospered and were intractable by nature, they became so ardent that neither the king nor his ministers were ever obeyed. Questions of law and order were ignored to the point that all Castile was replete with bandits. One could not leave a town or any large settlement without significant risk of murder. All the cities and castles of the kingdom were factious and divided, with daily, armed conflicts, murder, and bloodshed. Another ugly and reproachable infection of the entire kingdom was that it was replete with Jews and heretics. Most of the populace was besotted by this depravity found in all offices and stations of the kingdom in such numbers and power that if no remedy had been taken, in a few years all of Spain would have abandoned the Catholic faith.

Thus, there was the chaos in the very heart of the kingdom. Beyond its borders, Granada, a noteworthy Spanish province, remained in the hands of the Moors, incurring infamy and weakness upon the king. Despite all these scourges, the happy couple of Ferdinand and Isabel overcame every difficulty owing to their virtue and fortune.

First, after some time, steadily and without provoking damage, they plucked everything King Don Henry had inadvisably lost from the crown and given into the hands of the grandees, reducing all of them, little by little, to obedience before the king. Under the command of one man and one voice, everyone either obeyed or went to prison. Then followed the imposition of severe justice, with murderers dispatched by being shot alive with arrows. Under the order of Saint Hermandad,[6] if anyone claiming to have been robbed pressed charges at a location and provided information about the perpetrators, then those in said location were required to conduct a search for a given number of miles. If they found no one, then they had to notify nearby locations one by one, which would then have to assist in the search, and in turn give notice to others. Thus, detection became difficult to avoid. This meticulous dragnet, together with the severity of punishment, rendered the roads quite safe except for a few places, which owing to their characteristics are nearly impossible to keep clear.

In matters of the faith, they organized the entire kingdom under the authority of apostolic inquisitors who seized the goods of those found guilty and even burned people at the stake, dumbfounding all. In Cordoba, they burned between a hundred and two hundred people on a

---

6. Guicciardini is referring to the Order of Saint Hermandad, Spain's first police force.

single morning. Thus, many of those infected fled. Those remaining carry on by dissembling. However, the general opinion is that were the fear to subside, many would return to their accursed state.

Having tidied up these matters, they turned their attention to Granada. After waging war over the course of years, they conquered it entirely. After the king fled, they found his two small sons and had them baptized. Even if not obligated from this point, they issued an edict requiring everyone to convert to Christianity. Anyone who did not wish to do so would have to leave Spain. Thus, almost all the rich and powerful left for Africa, but those who remained were baptized. This earned them the title of "most Catholic Kings." Thus, throughout Spain today all the inhabitants are Christians, except in the kingdoms of Aragon where there are many Moors who keep to their mosques and ceremonies, which is tolerated by the kings because they pay extremely high taxes.

Nor in these actions should any less glory be afforded to the queen. In fact, the consensus is that everyone attributed to her the greater part of the credit, because all matters pertaining to Castile passed principally through her hands. She gave everyone her utmost attention, and in most matters, it was no less useful to persuade her than her husband. This was not because the king was in anyway unworthy, as evidenced by subsequent events demonstrating his virtues. Rather, one must say that the queen was so remarkable that the king himself would yield to her, since these kingdoms were in fact hers, and he was also inclined to achieve a positive outcome. She was reportedly a great believer in justice. In matters of her own person she was quite proper, and much admired and feared by her subjects. She coveted glory, was of a liberal and generous spirit, and is comparable to any remarkable woman of any period. They also say that even though the king was naturally inclined to gambling, out of respect for her, he played rarely, and in games that were quite ordinary. This may be proven because after her time, he took up gambling in larger and less honorable venues, spending more time than befitting a prince with the government of so many kingdoms upon his shoulders.[7]

Thus, they reorganized affairs in their own states and provided Spain with a strong and solid government, free from ancient servitude and infamy. Now let us return to the first topic of discussion. The glory of this nation has increased also because of the recovery of the state of Perpignan,

---

7. King Ferdinand II (1452–1516) survived Queen Isabel, who died in 1504.

which had been ceded to the king of France by King Don John in exchange for the kingdom of Naples. They also won and conquered many important places in Africa, along with newly found islands Hispaniola, San Juan, and others from where they extract gold. One fifth of the gold goes to the king, the rest to whoever does the extracting. Thus, in our times Spain has become enlightened and left behind its traditional darkness.

Certainly, whatever has been said of the queen, when speaking of this province, also applies to the king. There is no need to mention the grandeur of his current glory, his behavior and customs after the death of the queen. What he has done is known to the entire world. He has been able to retain the kingdoms of Castile not as king but as regent for his daughter Joanna, who is out of her mind.[8]

The works that he has undertaken, his words and demeanor, and the common opinion therefrom, demonstrate that he is a very wise man. He is extremely secretive and divulges nothing important unless out of necessity. He could not be more patient and lives in a very ordered manner, spending time in the desire to understand and have a hand in all the great and even petty matters in his kingdom. Even though he appears willing to consider everyone's opinion, he is the one who decides and handles everything. He is commonly considered avaricious, although this does not proceed from his nature. He has become so because of an income small in comparison to the great expenditures and important enterprises he undertakes. He thus places limits on expenses as much as he is able. He has been adept at arms before and after becoming king. He speaks with great reverence about divine matters, with demonstrable religiosity in duties and at ceremonies, which is a characteristic of the entire nation. He is not educated but displays great humanity, handling audiences easily with appropriate responses and grand demeanor, so that very few are left unsatisfied by his words. He has a reputation for not keeping his promises. Perhaps he promises without intention of keeping his promises, or perhaps events cause him to change outlook, after which he does not consider what he said previously. I believe that he can dissimulate above all other men, although I am not sure this is true. A reputation for being wise always creates suspicion that it results from artifice, backtracking, or that everything is performed out of self-interest. However, such charges

---

8. Joanna of Castile (1479–1555), also known as Joanna the Mad owing to her mental illness, which was reportedly exacerbated after the death of her husband, Philip I (1478–1506).

may be unfounded for he is a quite able and remarkable king with many virtues. Nor can he be accused, truly or falsely, of being illiberal, nor a poor keeper of his word. For the rest, he acts with great decorum and moderation. He is not boastful about himself, nor does he allow anything to leave his mouth except words that are weighted and appropriate for wise and good men.

Nor out of so many virtues has he lacked fortune. To the present date, he may be considered amongst the most fortunate. He went from being the second-born son of a poor king of Aragon to become firstborn. He had a remarkable wife with many kingdoms as dowry, and he never lacked fortune in any enterprise he undertook. Besides much success, he was also presented the opportunity to start just wars in Granada, in Africa, and lastly in this war against France over the succession in Naples.[9] This involved a very close relative of his to whom he had given hope of sending aid after facing opposition. Nor is it just a convenient justification to say that that kingdom was his by inheritance, since his uncle, King Alfonso, died without legitimate children and had acquired it with Aragonese forces. Had he acquired it as something not belonging to Aragon, then this king could never have had any cause for dispute. What is a less justifiable reason, invoked at the time by himself and the queen, was that they acted to prevent the kingdom from ending up in the hands of the king of France. Therefore, it seemed better to them to have some part rather than nothing, an explanation that seems more self-serving than honest. His fortune was lacking only when it came to children. The only male died shortly after being married. As for the females, they were married to the firstborns of kings. Yet, the first, the wife of the king of Portugal, was soon widowed. She was remarried to King Don Manuel but died shortly thereafter in childbirth, leaving a small son who would have to rule these kingdoms, although he also died shortly thereafter. The second, who is queen today, soon lost King Philip, her strong and powerful husband, and then she lost her wits. From the third, who married King Don Manuel, he had no further unhappiness. The fourth, married to the firstborn of the king of England, soon lost her husband and had to marry the second-born. Even to these misfortunes may be credited some positive outcomes, because if the male or the first of the females were alive, or the second were in command of her faculties, it would have been

---

9. A war between Spain and France over control of Naples, 1499–1504.

easy for him to retire to Aragon. In everything else, he has had perpetual fortune, except when King Don Phillip came to Castile, when he jokingly thought to have caused some offense.

Today, there is great strength in these joined kingdoms of Spain, especially for the number of armed men and good horses, of which the real fiber lies in Castile, and from whence comes the main source of tax revenue. In fact, the kingdom of Aragon is of little financial use to the king, because owing to ancient privileges, the nobility pays nearly nothing. Not only do they have immunity from payment, but in civil and criminal matters they may appeal to the king, who cannot control them. Queen Isabel was so annoyed by their privileges and freedoms that she remarked, "Aragon is not ours, we should go forth and reconquer it." Castile is not like this, for the people pay quite dearly and the word alone of the king prevails over all the laws. I do not know the details of their entire budget, which cannot be that large and is overwhelmed by many perpetual and continuing expenses, provisions, and salaries. Thus, the greatness of the nation has impoverished the king. Without Castile, he would be a beggar because from the kingdoms of Aragon he receives almost nothing, except when there is an outbreak of war and they are required to provide six hundred men-at-arms for the defense of the realm. Even if sometimes they voluntarily provide some aid, it is irregular, and they cannot be forced to do otherwise. The king depends upon extraordinary revenues, stipends, confiscations from the Inquisition, and the apostolic licensure of the tithes of priests, which all come out of Castile.

The king regularly maintains men-at-arms for deployment in Italy, referred to as men of arms of the guard. He gives each one eighty ducats per year. He also has another type of combined militia, which maintains men-at-arms and light cavalry to whom every year he gives a small provision. They are each obliged to maintain a horse, whether for a man-at-arms or a lancer, and to be ready for the wars on this side. He may command them as he pleases, and when he uses them, he gives them a daily allowance that amounts to four ducats per month or thereabouts. This policy provides many benefits. First, with little regular expense he always may count upon a certain number of men-at-arms and lancers. Second, when he must deploy them, he does not have to pay more than a month or two in advance. Third, he may disband them when he deems necessary. However, if he needs them for two months, he may pay them only for two months. Thereby there is no need to hire any others for at least a year or two. These men-at-arms in the combined militia, as was said, do not have more than one horse apiece.

His guard numbers one hundred pikemen, to whom he gives a bit less than three ducats each per month. I believe he keeps about one thousand five hundred infantrymen in the guard, under the same terms. When they are not engaged in war, they are stationed about four or five leagues from the court, which is usual procedure for this king, following the return to Italy. The other infantry he requires are recruited day by day, without, I believe, much expense, owing to the general poverty of men and their inclination to take up arms, which can provide him numbers that are quite large. Therefore, he has enough of an army and enough subjects in his lands. Although verily, the men-at-arms are not adept on horseback, nor are they considered so. The lancers are excellent because they are well trained and have good horses. However, these lancers remain one-dimensional since thus far they do not use the pike on horseback, just lances. The infantry has a good reputation, especially for conquering territory, but they are rather poorly armed. Most have only a sword and a buckler. These soldiers have the quality of being extremely patient in the face of discomfort, and they know how to live on very little when required.

Besides these militias, Spain also provides militia for the Christian religion. Because of the former oppression by the Moors, three orders for knight commanders were instituted in Castile: the Saint Jacob, the Alcantara, and the Calatrava, which are similar to the Knights of Rhodes in terms of stipends and benefits. They have considerable income and are obliged to combat any Moors coming to Spain. Some of these orders, like the main one, the Saint Jacob, have no other duty. These knights may marry and live secularly in every aspect. Each of these orders has a grand master serving for life who comes from the knights of the order. This grand master confers all stipends according to his prerogative. The king and queen obtained apostolic authority to control these officers and their stipends, so today they are subject to the king. By account of revenues, all three of these stipendiaries amount every year to more than 120,000 ducats. These stipends may be distributed as deemed fit to apprentices and favorites. Their initiative to demote the Castilian nobility was also useful since these stipends often went to the grandees. Having such revenue, and the ability to confer such hefty incomes, allowed them to draw the entire Castilian nobility to their side.

The court of the king functions by providing for those who render services and are officers in his house. They all live in houses of their own possession, with provisions made according to the nature of the people and locations administered. He eats alone in the presence of many others, except on great or solemn occasions when the king and queen eat together. Others do not eat with him, except when he wants to bestow supreme recognition on some great lord of his realm or upon some important ambassador, which rarely occurs. Anyone who wants to address him when he is seated must kneel without rising, unless commanded otherwise by him. In private, he allows men of quality to be seated. In public, when he is seated no one else may be seated, except ambassadors. The custom is to kiss the hand at first encounters or upon taking leave, although he, like the ambassadors, or others of similar rank, resists offering his hand. If he offers directly upon entry or departure, then the custom is to be observed. However, out of kindness he does not always offer his hand. The Spaniards are pleased when their king demonstrates kindness, so long as he maintains gravitas and majesty. The court moves frequently from site to site, and whoever follows the court is assigned lodging in the homes of others. It is up to the master of the house to provide from their household or farm. This is the custom only in Castile because the kingdoms of Aragon have the prerogative not to provide lodgings unless they so desire.

With all of this, as stated, this nation is universally poor. Not even the grandees, as much as I can tell, live splendidly with great sumptuousness, not just in furnishings, tapestries, and silverware, which are also found among the people who have such possessions, but in every aspect of their living expenses. There is a considerable number of courtiers, who are commonly provided for, although many live scattered about. They always accompany the lord when riding. Some are allotted housing expenses, others receive daily board for themselves and their horses, which they call a spending ration. This is also the practice when wanting to honor a foreigner. Many of the foremost lords maintain a couple hundred pikemen and lancers—some more, others less, according to their capacity—who are allowed use of land. They set great tables with hearty meals and are served with great pomp and ceremony as if they were kings. Men kneel to speak with them. They make themselves objects of adoration in an indication of the natural tendency toward pride in this nation. During the reigns of other kings, these lords of Castile governed everything and were not very obedient and did not allow themselves to be managed by the king. The king and queen reduced them to their present state, so they no longer have their usual grandeur and authority. Nevertheless, there are many dukes, marquis, and counts whose revenue does not exceed forty thousand ducats, and few who even reach that much.

Even though they assiduously keep to ceremonies, displaying reverence in matters concerning God, the practice of the divine cult does not flourish, nor is it practiced in an orderly fashion. In fact, there is much disorganization. Nor can one find any monastery or convent with a reputation for holiness or exemplary living. In truth, there are many bishoprics with ample revenues, which have a temporal as well as spiritual role. They say that the bishopric of Toledo reaches fifty thousand ducats. Seville and Compostela surpass fifteen thousand. There are many others with six, eight, and even ten thousand ducats. There are many fine churches and abbeys. The wealth of these ecclesiastical sites is due in large part to the tithe paid by the people, who give one-tenth of everything they have, whether in livestock or possessions, which amounts to a great deal. Of this tithe, about two-ninths go to the king; the rest is partly distributed among the clergy, and partly to the bishop of the diocese.

The revenue of the entire realm may be calculated thus, as far as I can tell. The kingdoms of Castile provide a little under three hundred of about eight hundred thousand ducats, of which about half goes to courts and obligations separate from revenue. Then there are nondiscretionary provisions and salaries; from these the king does not see a cent. Of the remaining four hundred thousand, there are the expenses of his court, officers, the expenses of the houses of the queen, and fortresses, which does not leave much. He has revenue from the stipendiaries, added to which are expenses from matching funds and obligations. So, there is no surplus, and he declares that there is nothing left. He does take revenue from these newly found islands. One-fifth of all the gold taken is his, said to amount to about fifty thousand castellanos[10] each year, some say seventy thousand. In the past, he took a great deal from the Inquisition, because every sentence, whether a matter of life or something else, included the seizure of goods. Even if much of this was in real estate, he still took a good profit, whereas today there is little. He also has regular seizures from other crimes, which are not numerous.

---

10. Gold coin minted under Ferdinand and Isabel.

From the wars against the infidels and in defense of the church, he gained apostolic licenses and tithes of the clergy. Thus, he obtained jubilees, indulgences, and the possessions of those who had contraband or had committed other crimes. Corresponding to this, besides expenses listed above, he had nondiscretionary expenses for the guards at Orano, Mazalchibir, Béjaïa, and other places on the Barbary Coast. Thus, adding everything together, one could judge that the expenses come very close to revenues. Even though there are rumors that he has a great treasure in Aragon, those who are well informed do not believe this to be so. The revenues from the kingdoms of Aragon, Sardinia, Majorca, and Minorca are a trifle, nor does Sicily offer much. Much of the revenue from Naples, some sixty thousand, is given every year to the queens. Much of the liquid earnings are assigned to Aragonese lords whose estates were ceded to the Angious[11] under the terms of surrender with France, so that these lords receive the equivalent either in currency or estates. Because of all these expenses, as well as those for the men-at-arms whose provision is a continuing outlay, or guards of fortresses and galleys, it is reputed that he does not regularly receive more than thirty thousand ducats a year.

Besides the revenues above, he has apostolic privileges, collecting ecclesiastical fees of about one-tenth and sometimes two-tenths in his kingdoms of Castile and Aragon. However, the one that provides the most is Castile alone. This is because when the kingdom of Aragon provides some subsidy to the court, there are always exclusions whereby for a period the clergy does not have to pay any form of tithe or subsidy under what the king received from the pope. Thus, the burden falls only on Castile, which determined of its own accord how much tithe to pay, arriving at the amount of about sixty thousand ducats. He also obtained an ecclesiastical subsidy from the wars against the infidels, called crusades, out of which there is much booty for those who take it, as well as the authority to absolve almost anyone in trials in matters of life or death, for a fee of two *reals* apiece, a coin that is eleven to the ducat. Under this bull, he also had the authority to decide many cases of usury, which involve lesser or greater levels of restitution according to the nature of the cases. Thus, everything having to do with war against the infidels must pass through the king. According to this royal privilege, he chooses ministers to help

---

11. The surname of the French kings.

him in every possible manner, direct or indirect, to divide and extend to an infinite number of cases.

This authority was first conceded for a determined period, after which the king obtained extensions from time to time, which he retains to this day. He obtained much at the outset, since it was a new operation. Reportedly, the year in which the king took Malaga, he received eight hundred thousand ducats. Afterward this decreased, because only a bit came from the cities, whereas much more came from surrounding counties, which were perhaps motivated by fear, so that today he regularly takes three hundred thousand ducats. The popes may think that they are conceding him a pittance. However, the revenue has been consistent enough so that without these subsidies this king would not have retaken Granada nor any other foreign kingdoms, and would have had difficulty retaining Aragon and Castile. Therefore, a prudent pope, who understands matters well, would allow concessions that greatly profit the church, since there is no king more obliged to help the church than this one, since by her authority he has profited so much. The popes still please him by conferring bishoprics according to his designs, in particular in the kingdom of Granada where Innocent[12] conceded tutelage not only of bishoprics but also of parishes and all their benefits, leaving to his discretion the assignment of their earnings and income as he deemed fit.

---

12. Pope Innocent VIII (1432–1492).

HOW TO ENSURE THE STATE FOR THE HOUSE OF THE MEDICI

The return to Florence of the Medici brought momentous changes for the entire city. Except for a desperate and ruined few who desired their return out of dire need since they had no other path to prosperity. Their return pains not only their enemies, but the entire population, which would have willingly remained with the popular government. Even their friends who had been satisfied with the state before 1494 were not overjoyed. From their decreased status, they would now be forced to travail for the city, incurring ruinous burdens for themselves and for others. Then came the miraculous elevation of Cardinal Medici into Pope Leo X, which immediately changed everyone's hopes and plans.[1] The general opinion is that this pontificate removed the Medici from a state of neediness or suspicion and put our affairs into an advantageous position. Those who were hostile were reassured they would be able to live in a reasonable manner. Those who were supporters threw themselves into service of the state with heated vitality. The people hoped for the sweetness of peace without the burden of taxes. There was the expectation of the reform of public revenue and bonds under the assurance that everything would be administered properly, and the grandeur of such a young and powerful pontiff would improve conditions. However, now that we are already at the end of three years of the pontificate, there have not been results supporting these expectations. The partisans are not content; in fact, they are distant and detached. The people are even more discontented, laden with jealousy and suspicion. At

---

1. Giovanni di Lorenzo de' Medici (born in 1475) ruled the Papal States as Pope Leo X from 1513 to his death in 1521.

present, the city is in a miserable condition with everything harmful to the state, because it is difficult for a government to have a hostile people and to lack powerful partisans.

That the grandeur of the papacy does not allow admission of such setbacks is not a sufficient reason to dismiss them. Since times and moods change, to rely on the life of a single man is a weakness. Should he die, the consequences of this chaos would become apparent. Even while he is still alive, many issues could arise that could determine behavior. There was a taste of this last summer with the arrival of the French.[2] Confusion multiplied to such an extent that at every disruption, nobody thought to resist for the benefit of the city or of the state; instead, everyone thought only about themselves. Prudent sailors in port or in a calm sea prepare their vessels and instruments to resist a future storm. Similarly, while in a state of leisure and comfort, the one with a hand on the helm of this state should put things in order and arrange all the parts of the body politic so that if there were to be some incident, then one could rely upon all its strengths and virtues. Certainly, whoever carefully considers the causes and the origins of these ills should not rely, without great misapprehension, on the service of such a sickly patient who is not in optimal nor even in stable condition.

The first basis for cure is for the one who has the state to want to make it more powerful. He must be convinced of the profit and fruit to be gained thereby because nobody puts time and effort into an endeavor that offers no satisfaction. Nobody should have any doubt that this is part of their plan, except those who would be better served if they had no doubts, which are the Medici themselves. For by having such a young pontiff, they have placed their sights so high that the government of this city seems but a trifle to them. One can see that it is among the least of the capital they possess. First proof of this came from Giuliano,[3] who was still without prospects and yet rejected it as a meager posting of little pith and moment. Nor was Lorenzo far from this line of thinking as much as may be understood.[4] However, this opinion was quite unfounded because retaining this government means having authority as owners of this city and its entire dominion. Between them and any lord with any might, there is no real difference expect the manner of commanding. If

---

2. The invasion of Italy by French king Francis I in 1515.
3. Giuliano de' Medici (1478–1534), later Pope Clement VII (1523–1534).
4. Lorenzo di Piero de' Medici (1492–1519), to whom Machiavelli would dedicate *The Prince* (1513).

the words of one lord impart laws and determine discussion, then here they also do as they please, acting through others or magistrates who are their creations and obey their slightest gesture.

Commanding a city and dominion of this breadth, one of the main states and cities of Italy, affords great power and reputation. While the pontiff is still alive, they could take advantage of the opportunities and power to acquire states and achieve their goals. Once the pontiff dies, who would not realize the importance of planning to maintain the position they had acquired? For then it will be difficult, quite difficult, for them to retain other states. They will encounter powerful opposition either from neighboring states, from those who claim some title, or from the opposition of the people. If they organize themselves properly here, then once they are well established, they will have no difficulty maintaining themselves because their rule over this state will not offend or take anything away from anyone except the citizens themselves, and satisfying them, as will be explained below, is not difficult.

This manner of reasoning is so clear that there is no need to support it with examples, yet if examples are needed, one does not have to go very far. Their first attempt at acquiring a dominion was in Lombardy, where they were already forced to abandon Parma and Piacenza. Their position in Modena and Reggio is also uncertain and weak, affording little or no profit, not to mention Ferrara, which they have thought many times to return to the Duke of Ferrara. Florence offers them a steady foundation where they can establish themselves. Without Florence, anything they do will ruin them over time or at the first encounter with adversity. To retain Florence would be a solid move toward retaining all the other places. For if they were to relinquish all the others but retain Florence, they would still be considered powerful for having a state of such quality, especially by those who will recall how they received everything from a pope and are therefore not the natural rulers, but rather citizens and descendants of fathers who were powerful, but who had always lived as private citizens.

I do not want to use this forum to discuss whether it has or has not been duly considered that they have the courage to take advantage of the opportunity from the papacy to make themselves into great lords. I will say only that we have the example of the relatives of Callistus and Pius,[5]

---

5. Alfons de Borja (1378-1458), later Pope Callistus III (1455-58). Enea Silvio Bartolomeo Piccolomini (1405-1464), later Pope Pius II (1458-64).

for whom it was enough to have plucked from the pontificate some rather convenient but unremarkable holdings, which not only did they enjoy, but which they perpetuated for their descendants to the present day. To the contrary, there is the example of Valentino, which reveals how difficult it is for a private citizen to acquire a great state, and even more difficult to retain it.[6] There are infinite difficulties that come with a new principality, particularly for a new prince. Only Francesco Sforza was able to retain the state of Milan, for a variety of reasons.[7] First, he was a man of great virtue. Second, he was a great military leader of the period. He found the line of the Visconti, the natural lords, lacking. Thus, he did not have to fight anyone claiming a title. In fact, his rule seemed just since he had taken as his wife Madonna Bianca, the daughter of Duke Filippo.[8] She may not have been of legitimate birth, but she was the only one remaining of the ducal line. Added to this, he found a state that enjoyed some freedoms but was accustomed to rule by others. Thus, they were as unaccustomed to freedom as a free people would be unaccustomed to servitude. All these conditions greatly facilitated the process for retention. Rarely are those who acquire new dominions beaten, except for the greater part who are removed by free peoples or natural rulers. One could say that he came to occupy a vacant inheritance without taking anything away from anyone. In fact, the people deemed it beneficial for him to take over, because in this manner they were delivered from the jaws of their natural enemies, the Venetians.

Returning from this digression to our main topic, the second reason for the necessity of this approach is that the Medici must be persuaded to establish many, good, faithful, and trustworthy friendships in Florence on which they may rely and direct toward important endeavors. This would result in two good, healthy, and even necessary outcomes. First, when men of good reputation receive credit, authority, and benefits, they may become staunch supporters and reliable instruments for the maintenance of the state and power. Every state and eminent power needs dependents of different stations holding different offices, just as a head needs its various limbs for support and service. Alternatively, since they are young and were raised abroad, they are unaccustomed to our ways.[9] They are not

---

6. Cesare Borgia (1475–1507), illegitimate son of Pope Alexander VI.
7. Francesco Sforza (1401–1466).
8. Filippo Maria Visconti (1392–1447).
9. Lorenzo di Piero de' Medici (1492–1519) and Giuliano di Lorenzo de' Medici (1479–1516), the first Medici lords of Florence after the fall of the republic in 1512.

ready to lead and had other plans and thoughts. They have insufficient understanding of our ways and of the things specific to us for them to be able to rule this city properly. To the contrary, many times they make decisions and issue commands that cause damage and chaos, which they would not have done had they understood what was at stake. However, if there were some citizens in whom they had faith and with whom they could confer, and to whom they would allow the ability to speak the truth freely, then they could be forewarned of the importance of such matters and would not err unless they purposefully wanted to make mistakes.

Wise men with broad experience and maturity profit from the opinions and counsel of others. This is especially the case with the young and inexperienced and would allow for their natural talents and disposition to serve them well. Such deputations must be considered carefully if one wants to profit from them. That is, citizens of excellent quality in the city should be chosen who are their friends, are intelligent, and have good intentions. The way to win them over and to retain them would be to entertain them in deed and with facts, communicating with them about matters occurring in the city and in the dominion in a manner so that they may be sure that they are being trusted, rather than as some perfunctory outward ceremony. Anyone who discerns truth and love from others will necessarily return that love.

Those who ran this government until now must have believed their power was as great as others' was meager. They intended to command all the affairs of the city and its dominions on their own so that all citizens and subjects would know that nobody was so capable and that there was no need to make leaders of any other citizens, but to rely solely on them. This reduced the reputation of those within the state and benefitted nobody. It is good for it to be known that every matter depends upon a ruler and that the citizens of the state are nothing without him. However, to retain friends, one must grant favors and be recognizant, and not think that that one may be satisfied by the mere title of magistrate without any administrative duty. Instead, such functionaries must be contented by allowing them to control something. What use is it for a citizen to be an elected official, if a magistrate does not have the sway to act as one of the rulers? To appease them and to allow them space in such matters can turn citizens into supporters who will then bring in other supporters and friends to serve and benefit the state, even though, as will be stated below, nobody should be made powerful enough to pose a danger or create suspicion.

This largesse and faith must, as all things, be exercised in moderation. That is, it must not become common knowledge, nor followed blindly, as if it did not require careful consideration. Instead, a firm hand must be kept on the bridle to appraise and understand opinions with an open mind, ready to follow or to ignore like someone who listens to everything before arriving at a decision. As with the other topic, it may be said that they should not be allowed to rush in, oppress, and usurp the weak and impotent in an overbearing manner, which for them, would not be difficult. Yet, it was necessary for their supporters to profit, so one must consider this as well. Lorenzo had difficulty because he did not want to usurp the belongings of others. Yet he did so anyway. Thus, through the honest profit that the city could give him, in reputation, he attributed many things to himself that are reasonable and convenient. However, they could obtain even better results by arranging to satisfy friends through Rome by way of the sort of compensation often allotted to others, and even to some from whom they receive little profit or benefit. Such appointments were made some months ago in a manner and with ceremony that served neither them nor their friends. Organizing as described above would achieve results that would work as a buttress to provide a solid foundation for the defense of the state.

I am certainly not saying that they are unaware of such reasoning, at least in part. However, among other factors preventing them from following through has been their lack of faith in us. I think this is due to two factors, better explained under two headings. First, they doubt the goodwill of the citizens, who to maximize their own interests and advantage would harm the state. This doubt is unreasonable because Florence, like all the other places, has good and bad men: wretches focused on their own desires, as well as those who love the city and its general welfare. However, this difficulty could be entirely or at least partially resolved by two remedies. First, by making prudent and competent choices. The other would be not to involve them completely, as stated above, but instead at times seek to understand and guide their actions, lending support or opposition according to their behavior and merits. The second doubt, which I think is more important, even though they may deny it, but is evident upon observation of their daily management, is that they do not trust us. They do not believe that we love them enough for them to base the well-being of their state on us. They remember being expelled in '94 and the experience of having few friends during a long exile. Their return came with the support of foreign forces and not by anyone here, except for those few whom they would naturally recall as their enemies, and from these they expect nothing but fickleness and inconsistency. They understand well enough how desperation and extreme necessity determined their actions previously. Therefore, they judge everyone else by contrary disposition and with reticence, since they have no favorable experience of them.

That they hold such opinions is certain death to us, allowing no consultation, participation, or acclimation, which means being perpetually on guard and reserved. Although, if I am not deceiving myself, this is unfounded and quite false. Citizens who would find themselves entertained and raised in reputation, prestige, honor, and profit would doubtlessly become passionate supporters. Even the attitudes of those whose positions are not completely ironclad could be transformed by benefits and displays of gratitude. They would be influenced above all by their personal interest, which is the guide that drives all men, and which could turn them into stalwart supporters.[10] I do not deny that what may prevail are certain natural inclinations toward hatred or love, which can be powerful, effective, and not easily erased. These are no longer the times of the ancient Greeks and Romans and their generous drive and perpetual aspiration for glory. There is nobody in Florence who loves liberty and popular government enough that if they were to gain a higher standard of living, they would not think about what they had and would not devote themselves with all of their being, especially if they were to be affected by a change in the state. They would not just lose their advantages but could even risk complete ruin. At least they would not be satisfied, for the popular government that ruled from '94 to '12 was at times close to becoming a truly free republic, especially under the principles and rule of Piero Soderini.[11] However, when the republic proceeded to enlarge and deform, it expanded and transformed without any hope of reform. By the end, it worsened every day into a state of muddled confusion. Nevertheless, it was sweet as sugar compared to what would have occurred if there had been another change of government. In my opinion, from

---

10. Echo of Guicciardini's *ricordo* C28.
11. Piero Soderini (1452–1522), *gonfaloniere* of the Florentine Republic (1502–12).

the expansion or representation in that period to what may have been introduced later, there is the same difference as the restrictions of access of today compared to the time of Lorenzo.[12]

However, this would have raised suspicion, rage, and ignorance in the men coming into the state. For no one should think the situation is like what occurred in '94, when the friends of the Medici, the flower of the city, were protected and after a few months participated with the others in government. Today such a course would be dangerous if not undertaken with some cruelty. For those who thought they enjoyed grand and beneficial status with the Medici understood reversal could bring the risk of exile, loss of goods, and similar ruin. It is believable that they would run to preserve and defend the Medici with all their spirit, might, and vitality. For, in all truth, it would be the same as preserving and defending themselves. Nor is there the risk that the empowerment of these would suffice to raise suspicions among the Medici, for they now control the state so absolutely that there is no citizen strong enough not to be ruined and diminished by a nod from them. Nor should there be concerns as in '66, when the Medici had to fight those who had been their friends in '34. For there is no house in Florence with either the authority or presumption of power to match them. Nor is there any citizen with a beard full enough that a bit of wind could not knock him over. Undoubtedly, conceding favors to anyone has risks, especially if they are indifferent to what could benefit the state. There is the example set by our ancestors, who acted out of self-interest so that they would be well connected with the government of that time, whether in '58, '66, '78, or in any other occurrences involving the state, and who were as ready and as committed as could be desired to provide supplies, followers, arms, and supporters.[13] Nor should anyone dismiss my focus on '94 because the malevolent behavior and poor policies of Piero alienated friends and ruined everything.[14] Returning to consider from this perspective, I believe that a deputation of many well-chosen friends, handled discreetly, treated with care under the parameters described above, would not lack in faith, love, and commitment for any need of the state and, in fact, would bring great profit and benefit to the state.

---

12. Lorenzo de' Medici (1449–1492).
13. Guicciardini lists the dates of attempts to free Florence of Medici rule in 1458 against Cosimo de' Medici, in 1466 against Cosimo's son, Piero de' Medici, and in 1478 with the Pazzi conspiracy and murder of Giuliano de' Medici.
14. Piero di Lorenzo de' Medici (1492–1503).

The third approach would be to aim for the entirety of the city to remain as contented as possible. This is problematic because popular governments are pleasing to most and contrast with the grandeur and absolute authority that they have assumed. Here outward appearances can be damaging, because if it had been possible to live and converse with them more civilly and equitably, in the manner of old Lorenzo,[15] then this grandeur would bother the people less than is presently the case. However, their manner of living cannot be moderated. Therefore, one must figure out how to satisfy men in other things as much as possible for them to remain content. If their displeasure cannot be entirely removed, then at least let it be somewhat reduced. If everyone cannot be convinced to love them, then at least the greater part might come to do so. Where there is no love, at least be sure that there is no hatred. If there is hatred, at least let there be no desperation. This is something that anyone who has ever taken things into consideration should be able to understand. Of all these issues, the three most important considerations are the treasury of the commune, justice in civil matters, and that the weakest and least powerful should not be oppressed by the stronger and more powerful.

The matter of the treasury is quite important because everyone understands that when the municipality lacks funds, expenses must be taken from the wallets of the citizens. This means the imposition of taxes and withholding interest payments from the bond fund,[16] which has been administered in a manner to make everyone suspicious. There was a reduction in the administration of the treasury and deposits, held quite tightly, so anyone reviewing accounts did not do so blindly. Yet everything came to a head with Lorenzo, whose court ran unsustainable expenses despite expectations that taxes would be reduced, or that the bond fund would be aided. Instead, there arose new forced loans and taxations implemented and distributed under malice and partisanship. These occurrences and the way they were conducted led everyone to believe that their superfluous expenses would force them, even against their will, to abuse the public revenues. Between this and the malice of the officials managing public revenues, regular taxation did not suffice, and instead they recurred to the necessity of adding new taxes daily.

---

15. Lorenzo de' Medici (1449–1492).
16. The *monte di pietà*, translated literally into English as "mount of piety," was a chartable pawnbroker institution.

That they were going to behave in this manner became known when wise men realized that they had gotten the idea into their heads to abuse the citizens. This immediately led to much jealousy and suspicion in the disposition of the entire city, so that they immediately ceased all business and exercises. Everyone was so astonished and immobilized that the city almost came to a halt. This worked to our advantage during the passing of the French, when everyone feared a change in government as a main and powerful result from two very negative consequences. The first was universal hatred and even desperation against the Medici. The second is that by ceasing and slowing life, business, and enterprises, the city became weak and poor. As the city weakened and lost power, its masters lost power as well. The grandeur and reputation of the one holding the state derives from the wealth and reputation of the city, for he is only as vigorous as what he commands. To befriend the popular faction and to enjoy increased prestige throughout Italy, monies must be well managed, with expenses and revenues of the commune properly and usefully distributed. Once the minds of men are reassured and they understand clearly, then jealousy and suspicion depart. Everyone can safely attend to business, enterprise, and earnings when men are unburdened by taxes.

To this second part may be added the justice of civil matters. I am not referring to civil matters to exclude criminal matters, for justice must necessarily be observed, even if at times discretion may be applied. However, civil matters require the reckoning of a tight and solid order, so that matters proceed properly and sincerely, without burdening whoever has the state in their hands. For this is another factor that greatly determines security. Men expect judges not to take away what is justifiably theirs, nor to impede the restitution of what was illicitly usurped by others. Therefore, two things must be done. The first is for civil matters not to be separated from regular proceedings and transferred to extraordinary venues like the Signoria or similar locations owing to favor or influence. The other is to leave suits of ordinary administration and commerce to the chief magistrates who are the principal judges of this city. When justice is done, they are at the helm as the guarantee of life and security for all. One must be wary not to interfere directly or indirectly with them through any spirited or even general intercession. In their opinion, the habit of interceding in regular cases does not seem like an offense to man or God. However, nothing could be more pernicious, because the spectacle of their ministers entering municipal buildings foments and generates universal suspicion under the assumption that they will receive preferential treatment. Furthermore, judges who acquiesce to an intercession on someone's behalf contrary to ordinary justice will become hesitant to the point of not being sure when a nod is really an order. Therefore, every intercession, special appeal, or ceremony must be entirely eliminated. Judges must be helped to be diligent and to lead us according to their good reputations and abilities. For when they are allowed to behave in such a manner as demonstrated with the results confirmed in their guilds, then this extends to the perception that those who govern desire justice to be impartial.

For these same ends, there must be vigilance of the sort of subjugation that may occur in the city's dominions through our rectors and officials, who think of nothing but how to enrich and fatten themselves by being unjust and stealing at every opportunity. This is something that could not be more shameful and damaging to the state. It creates a negative attitude among all subjects, on whom, God willing, we may have to rely in a time of travail, when the fruit of these wretched seeds will be seen and tasted. To remedy such disorder, it would be quite profitable if those who govern could be seen to understand the behavior and lifestyles of men, and to make a discernable distinction between the good and the wicked. When this is not undertaken, as is presently the case, by those in the surrounding areas who by nature value honor or are well behaved and are few in number, then others will always act to the worst of their knowledge and ability. Therefore, one must prepare for the behavior of our representatives in the hinterland who may feed off their neighbors under the power and the authority of the state, leaving the country without money and capital. One might retort that if the representatives of the state have nothing to feed from, then they will not be firm supporters of the state. In response, no course of action could be more damaging and disgraceful, creating many enemies not only among the subjugated, but also all those who are in the proximity and observe dishonest behavior. These days, more than ever, the citizens in power will not lack means while they have the pontificate in hand and may bestow advantages legally and without obstruction to make supporters and well-wishers not only of heads of state, but also of upstanding men of quality. For when the pope decides to bestow benefits with the degree and distinction in which prudent men undertake affairs, he can create vibrant and healthy support for his house upon every occasion and occurrence.

These are the principal matters requiring consistency in law and behavior. In my opinion, these issues may be resolved without much difficulty if the one carrying the burden of our affairs is willing to expend the necessary time, diligence, and effort. If they consider the quality and foundation of this city and its government, then they should reasonably value it enough to keep it in good order. They will realize the advantages of the great profit that comes by understanding that the foundation of their strength and permanence lies here. If they do not capitalize, as has been the case thus far, and do not deem it worth the effort, then I do not know what else to say except let them turn away. In the end, results will speak for themselves. If the outcome is positive, then they will value it even more than has been expressed herein. If it is otherwise, then they will be displeased. They should realize that many doubt that their downfall would also bring ruin to the entire city or even to those who are currently considered their friends or are favored by them.

These arguments should help and lead them to demonstrate to the people that they are humane, grateful, and will be able to peacefully coexist with all by managing their ministers and chancellors in a manner that does not lack respect for the city. To act with insolence and venality without consideration or understanding of our way of life can only incite disorder. Thus, it is important to allow men freedom in their marriages. The desire to abuse authority to impede consummation produces little profit and incites hatred. What would find great favor with the people is, on some occasion, if they were to think of the welfare and comfort of the city by aiding the public bond fund or enterprises on which the city depends, or by reforming with sound laws the disorder that exists in the offices and among officers. Or, by reforming the manner of dress of men and women, in which the city has gone so far beyond itself that there can only be the most negative consequences, both in private and in public.[17]

When they are seen to turn their attention to such matters, in which they could be helped and advised, the result would be that they would gain affection and be loved as fathers of the city. Now the perception is that they ignore everything as if our well-being or troubles had nothing to do with then. This only adds weight to arguments of the poor disposition that is expected of us. If these things were to be done, I would hope

---

17. A seeming pro-Savonarolian statement by Guicciardini—one of Savonarola's policies was to curb ostentation in dress.

that not only the city but their government would profit. If they do not act so, then I can say only that poor governments usually do not bear satisfactory results.

I do not want to overlook that there has been no lack of those who think, or perhaps have been persuaded, that it would be more secure for them to assert absolute dominion over the city in fact and in title than to keep this city under the presumptive shadow of freedom and civility. This is not something that I intend to discuss now. However, I will make the judgment that nothing could be more pernicious over time for themselves, for us, and for their administration, nor more replete with difficulty, suspicions, and every cruelty.

ON THE USE OF FORCE

Whether it is right to lead the people to good laws by force if there is no alternative

At first glance, this matter does not seem controversial and should not present much difficulty for discussion. For nothing is more contrary to the law and freedom of the city than the use of force. The aim of the law is to eliminate the use of force and ensure that the will of a single individual is not more important than reason. A city free to choose is presumed able to determine for itself according to its own opinion. The use of force presumes that it must be controlled in every aspect according to the discretion of others over time and in practice. Anyone who wants to lead the people by force acts contrary to the essence of liberty, and even by wanting to maintain law and well-being, will ruin both. There is nothing more abominable and vile for a free city than the realization that it is coerced and violated, because that removes the glory and splendor that comes from the status of living in liberty. There is no benefit, therefore, to resorting to violence since it deprives one of honor, like a doctor who tries to cure the sick by administering a harmful medicine. An additional concern for those governing a republic is how the introduction of something by force, which may even greatly benefit the city, sets a poor example. In the future, anyone who may want to change the government of the city will be afforded an opportunity by the precedent whereby arms and violence may be used against those one is supposed to love. All poor examples originate and gain authority from honest beginnings. Whosoever resorts to violence perverts the law and liberty, is an embarrassment to the city, and affords an opportunity that shields anyone in posterity who may want to do ill to the homeland.

On the other hand, if a republic is in a terminal and irreparable condition headed toward certain ruin, or if the city is so divided among its citizens that no remedy is possible except coercion, then it is surely better to provide for public safety through extraordinary measures than to abandon it to a course set for perdition. If the laws could speak for themselves, they would concur in a case whereby a single infringement would yield their perpetual preservation, for the laws usually do not prohibit exclusions in cases of necessity. Certainly, anyone who does not break the law but allows the same law to perish cannot be said to respect the law. Nor can anyone claim to be a lover of liberty if they allow it to be lost because they will not have it infringed. All the actions of men may be defined as good or bad according to their outcomes. Therefore, one may only define something as good and legitimate, which has as its outcome the removal of coercion. No law of nature is stronger and more binding than the union between body and soul, as demonstrated by observance of the difficulty and bitterness of their separation. Many illustrious men in ancient times broke this bond by violently depriving themselves of life by their own hand in order not to be reduced to bondage and not to see their homeland lose liberty.

Some revered authors say that the way to proceed according to God and the natural order is that when a desired outcome cannot be reached by ordinary means, then that leaves only the extraordinary, or the perfection made possible by miracle or the supernatural. Thus, a proper citizen, seeing his homeland in perdition and understanding the solution required, must understand, above all, if it may be introduced with the sort of arguments and civilized manners expected of republics. However, when these are ineffective, and force is necessary, a slight infringement of the law to preserve freedom in perpetuity is indicated rather than the abandonment of everything. That this line of thinking is true can be reasonably demonstrated by the example of that most holy and admirable man, Lycurgus, who without any consideration for himself, but driven only by a desire to benefit the public, would not have taken this path if he were not sure that it was legitimate and permissible.[1]

---

1. Lycurgus (800–730 BC) is the legendary founder of ancient Sparta's totalitarian, militaristic society.

I conclude, therefore, that this ruling is so true that it should be copied by all good doctors who find themselves unable to heal a wound with ointments or soothing medicines and must resort to fire and iron. I also conclude that no free city must allow anyone to assume enough authority for themselves to be able to decide when to follow the law or when to resort to violence, even if they were known in the past to be good and faithful to the homeland. For all men are false, and power creates desire. The best safeguard against someone who may do harm is not to focus on capability but rather on desire.

ON SUICIDE FOR POLITICAL REASONS

If killing oneself in order not to lose liberty or not to see one's homeland in bondage derives from magnanimity or cowardice and whether it is praiseworthy or not

To approach today's discussion without hesitation, there must be a recognition that Christian law prohibits anyone from performing violence upon themselves or ending their life before the time and manner fated by God. Nevertheless, because of a desire to examine the question according to natural reasoning and placing our reverence for the Christian faith aside, one cannot deny that considerable doubts could be raised. The schools of the ancient philosophers, as well as learned men including Cicero and Cesare, among others, raised the question vividly and at length, with clear and sharp reasoning. This question is also raised by the examples of the greatest of men who, by killing themselves or by waiting for better times, rendered the issue even more dubious and unclear. Undoubtedly, it merits discussion by fine intellects accustomed to the study of philosophy, of which I have never read a book. However, since I am giving this speech as an exercise for my own benefit and not to profit anyone else, it will be sufficient for me to speak ostensibly, employing only those arguments occurring to me naturally.

Nor can it be denied that anyone who killed themselves in any of the known cases did not do so to avoid something that he thought evil, or which caused him fear. For example, someone who kills themselves in order not to see their homeland or their own person in bondage does so out of an estimation that bondage will be bad and in fear of its inconveniences. This lack of consideration allows fear to force them to deprive themselves of life and remain senseless, rather than to feel and to taste the evil it is presupposed to contain. The root and origin therefore of suicide is mostly based upon the fear of evils that can be avoided by killing oneself. However, it is necessary to state that this is a result of cowardice and a lack of the spirit needed to dare to suffer the evils believed to exist in bondage. Nor may it be said that it is not fear but love of liberty that persuades someone to the act, because this love of liberty is necessarily based upon a hatred of bondage. This implies a relationship between love and hatred where one cannot exist without the other. Thus, it may be presumed that to have love for one thing implies having hatred for its opposite and vice versa. However, anyone moved by a love for liberty and at the same time by a hatred of bondage loves what they judge to be good and hates what they judge to be evil. Where there is hatred, there is fear of what men hate. Consequently, it is necessary to admit that there is also the fear of bondage and of the evils expected to come with it. From here, it necessarily follows that anyone who kills themselves to avoid bondage for themselves or for their homeland is originally motivated by fear and dread, and one can state that this is cowardice, not magnanimity.

This is vividly confirmed since there is no doubt according to commonly held beliefs that no evil compares with death, which separates body and soul, the greatest and strongest relationship among men. Philosophers have said that death is the worst of all terrible things. Certainly, poverty, shame, and bondage are lesser evils than death, because men have a natural appetite for existence. Take it from someone who speaks reasonably, it is preferable to be than not to be. A revered author once said that the damned in hell who have no hope of redemption in perpetuity would not change their condition to one of not being. So great is the natural appetite among men to exist. It therefore follows that anyone who chooses death out of a repulsion for bondage chooses a greater evil to avoid a lesser one. This derives from an estimation that bondage is a greater evil than it is. To have more fear of it than one should is not reasonable. One may not declare that this derives from a generosity of spirit because the prime characteristic of a spirited man is not to make something out to be more terrible than it is. Anyone who displays such a shortcoming lacks spirit, and it must be said, they necessarily have an oversupply of timidity. By this line of reasoning, one may conclude not only that they lack spirit and are fearful but that they also lack judgment because they deem something to be a greater evil than it really is and thus choose a greater evil over a lesser one. It would be like comparing someone who wants two wounds to someone who wants only one, which would doubtlessly give them a reputation as an idiot among all men.

This conclusion may be confirmed by another argument. Anyone who finds either themselves or their homeland in bondage may hope to regain their freedom, finding that the sorry state was temporary. They undoubtedly choose bondage in the expectation that it would end. Death, on the other hand, is understood to be an evil that lasts forever. Killing oneself for such reasons is a form of desperation that results from a lack of spirit and from an excess in timidity, especially when one loses hope that circumstances, which usually never remain constant for long, can change. We see how the affairs of men and especially of states change every day. Where today there is victory and empire, tomorrow there could be defeat, bondage, and vice versa. Moreover, such revolutions and storms often arrive in times without warning and contrary to the opinions of all men. However, whoever loses hope to an extent that is unreasonable must have either been born too timid or too fearful.

Finally, one cannot deny that suicide removes any chance for a person to return to the condition they desire. The removal of life harms others especially when a man commits suicide to avoid seeing his homeland in bondage. It would be more advantageous to live and to await an opportunity to reclaim a tradition of freedom. Therefore, I do not know how someone may be called a lover of his homeland who harms himself and removes any means to ever be able to help. Nor how this killing can be praised when it derives from lack of spirit, an exaggerated fear of bondage, and poor judgment that does not give enough weight to how great an evil death is, which harms not only them, but others as well. Someone who spiritedly endures the difficulties of bondage is more praiseworthy, for they preserve their ability to enjoy freedom at some point in the future.

On the other hand, one reads how in ancient times many men thought to be great and generous killed themselves unexpectedly. They acted not only to perform a service to their homeland, as was the case with the Decii,[1] who should not be discussed since they do not fall within the terms of the subject under consideration, but under circumstances that did not benefit the public at all. They wanted merely to avoid bondage, so they

---

1. Illustrious ancient Roman family that represented the Plebeian class during the early Roman republican period.

would not have to live in a homeland that was not free. Among these, there was a leader of the Romans, Marcus Cato,[2] who killed himself in Utica. He was a spirited man of unique virtue and consistency who held in low esteem the opinions of the masses evidenced by practices such as internal exiling and other civil infamies. He made many enemies in the city since he did not want to live in a country reduced to serving others. Following him, Marcus Brutus, his nephew, a man learned in the study of philosophy, was so prudent and serious that he was considered the epitome of Roman youth. When Caesar attained the top of rank in the city, Brutus put himself at the head of a conspiracy because he did not have a spirit generous enough to accept that the homeland would be servile. Once the Roman people were reduced to servitude because of the agreement between Marc Anthony and Octavian, he was defeated in battle against the tyrants on the fields at Philippi. Despite everything, he endeavored to escape and hoped to raise new armies or at least take refuge somewhere in the east not under Roman rule. Owing to his friendship with Anthony, he also had some hope of reconciliation with his enemies if acceptable terms could be reached. Instead, he decided to take his life rather than to live under servitude and to see his country continue under uncertain hopes.

These were very prudent men, and it is hard to believe that they did not discern the greater of evils between death and bondage. Nor is it believable that after having lived always displaying great spirit that they would decide to kill themselves out of timidity, especially since death is, by its very nature, so terrible and contrary to the natural desire of all men who call out in unison to life. Nor is it believable that someone who does not fear death should fear anything else. Therefore, it cannot be said that such excellent and generous men abandoned themselves to death out of fear and without the courage to endure the evils that they had been prepared to face while alive. Rather, they were so accustomed to living freely and honorably and driven by a certain greatness and generosity of spirit that they vehemently disdained life under bondage without the glory and liberty in which they were born and raised. Life is something that must be desired and abandoned only when that desire no longer exists. Since life is impermanent and everyone must die, a short and honorable life is preferable to a long and ignominious one. Someone who is accustomed to living gloriously, depending only on themselves, must flee from the

---

2. Marcus Porcius Cato (234–149 BC).

loss of that glory with every effort rather than bow and be humiliated by others, contrary to what is reasonable. Nor is this appetite born out of fear of not being able to withstand the evils of what may be avoided, but rather not to sully the glory and generosity under which one has lived.

Cato, Brutus, and many others did not lack the talent and the ability to know how to live in bondage, nor did they lack the skill and industriousness to humiliate the tyrants. Nor did they fear or want to avoid the loss of power, abuse, and torment. Nor were they so naïve in the ways of humanity, especially since they had witnessed in their own time so many changes in their republic, that they did not understand that these were evils that would not exist in perpetuity and that by living one day they might see a return to liberty in the homeland. Nobody has the power to preserve their lives forever. Yet one may preserve one's honor and glory. It would be a great opprobrium to obey and to serve someone who by the laws of nature and society becomes their equal, just because of poor fortune. Thus, by wanting to preserve their glory, they took their own lives. This was not because they lacked the spirit to withstand bondage but because they valued retaining their glory and honor forever, rather than their lives for however brief a time.

Here one could argue that it is not their place to judge how much opprobrium and shame would result in obedience, by no fault of their own, owing to the dictates of fortune. However, given that to them it would have been hateful to live in such a manner, then one cannot, in my opinion, question whether they lacked spirit. To the contrary, they demonstrated a high degree of generosity by valuing glory and reputation more than life, since these qualities are perpetual, whereas life is temporary. One can control one's own virtues, whereas life is controlled by nature. Since death is the greatest and most terrible of evils, then it is even more praiseworthy to admire the consistency and greatness of those who do not fear it to preserve their glory. Nor should the possibility of hoping to regain liberty be taken into consideration, as if it would redeem the glory defiled by living in bondage under a tyrant. Glory cannot be recovered with the return of liberty after the humiliation required to withstand obedience and existence under a tyrant. There are arguments for one side and for the other. In my opinion, one cannot deny, as demonstrated by the example of so many men, that it does not derive from the greatest generosity of spirit, although one could argue whether that generosity was properly used.

ON PROGRESSIVE TAXATION: THE SCALED TENTH

At the time of the wars with Pisa, a tax called the scaled tenth was introduced in Florence. It worked in such a way that whoever was assessed a tithe of five ducats or less paid one-tenth of his income, and whoever was assessed ten ducats paid one-tenth and a quarter, and who was assessed fifteen ducats, paid one-tenth and a half—and so on. The rate increased by one-quarter every successive five ducats, with nobody having to pay more than three-tenths. When this measure came before the Grand Council but seemed not to be winning, those in favor spoke thus:

Most honorable citizens, all the provisions before you must be considered from two points of view. First, whether their outcomes are such that they deserve approval, and second, whether the proposed means are reasonable and conducive to the desired goal. On the first point, the speakers preceding me have said quite enough. They have demonstrated that the provision of funds is necessary for the preservation of liberty and your sovereignty. There is no need to dwell on this point any further. However, despite having satisfactorily argued the first point, they have failed to establish the second. To convince you to support this measure, they needed to prove that it was appropriate and reasonable, which they have not done. I do not think this is because they lacked true, convincing, and plentiful arguments for persuasion, but rather because they did not want to offend those powerful, leading men in the city who have spoken out against this measure. I also would prefer not to offend these men. Yet, I am overcome by devotion to the republic and the desire to do my duty. Let others do what they think is right. I want to conduct myself as a good citizen and as a son of this council, which today, by the grace of God, is the lord of this city and has done me the honor of calling me to serve as one of its esteemed colleagues. This means nothing less than safeguarding the common weal against the will of the powerful. Therefore, I shall speak freely and state what I think is right for the good of the people without deference, because I am their son and servant.

Those who oppose this measure cite two reasons. First, that it is unjust. Second, that it is harmful. They claim it is unjust because it would be fair if taxes were to be the same for everyone, whereas this tax is unequal since many will pay only one-tenth and a quarter of their income, while others will pay one-fifth, one-quarter, or one-third. They claim it is harmful because it impoverishes the rich and harms the city because the rich honor the city and come to aid in times of need, helping the poor in many ways. Furthermore, sound government should not seek to alter anyone's condition but allow everyone to retain their station. Upon precursory consideration, these reasons appear venerable, true, and fine. However, anyone who examines them more closely, without allowing themselves to be deceived by the appearances, will find these reasons fallacious and replete with vanity.

I say that this scaled tenth tax is just and equitable and whatever injustice or inequity it may contain harms the poor, not the rich. For a tax to be equitable, it must tax the rich as well as the poor. When a poor person pays one-tenth of his income to the commune and a rich person pays one-tenth, it is not merely a matter of the rich man's tax yielding more than the poor man's, but that it is much more damaging for a poor person to pay one-tenth of their income than for a rich person. The fairness of a tax does not mean that all should pay the same rate, but that the payments be such that they encumber one person as much as another.

The expenditures citizens undertake are of three types: some are necessary, some are for general comfort, and some are superfluous. A person with an income of fifty ducats or less does not have enough income to meet their needs. Requiring them to pay one-tenth of this income in taxes will mean cutting necessary expenses. The moderately wealthy, those with an income of one hundred or one hundred and fifty ducats, have more latitude and can pay one-tenth and a quarter or one-tenth and a half by cutting down on expenses or comforts without cutting back on necessities. Someone with an income of two hundred or three hundred ducats, even if they were to pay one-quarter or one-third in taxes, would not have to cut back either on necessities or on comforts. He could pay out of monies that he would otherwise have wasted on superfluous expenses or had accumulated in savings. Therefore, the rich cannot complain about this progressive tax nor call it unfair, because paying it does not mean having to forgo necessities like the poor, nor comforts like the moderately wealthy. Nor should those in the middle have any recriminations, keeping in mind that this tax does not deprive them of necessities as it does the poor. If anyone can call this tax unjust and unfair, it is the poor. This tax does not harm the rich as much as the poor when it comes to necessities. The poor have grounds to take issue with the tax's proponents who respect the rich but have no compassion for the poor. For we are all citizens and members of this council just like them. One might even add without offense that we are more attached to a leisurely existence than they are. My peers and I may have only one servant, so that when we want to go out to the country, we harness our one horse to the carriage ourselves. When the weather is fine, we may even go on foot, lightly shod with nothing more than a single cloak and mantle. Often it happens to me that when the weather calls for a cloak, I had already lent out the mantle. Yet, nobody pities us for such concerns and thus deem it fair for us to pay the tax. However, the rich make a great uproar when paying the progressive tax means having to dismiss one out of their three or four servants, or having a page instead of a footman, or being forced to sell either the mule or the horse in a stable to keep the other.

Just as we are all citizens of the same city, taxation would be equal and fair if everyone today were reduced to the same standard of living. I do not see why going on foot to the countryside should cause more hardship for the rich than for me. Nor why the rich should be more ashamed of having only one coat like me. I was born in Florence just like them. Why should there be such a fuss about being reduced to having only one servant? The rich will have to take their boots off by themselves at night before going to bed, or have their wives or children help them. If they would understand who we are, and realize that there are incomparably more of us than them, and today each of our votes counts as much as any of theirs, then I am sure they would make less clamor. They would realize that we might open our eyes and impose a fair and just tax that would hit them where they live and not only touch them slightly like this tax, whose injustice lies in weighing down the poor much more than the rich.

They claim that it damages the city because they honor the city with their wealth, helping the needy and covering expenses for many of the poor. This is a manifestly fallacious argument because their riches do a hundred times more harm than good to both the public and to the individual. I say that it would be of the greatest benefit to the city if we had a law to the effect that no citizen could have an income from his properties exceeding one hundred or at most one hundred and fifty ducats. Since there is no law to prevent it, measures like this progressive tax should be introduced to force anyone possessing more than such an amount to sell when their income exceeds what a decent man needs to lead an honest life. Anything above this amount is wealth that is offensive in so many ways. As you know, the territory of our city has limits, meaning that there is barely enough for the needs of all citizens. If someone has too much property, it is bound to be a detriment to others. If someone has more than they need, others must have less than they need. It is as if there were a length of cloth sufficient for ten good coats. However, ten people cannot each have a coat if the first two or three coats were cut too long with more material than required without leaving enough cloth for the others. If everyone had a fair allotment, our territories could yield enough for two thousand citizens. However, it would not suffice for, say, one thousand five hundred, when some have more than they need. Excess wealth in property harms others by depriving them of their share. The cloth that could have clothed everybody decently is poorly distributed if one man has a cloak so ample that he could wrap himself up in it three times, long enough for two arm lengths to trail on the ground, when others do not have enough to be clothed like a beggar.

Do not think, most dear citizens, that I am just inventing these things, because in prior times these matters were proposed and acted upon by masters in the art of governing cities. Of all the republics of Greece, none was ever more virtuous and well governed than Sparta. Of the republics of Italy, none was nobler, worthier, and better ruled than Rome. Both had discussions like ours. However, when the Spartans organized their government, which was highly esteemed, they divided all the lands of their country equally among the citizens. Rome did not enact equal distribution so rigorously but did provide a law whereby no citizen could have more than a certain amount of property and anyone having more contrary to the law would have the amount above taken away and would even be sentenced. I would support the first of these two provisions, but since our way of life is more corrupt and cannot withstand surgery or strong medicine, then let us at least apply a more soothing ointment and not take away property from someone who already has it, or ruin or sentence those with more than their due. Instead, let us apply a tax that is reasonable, so that to pay, they must sell. Or if they arrogantly insist, the tax should be so onerous, and here I do not wish to say what perhaps I should, that they would croak under it, but at least they would be forced to give what they have in excess for the needs of their country.

Assuredly, most honorable citizens, if you put feelings and vain arguments aside, and truly ponder the nature of things, you will find that this city has no more useless and pernicious citizens than those who live on the fat incomes of their properties. Besides the reasons stated beforehand, what they have in excess deprives others of basic needs. Where do famines originate if not in large part from those who have no other thought than the price of grain and how to store it until the time when they can sell it for the price of an eye out of a man's head? These corruptors of the city were mostly born and raised wealthy, from wealth and property requiring neither toil nor industry to maintain. At home, they are used to living soft, pampered lives. Outdoors they ride handsomely mounted, flaunting their outfits. They harm the city by raising pampered children to be like themselves, incapable of doing anything, unable to further the public interest by counsel or action, because what they have in common is a lack of industriousness and experience. They harm everyone through their example, because any citizen of this very city who is wellborn is ashamed of not being able to appear well heeled, whether at home or in public. Thus, they live beyond their means, and keeping up appearances leads to the ruin of illicit and irregular ways of earning money, which is the root of countless evils. Believe me when I say that the city has no greater stain or problem than the superfluous expenses that originate mostly with them. Because when men are unable to sustain expenses beyond their means as instigated by these types, they think more about profit than virtue. They esteem property more than honor, and count money above their very soul. They become dishonest and venal, and usurp what belongs to neighbors, church, hospitals, and community. Whenever they see a chance to profit or theft, they make short shrift of virtue, honor, country, and God.

Observe, now, for I have placed your very hands on all the evil created by citizens with excess property. Yet, let us go even further. They are satisfied only when well clothed, respected, with large and secure incomes requiring no effort or work. They are not concerned by the constant care required to earn a living and to maintain their property. Do you know what they think about? As always, they think of how to become even more important, how to change the status quo, how to introduce tyranny to the city. They are our enemies. I do not mean all of them, for there are some honorable men in any group. However, when it comes to freedom and popular forms of government, for the most part, if they had modest incomes, then they would become honest and earn enough to maintain their households and to marry off their daughters. They would have neither the leisure nor the opportunity to wrack their brains about how to reduce representation in government. By this manner of thinking, they are companions to the ambitions of those impoverished and ruined by wasteful spending. As I have said, this is largely due to the example set by those who, when they realize they cannot put their affairs in order by ordinary means, must therefore always wish for and think of new strategies. Thus, one may observe how many evils result when things are poorly distributed.

I will even go so far as to say that this state of affairs is harmful to the rich themselves. They and their children grow up in luxury and idleness, unable to earn an honest penny. If ill fortune befalls them, as often happens to men, they have neither the industry nor the know-how to protect or sustain themselves. Thus, they fall quickly into such distress as to evoke pity. Furthermore, their children were brought up rich under the security and vanity of great holdings and often take up poor habits and licentious living so that even without adversity they become disorderly and poor owing to their own vices. When they descend into poverty, they cannot endure it, because they are unaccustomed to hardship. They do not know how to live only on what they need like those born and raised in poverty who know how to thrive under a way of life that would drive others to despair. Even if they do not fall into poverty because of misfortune or their own fault, their waste and extravagance shortens their lives and always makes them unhappy. Look at rich men thick with gout, phlegm, and kidney stones and a thousand ailments, which cause them to die sooner than the rest whose lives they make miserable. Any common, unavoidable ailment, which would normally not be much trouble, wracks them with a half a dozen fevers.

Do not allow yourselves to be persuaded by the argument that those who have much property are useful to the city because they help in times of need, as it is quite to the contrary. By God's grace, owing to their wasteful way of life and because their income is irregular and dependent upon the weather and shortages, these people never have a penny. I do not want to mention names; but go and talk to those who live off their property. Most of them usually are in debt, spending most of their time trying to straighten out their accounts and never paying anyone. They do not honor the city, because the honor of the city does not consist in seeing them strut about the square or market in richly embroidered capes or gleamingly lined mantles. What honors the city are those citizens who know what to do and what to say in every circumstance and in every occasion, who love their country and whose counsel and experience holds up under scrutiny, whose services the city can rely upon during any foreign or domestic hardship that may occur. These are the ones who honor a republic, who preserve it, and make it great. In Roman times, it often happened that some poor citizen, who in his poverty was alone toiling in a field, would be made consul or dictator and, after having received the news, would go into the city to assume office. Nor should you think that they sent a carriage to meet him, for he would come by foot, as I, collegial as I am, often do from the countryside.

Nor is it true that the rich support many in their needs. On the contrary, as I have often said, since they do not pay their debts and keep what belongs to others, they do not give anything of their own. What they have is spent on laborers, retainers, and servants (who are either foreigners or peasants), or on horses, falcons, and hounds. Not only is this of no use to the city and its people, but it is harmful, taking the bread out the people's mouths and giving it to strangers and animals.

I could say much more, but the conclusion is that having too much property does no good whatever, but rather wreaks havoc on the city and its citizens, as well as upon those who possess it. If I came to understand how excess wealth is harmful, then a way should be found to tax not only those who have too much property, but also those rich merchants and men of money who draw large interest from the city's bonds and mount of piety financial institution. In regard to the latter, let me repeat what I said about property, because the reasoning is the same. Something might be done were it not for the respect due to the pledges, the faith of the people who believed or invested, which would be too great a failure not to honor and to sully. For the merchants, these arguments do not apply. This is not a simple matter since it is much easier to act against realty and property that is visible than against other forms of wealth, which are uncertain. Often, someone who seems to be a rich and grand merchant is poor, on the verge of bankruptcy. There are other reasons as well. The wealth of merchants does not harm others because it does not deprive anybody of anything. The money that one of our citizens earns either by going abroad or by sending his merchandise to various locations and making a profit thereby does not affect the city nor the purses of other citizens. Indeed, a merchant does not take this money away from other citizens to enrich himself but rather acts for their benefit by bringing money into Florence. If a merchant earns well, this does not prevent anyone else from earning. Nor are merchants responsible for famine by hoarding grain. In times of scarcity, they create abundance by importing grain from abroad. Merchants are people accustomed to earning a living. For that reason and because wealth founded on trade requires continuous work and industriousness, they do not give themselves over to idleness nor do they keep their sons in idleness, but mostly raise them in their own businesses. They do not spend the money they earn from work as lavishly as those accustomed to living on the incomes from their estates. They do not strut about nor set a poor example. If they did not in turn buy many estates, which they would not do if we had the scaled tenth, they would be much more frugal and modest, for the estates are what spoil them. Merchants and men with money want the city and the world to be at peace, because otherwise their merchandise is worthless. They spend their time in business and profits so that they do not harbor ambitions nor seek new ways to limit the access or participation in government. These are men from whom the city and the people derive honors and benefits. Merchants with great earnings are constantly enterprising and active. Rather than remaining idle, they build palaces, churches, and workshops that honor the city. They provide the poor a way to earn a living. They are the ones who lend money to the city when needed by having good credit abroad through their contacts in many parts of the world, which are also quite useful for gathering news and information. They do the city great good in many ways. By sending your sons abroad, or by employing them here in workshops, they pay the expenses for your sons who are brought up in virtue rather than in vice. They pay the expenses of a considerable number of artisans and common folk who are also part of the city. Therefore, we should think of how to help our merchants who are useful both to the community and to private citizens. Those who have too much property should be forced to cut back, for it is harmful not just to the city and to the others, but to the owners as well.

Honorable citizens, let me praise the modesty and the goodwill of those who lend credence for some vain reason to the notion that this tax is unjust. They have not defeated it, although it would have brought profits to their own purses. Now that everyone understands what is just and right, let me encourage them and the others not only to support it, but to expand the scaled tenth so that those who have too many estates can be rid of them. By doing so, not only will great profit and well-being follow as I have explained, but everyone will be equally secure in their station. For we are all citizens enjoying the same rank, so let us all become true equals, as we reasonably should be.

DISCOURSE AGAINST THE TAX, FOR THE PREVAILING OPINION

Let me dare state, most honorable citizens, that I am justified in saying that in all truth, this city has never been as close to either well-being or ruin as today. By the grace of God, the city has adapted to the liberties of a government by the people, as is its proper and natural condition. There can be no doubt that if we continue this way of life in an orderly and sober manner, increase the happiness of the people, and understand how to keep everyone content in their station as much as possible, then this city will prosper in peace, unity, and wealth. On this firm foundation, the city not only will free itself of external difficulties and retake Pisa, but also will expand dominions and become renowned beyond anything achieved in the past. Contrarily, if it becomes disorderly and licentious, insisting on clouding any distinction and rank between citizens, and allows vain and savage opinions to prevail, then certainly the confusion and division between us will lead the city to a situation where not only will it be unable to overcome present dangers, but it will undoubtedly arrive at the brink of great calamity and destruction. Therefore, it is necessary for you, honorable citizens, as rulers upon whom the city's good or poor fortune depends, not to lend your ears more than is unavoidable to rash and licentious men, nor to allow yourselves to be easily persuaded by strange and extravagant ideas, nor to open the way to the subversion of our ancient way of life. Instead, you should proceed prudently and soberly in your deliberations, for the development and consolidation of civic unity rather than the creation of chaos that will lead us all to our deaths.

No one can deny that the measure before you is not only dishonest, but so extreme in its dishonesty that I am astonished by how it was presented here by our honored colleague. If he could recall that this council was created to preserve the liberty and unity of the city, the peace of everyone, and not to become the source of discord, pernicious laws, and regulations, then perhaps he might have restrained his tongue rather than so inconsiderately encouraged and invited your honors to pursue a destructive form of government. Yet, for his actions, he deserves our thanks, because if his intention was to sow discord, he did so with such abandon and lack of discretion and implicated himself by so many contradictions and impossible propositions that anyone not blind could easily see how far he is from the truth.

I admit that as the foundation of liberty, equality is a good, even a necessary attribute in a republic. However, true equality consists in not permitting one citizen to oppress another, so that everyone is equal before the law and the government, where the vote of every able person in this council counts as much as any other. This is what equality in liberty means, not that everyone should generally be equal in every category. To uncritically understand liberty and equality in that manner would mean that we should heap everybody's possessions and money together and divide it *pro capite* (by head) so that the poor have as much as the rich. Public offices would also have to be distributed like anything else. Thus, the ignorant, the wicked, and the inept would have a turn at being *gonfalonier*, a member of the Dieci, the Balia, an ambassador, or a commissar as readily as the wise, the worthy, and the good. If we were to proceed indiscriminately, we would destroy all industry and extinguish all virtue and goodness, creating such immense chaos that would soon ruin not just one city, but the world. In this manner, your artisans, subjects, and peasants would want to be your equals in everything. Since they would realize that they are far more numerous than you, they would force your acquiescence. To live freely, it is necessary that equality be loved and respected in moderation, without removing every rank and distinction between citizens. Throughout the entire world, God made men and things diverse as recognized by laws the world over. To distinguish what is yours from what is mine is necessary to maintain the general welfare. If in a city one or more citizens have more property than others, then it is due either to good fortune, or their industry, or the industry of their forbearers. This is provided for the laws and universal customs of the world because there are distinct ways of earning by which one may legitimately accumulate wealth and property. Those who want to take properties from owners by law or taxation would subvert the world order and commit an injustice and iniquity suited to pirates and assassins. Proper and well-ruled republics usually punish such villainy, which our colleague, who seems to me like another Solon,[1] wants to introduce as a law. He does not realize that our liberties were established for no other reason than so that everyone might securely enjoy his own and not be usurped by someone more powerful. Yet, he wants to use our liberty to steal and divide the belongings of those who legally possess them. He abuses your patience by defining as just a law that is the height of injustice and iniquity.

It is reasonable to state that the rich should help the city more than the poor. I admit this is true. However, let me also state that someone with an income of three hundred ducats paying thirty helps just as much as someone with an income of one hundred who pays ten, or fifty who pays five, because when considered carefully, equality or inequality is measured according to the proportional rate that everyone must pay. By paying the same rate, everyone is equally burdened. Nor is it fitting for everyone to pay the same amount, but to pay different amounts according to condition and capacity. If a poor man has only one servant and only one coat, he is not criticized for it. Yet, he would be criticized if he were to spend beyond his means. Similarly, a rich man who spends meager amounts would be reproached, attacked, and censured by everyone. The explanation is that men keep to different standards according to their abilities and their kind. Even in a free city, everyone must live under the same laws and government. There may be various kinds of men, because one is of nobler birth than another. The desire to eliminate such differences is like wanting to put all the apartments of a house on the same floor.

Therefore, I say that the rich suffer as much from the loss of one-tenth of their income as the poor because it upsets their necessary expenditures just like the poor. Necessary expenditures are not the same for everyone, but different according to each man's station. It is necessary for the rich to spend much to maintain their station, just as it is necessary for the poor to spend little, or for me, a man of moderate means and property, to spend moderately. Anyone who takes away the ability to make such

---

1. Solon, Athenian statesman, died 558 BC.

expenditures disrupts not what is superfluous, but what is necessary. If they are to be deprived of something, there are other more honest ways of taxing the rich somewhat more than the poor, even proportionally. In recent years, taxes, fines, and assessments have been levied that could be more honest and more useful to the city than tolerating the inequality that comes with such a ruinous tax. To take away from what is someone's by right in anger is, not only according to the laws of this city but by the universal laws of the entire world, an injustice and iniquity beyond compare. Have you not considered what is at stake, of the level of harm done to the state by making so many richly endowed, notable, and noble citizens of good reputation despair? This is nothing less than the path to civil strife, an instigation of those who want to change the government and open the door to Piero de' Medici.[2]

The first consideration for those planning to organize a state is to arrange matters in such a way so that everyone is reasonably satisfied in their station and that nobody is given just cause or need to desire a new order. The city is a single body of all citizens, and when one member is dissatisfied, the rest of the body cannot feel well. Nor can it be called liberty if one part of the city is oppressed and treated poorly by another. This was not the reason why we restored liberty, but rather so that everyone could be sure of maintaining their station. Otherwise, it would be licentious tyranny or tyrannical license, which is wicked while it lasts, but which does not last for long owing to the discord and evil effects it generates. Whenever one faction is discontent, divisions arise. Where there are divisions, there cannot be stability. As the Gospel says, a house divided against itself cannot stand.[3]

Our colleague says that those with property harm the city, because to him they seem powerful and aim to restrict access and participation in government. He demonstrates his passion on the subject but is ill-informed in the ways of the world because the situation is exactly the opposite. As the proverb states, if you are dealt a poor hand, reshuffle the deck. Those who are badly off are the ones who expose themselves to every danger out of desperation. Anyone who is doing well will not willingly put themselves in jeopardy. In particular, the rich, whose wealth

---

2. Piero de' Medici (1472–1503), eldest son of Lorenzo de' Medici and ruler of Florence from 1492 to 1494.
3. Matthew 12:25.

consists of property they cannot take with them, will be very careful about placing themselves in a situation where they could lose what they have. Unless I am fooling myself, they always tend to support whoever is in power, even though they may hope to fare well under a tyrant in a city like ours where everyone naturally despises servitude. I have no doubt that if we use our liberty moderately without overbearence among peers, then their present reticence will dissipate because they will be unable to predict whether confusion or order will prevail. However, when they see the government properly in order, they will keep their peace, since it is to their advantage not to live in fear or be subject to anyone.

It is therefore your duty to retain their friendship and support for this way of life, and not to turn them into enemies. If considered carefully, this tax cannot be expected to continue to raise much since soon enough its yield will diminish after hitting some heavily enough to destroy them, forcing them to sell their property. This demonstrates the iniquity of this tax and the bad faith of its proponents, because to the public it will do little good and to the individual it will cause great harm.

I do not want to reply in detail to speeches that he admitted are born from excessive zeal, since most of his arguments on the matter are irrelevant and blatantly false. It is true that wasteful spending is a great affliction on the city, but this originates more from those with ready cash than with property. For they can spend their money with little inconvenience. They may be rich, but, as the saying goes, they are not comfortable and are more interested in comforts than ostentation, so they do not have the means to create civil discord. Truly, if wasteful spending is harmful, it is harmful to those who spend too much and set a poor example thereby. However, that is no reason to confiscate lawfully held possessions. Instead, like other cities, we should try to quell excess spending with laws and proper ordinances. If someone unjustly gathers or appropriates too much, let recourse come through laws and sanctions; but let us not out of spite take from a man what he has lawfully and reasonably acquired. Nor is it true that some having too much property is the reason others have too little. I have never seen anyone who had money lack property. Too often, either owing to misfortune or their own fault, owners are forced to sell. People do not have property because they do not have money. Nor should you hope that this scaled tenth will endow you with property. It may force citizens to sell but will never force them to give it away. Whoever has no money to buy will have just as little after the scaled tenth as now.

Then there is the example of how the Romans and the Spartans divided property *pro capite*, prohibiting anyone having more than a certain amount. Half what he said in this regard is untrue, and the other part does not exactly describe how things were. The plebeians proposed the agrarian law, as the Romans called the division of land, many times. The very proposition of the law sowed much discord and created riots in the city. A law by which nobody could have more than a certain amount of land was adopted. However, in the end, it never went forward, either because it seemed useless or because it caused such discord. In Sparta, it is true that land was redistributed because the rulers of that city had another goal. They wanted to accustom their people to bear arms and to live in poverty so that the people would think of nothing else but military exercise and manly virtues. The government removed money for trade and commerce by which one could earn a living as well as all the comforts and pleasures to be had from wealth. They instituted a savage and harsh way of life. Now I do not want to criticize them out of respect for their republic. But let me say that either owing to the difficulties of this way of life or its failure to yield expected results, of all the cities and republics over many centuries thereafter, none has ever chosen this path again. In our times, it would be impossible to reduce people to such a way of life. To imitate it, one would have to take away not only property, but money, goods, all trade abroad, and all humane manner of living. This is not just a matter of property alone. For this example to be followed, it must be followed completely or not discussed at all. Anyone wanting to take this path would have to bear arms like the Spartans, otherwise you may believe you were doing well, but they only caused harm. Since you are not accustomed to arms, it would be difficult to persuade you to take them up and to abandon your trades and traditional way of life. How would you defend your state without the wealth that hires foreign soldiers and makes the necessary provisions for the defense of your dominions and liberty? These things are easy enough to consider, but difficult, if not impossible, to implement. For all of them together cannot be done, and implementing one but not the others will result in disorder, not order. Anyone who wants to do away with landowners but retain merchants and those with money, as our colleague suggested, contradicts themselves, because it is impossible to ruin one without weakening the others. If the merchant or those with money are prohibited from buying significant property and are thus unable to ensure the future of their descendants, this will inevitably cool their desire to do business. They will not be able to work for anything solid or plant their feet on a piece of land. They will lack one of the goals for which merchants work, which is to acquire enough realty so that every one of their children may maintain themselves honorably. Taking this away would be like cutting off their arms. They will have no place to unload their disposable income, since it is not possible to employ everything in business. Even if they could, men still like to put away some of their wealth to safety. So, they would either uselessly store the money away in the till or be driven to usury, which is a bad and pernicious thing. These are the purported virtues that will result from striking at property owners.

Let us say even more. Once this dishonest garnishment of property and wealth begins and extremist methods govern the city, what assurance will the merchants or anyone with money have that they will not be saddled with a similar tax later after their holdings have been leveled, especially since this contest over property will be decided after a few turns? As I already said, this scaled tenth is extremely onerous but yields little. Anyone who wants to proceed with this tax will be forced to return to it repeatedly. With good reason, they are aware of the risk that not only will the merchants reduce their activities to hide their income, but some will even consider residing elsewhere. One must also realize that our colleague would readily apply the same measure to those who receive interest payments from the state. If not for the profound respect for public goodwill, which he holds in high esteem, he might as well propose that anyone who acquires property according to the faith we have in our laws and our judicial system be robbed and despoiled as if they were abandoned on the highway. Once the road is open to these unjust and iniquitous ways and it becomes apparent that you, most honorable gentlemen, have begun to lend your ears to these agitators and these dissipaters of liberty, then the poor will not hesitate to rid themselves of such a tax burden or be concerned about taxing the rich inequitably and destroying them. These slanderers will appear every day to propose dishonest and extravagant measures that may seem to have a sweet taste but whose effect in the end will be poisonous. Because when one begins to resort to these pernicious inventions and govern the city by the appetite of the masses rather than by prudent counsel, then what follows will necessarily abound in confusion and disorder. Cities destroy themselves either through social strife or because men turn to evil ways and hope to acquire riches and honors from you by rioting and passing iniquitous laws. Virtue, industry, and work will give way to idleness, rapacity, indolence, evil words, and worse deeds. In such a situation, it will become impossible to preserve a tradition of deeply rooted and secure liberty, let alone ours, which is still new and ephemeral. Yet, there should remain some fresh recollection in the memory of men of the history of the Ciompi riots, which brought this city to the point of losing everything in a single stroke.[4] Do not believe that they started as anything more turbulent than this; if anything, it was more restrained. Such events have humble beginnings. However, if men pay them no heed, then problems quickly multiply and spread to a point where nobody is in time to act.

Remember the state of our affairs. We no longer have Pisa, the focal point of our dominion and one might even say the soul of this city. There is a powerful insurgent abroad, perhaps the greatest threat ever to the city.[5] He is from a house that dominated our government for sixty years and has the advantages of many friends and dependents among us and our dominions, and he enjoys high repute among foreigners. If you want to remedy these scourges, you must not foment them by creating discord among us with a government that is confused and increases the malcontents by making powerful citizens and men of quality despair. Fostering such disorder will not lead to the recovery of Pisa. Nor will it lead to an increase in standing among princes, among whom Piero de' Medici has ten friends for every one he has in this city, who will remain his enemies if you do not alienate them and they see civic affairs moving in an orderly and secure manner.

Honorable citizens, if you wish to preserve your liberty and peaceful way of life, if you want to restore this city to its ancient sovereignty and renown, then throw out those proposing riotous and confused measures. Embrace unity and harmony among your fellow citizens by conducting affairs justly and with discretion, so that everyone may hope to live under the secure protection of this government and preserve their wealth and capacity. Remove anything, such as this scaled tenth, that could terrorize

---

4. The Ciompi riots of 1378.
5. Piero de' Medici.

anyone who wants to live from their possessions. This tax will provide very little income for the needs of the republic but will be very detrimental by alienating the rich. If you act properly, everyone of quality will cherish liberty and popular government. Unity and harmony among citizens will be maintained. We can hope to enjoy all the happiness to which a republic can aspire at home and abroad. However, as I said at the beginning, if you begin to take another path, this poor city will soon come to ruin, and we shall lament because we, and no one else, were the cause.

REPORT ON THE DEFENSE OF PARMA

Of all the affairs I have managed to the present day, after the passing of the present year, I have come to realize that for me, none were more honorable than the defense of Parma. Thus, it seems that I should briefly describe what occurred there.

At the taking of Milan and the entry of the papal and imperial armies, I found myself in the role of commissar general of the field. I remained there with the most reverend Monsignor Medici on November 28th. On that day, a message arrived from Count Caiazzo informing that Signor Federico da Bozzolo and the French had left Parma, and that Caiazzo remained in the citadel, which he held in the name of our lord, who instructed me to go forthwith to maintain possession and to remain there until our lord could deputize a governor, which eventually he decided would be me.

Thus, I proceeded to Parma, and three days after having taken charge, news arrived of the death of Pope Leo,[1] which was so sudden and unexpected that it upset everything. It became necessary to delay the path to victory that would have ensued within a couple of months had the Venetians severed their alliance with the French, which would have meant the relinquishing of everything the French still retained in Italy, except for the fortresses of Milan and Cremona. To maintain our position until the election of a pope, Monsignor Medici, while passing through Parma and heading by relay toward Rome, ordered me to remain

---

1. Giovanni di Lorenzo de' Medici (1475–1521), elected pope and taking the name Leo X in 1513. He died unexpectedly on December 1, 1521, leaving Guicciardini in the predicament he describes in this report.

FIG. 4 | Tintoretto, *The Capture of Parma*, ca. 1580. Alte Pinakothek, Munich. Guicciardini's defense of Parma occurred on August 29, 1521. Photo: Wikimedia Commons / The Yorck Project.

for the defense of Parma. Iacopo, my brother and lieutenant in Reggio and Modena, remained at Reggio.[2] Modena was left entirely to the care of Count Guido Rangoni. At Parma, I had at my disposal just three companies of nine hundred and fifty infantrymen, whom I had no means to pay. The territory was in grave danger, without artillery, without weapons, and without ammunition. The walls had a breach on one side, which had been opened by a battery of our army the preceding September. The French were in proximity, occupying Cremona and the entirety of the area on the opposite side of the Po River, from the Adda River to Casalmaggiore, ten miles from Parma. I was informed that orders had been relayed to the bishop of Pistoia whereby one thousand of the three thousand Swiss from the canton of Zurich would come to Parma. Their presence would have secured Parma, especially since it was thought there would not be a delay in the election of a new pope. In the interim, the Marquis of

---

2. Iacopo Guicciardini (1480–1552), brother, collaborator, and confidant of Francesco Guicciardini.

Mantua—captain of papal forces at Milan—could descend with papal forces to Piacenza. Imperial forces on the opposite side of the Po River would be a sign of intention to take Cremona, which would deter the French from attacking along the Po. There were also two thousand Swiss with Count Guido in Modena, whose proximity favored the position in Parma. Signor Vitelli remained in Bologna.

However, all these plans were in vain. There was no way to pay the Zürichers, who decided to remain in the defense of Piacenza until the election of a pope. They refused to serve in any capacity in defense of the Papal States outside Piacenza. The entry of cardinals into the conclave went slowly for many reasons, including the capture of Cardinal Ivrea in the Milanese hinterland.[3] Thus, the cardinals were not making any decisions, especially regarding the defense of the Papal States. Following the advice of Signor Prospero and the imperial captains, the Marquis of Mantua did not cross the Po River. The idea of separating forces from those of the church seemed to them to be too much of a reduction of their capacity. Thus, they gave no indication of intent to cross the Adda, which would have caused the French concerns about having to defend Cremona, where they remained at leisure with their garrisons. The advance of Francesco Maria della Rovere on the road through Romagna to retake Urbino caused the departure of Signor Vitelli and his troops from Bologna. Upon the news that the duke of Ferrara was making preparations, the Swiss left Modena and went to defend Bologna.

Invited by these opportunities, the French persuaded the Venetians to lend support. They decided to cross the Po and advance toward Parma. They were encouraged by Signor Federico da Bozzolo, who had been at a garrison of Parma for many months and was well aware that he had a fearsome reputation. Following the preceding period of travail and servitude, the people were in a state of shock. They were also unarmed since everything had been requisitioned from them. Thus, he proposed that the venture would be quite easy, reasoning that Parma had only a few, poorly paid foreign infantry and a governor without military experience who was new to the city. They reasoned that since the papal seat was vacant, there was no way for anyone in Parma to know whom they were serving, and therefore neither the governor nor any of the others would want to place themselves in danger. Parma thus seemed to offer an inviting

---

3. Bonifacio Ferrero (1476–1543).

opportunity. The nearby city of Reggio was also poorly defended and could be taken just by blowing a trumpet. If the duke of Ferrara could produce a large deployment of artillery, they could also hope to take Modena and Bologna, news of which could be enough to turn Florence, which was already deeply suspicious because of Duke Francesco Maria, Baglioni, and the other malcontents from Tuscany. With these successes, they might be able to advance at will all the way to Rome.[4]

Having resolved to take Parma, they started through Cremona and began to slowly lay a pontoon bridge across the Po. This may have been done to allay suspicions, although it did not matter since they had to await the arrival of the Venetian infantry, which was amassing on this side of the Oglio. The construction of the bridge did raise suspicions about all the troops on this side of the river, although the nearly universal opinion was that they were not planning to besiege any city but had only done so to be able to pass through and to overrun the countryside. The general opinion was since so many were in the service of the church and the emperor between Milan, Piacenza, Modena, and Bologna that the French would not dare. Nevertheless, this bridge did arouse my suspicions. Although I was better equipped for fear than for taking any precautions, I decided to prepare in any way I could.

After the news of the death of Pope Leo, I arranged for a cannon and two artillery pieces[5] for Parma with a few barrels of heavy gunpowder, which the governor of Bologna had intended to send for engagement at San Secondo. Fully aware that the territory was unarmed and poorly provisioned of anything useful, I had a certain amount of fine gunpowder and one thousand pikes sent to the fortress of Reggio. Then, after expelling any malefactors, I convened the populace in an attempt to organize and to prepare them, without any confidence that I would be able to rely upon them. It seemed to me that spreading the word that the people had taken up arms to defend themselves would reduce enemy morale, especially if their plans counted upon our disorganization. Yet, these initiatives were insufficient, because as soon as the bridge was finished, Signor Federico left Cremona on December 18th at twenty hundred hours with his infantry and a company of light cavalry. He pitched camp on the

---

4. A similar course of events would occur in the years 1525–27 and lead to the Sack of Rome in May 1527, with the contending sides having switched alliances.

5. A *sacro*, a small artillery piece similar to a *falconetto* with a caliber of five to seven centimeters.

other side of the Po at Toricella. Then, with boats ordered from Casalmaggiore, he crossed the Po and headed toward Parma. That same night Signor Marcantonio Colonna, Monsignor Buonavalle, and Carbone left Cremona and crossed the Po with three hundred French lancers and the Venetian infantry, camping first at Borgo San Donnino and not heading toward Parma before the morning of the twentieth.

Immediately after receiving the news about the first encampment of Signor Federico and that boats were set for a crossing, of which I was advised by Signor Francesco Maria Simonetta di Toricella, I understood they were coming to take Parma. That night at ten o'clock, I convened the local leaders and communicated the danger and my resolution that we should defend ourselves. With them, I decided that the people should be armed, that pikes should be distributed, and everyone should be organized under different commanders. This came to pass. Then, having posted guards where most advantageous around the area, as day broke, I began to discuss with those interested if we should abandon Codiponte and retreat to this side of Parma or defend the entire territory. It was advised that we should abandon Codiponte, which encompassed a large area and would require many men. The Santa Croce gate to Piacenza would have also required a company on walls weakened from damage by our artillery the preceding September. We were comforted by the thought of the trouble defending it would cause the enemy, which would have to bivouac in the open, which in the season was quite unforgiving. Those with houses in Codiponte insisted it should be defended, offering to do much more than they would have been able, a normal reaction for people in such a situation.

I decided it must be abandoned in any event, because we did not have the means to defend it. This decision resulted from the example they had provided, for when we pressed them, they retreated into the central sections. It was recalled that when Signor Federico was stationed in Parma, if we had gained an advantage in the field, he would have based himself here. However, I concluded that we could retreat before the enemy started to notice by keeping close to the walls. Since I knew that the people were not well trained, if we had to beat a hasty retreat, there was the risk that the enemy could mix with us in the field. Owing to the foolhardiness of a few, this was quite difficult for me to accomplish and I to make them reenter almost by force. Nor did they act with enough expertise to avoid having some of the enemy on their heels and almost gain entry at the Pietra bridge.

As soon as Signor Federico approached the territory, he sent a trumpeter, who on behalf of Signor Marcantonio Colonna demanded the city in the name of the king of France. To queries about the troops and artillery at my disposal and other details, I answered that he should tell his masters that in their present position, they could request anything that was mine to give and I would willingly give it to them. However, if they asked for something that I had been instructed to care for by others, then I could not dispose of it without instructions from my superiors. I added that I wished to tell Signor Federico in particular that I did not want to be less courteous than he had been when we had been in the field. Since he had left us Codiponte, I had also decided to leave it to him in the hopes that he also would act with no less courtesy toward me than we had displayed toward him. Since we had not taken the territory away from him, we hoped he would be so kind as not to take it away from us. Thus, he entered Codiponte at twenty hours, and encamped his troops therein, except for the light cavalry, which he sent to Certosa and toward Enza to prevent the arrival of reinforcements.

The next day and night, nothing was done except the posting of a reliable guard. As occurs with a timid and peace-loving people, every slight cry caused great uproar and call to arms. Even after instructions that without my expressed order or signal, including that the bells should not be rung, it was impossible to restrain them. Thus, there were constant outbursts, and I was attentive to appear at the site of each ruckus. This was quite useful because my presence quelled much of the chaos. Making a show that I was not afraid gave courage to the multitude.

The following morning of the 20th, Signor Marcantonio, the French troops, and the Venetian infantry arrived so that Parma was surrounded by four or five thousand troops, five hundred Venetian light cavalry, and three or four hundred French lancers. Because they did not expect any resistance, they brought no artillery except for a couple of *falconetti* small artillery pieces. In their approach, they had captured Giovan Francesco Cerrato, a citizen and respected merchant of Parma, and had kept him with Count Cristoforo Torello, who was on their side. They persuaded him that they had five thousand infantrymen, expected cannons, and any defense of the territory would be futile. Then they let him go, and when he came inside, I realized that listening to him would be like taking poison. However, to refuse him entry would have been impossible. When he arrived, I spoke to him beforehand, instructing him about what he should believe in terms of what he reported. However, this was completely in vain, because he immediately repeated what he had been persuaded to believe about the situation. Thus, everyone became so frightened that I had to convene all the elders for what they call a *credenza*, which is just a counsel although not referred to as such. Everyone unanimously agreed that it would be madness to resist and that we should surrender. To justify themselves, they diligently sought my approval at every turn. I had to face arguments that seemed valid and assurances that they would not surrender if they could not save me, my soldiers, artillery, and belongings. I attempted to dissuade them, explaining that the enemy did not have more than three thousand troops, and without heavy artillery that would not be enough to take us.

Another difficulty was added when the troops requested to be paid on their payday. Since I was short of funds, I had planned to pay them half wages. I was short eight hundred ducats, which the day before the community had promised to put at my disposal. However, after their fears rose, they changed opinion, which was going to lead us to certain ruin. I argued that even if they were within an hour of surrender, they should pay, because this would always be the best proof a pontiff could have of their faith and devotion. After I received the money and was intent on paying, some incited by Francesco Salamone reneged, saying that they wanted to be paid in full, which was impossible. After much discussion and pleading, they turned toward the gates demanding to be let out into the French camp. I followed them, and they were stopped on the other side by their captain, to whom it seemed that the question had gone further than they had intended, so they wesre content to accept half wages. This was a narrow escape, because part of the walls had been abandoned, and in the ensuing disorder, the locals pressed me with great insistence to surrender, claiming that I obstinately wanted to cause their ruin by leaving them without troops. To these, I vigorously responded that since the troops had not left the area, nobody could tell me that I had no troops.

At this time, a messenger from Signor Marcantonio Colonna demanded to speak with the deputies of the city. When he was not admitted, this afforded an opportunity for some locals to make a motion for me to allow them to send a messenger to Signor Marcantonio asking him to excuse them since I was the one who had not let him in, not them, adding that in similar occasions his rancor had proven quite damaging for a city. What they were really trying to obtain was a pretext for negotiation. I refused vigorously, but they were unreceptive and at every turn pestered me with arguments and very serious complaints to the point that I came to a troubling realization. If I allowed the dispatch of a messenger, which resulted in negotiations that then engendered a surrender, the fault would be mine alone, because they could always retort in their defense that the messenger had gone forth with my approval. On the other hand, if they had the courage to send a messenger without my knowledge, knowing that I had forbidden it, then they might also have enough spirit to surrender without my consent.

All the difficulties arose from the fact that I had too few forces to defend the territory against their will, nor could I defend it without their aid because inside there were three companies of foreign infantry—Francesco Salamone with four hundred, Signor Francesco dal Monte with the same number, and Prete Bachione da Lerici with one hundred and fifty. From these were missing two hundred or so from the total, because for many days I had kept them to a *scudo* coin each, and captains who are poorly paid make a point of not parading so their number may be known. Two days earlier, fifty men who were quite useless arrived with the Marquis of Mantua, led by Messer Ludovico da Fermo, who however comported himself with prudence and valor. Given these reduced forces, one could not alienate the locals, who became more insistent with words of increasing alacrity every hour. Therefore, it seemed like a lesser evil to allow them to send this messenger. I delayed as long as possible until later in the day, with a written order that limited the message to an apology and an indication that any answer or offer received would have no official valence without my consent and that they were not to make new requests nor hear or review others.

The night proceeded with the same rumoring and chaos. Many of the locals were truly frightened. They could not be convinced that the enemy did not have cannons and were concerned that I wanted them to work like soldiers to repair the breach where it seemed the attack would come, if they did have cannons. However, it was impossible, even with all the remonstrances made with the elders, to procure the necessary tools. Thus, I was convinced that if they had cannons, then our situation offered no solution. Since the locals were convinced that they had at least two, it would become impossible to stop them from running out to surrender.

This fear and behavior in the locals was observed and understood by our soldiers, who were put into such a state of anxiety that I could not reassure them. They suspected the city would switch sides so that they would have to fight the enemy and watch their backs at the same time, before being completely abandoned. Since the guard had left, the fortress up to the Cavrazuca bridge was under Signor Francesco dal Monte, from there to the Bologna gate was under Francesco Salamone, and the rest under Prete Bachione were guarded by deputies and their squads. If they abandoned us, we did not have sufficient numbers to guard the entire perimeter and offer resistance in battle, which it seemed might break out in several spots. All these difficulties were exacerbated because I was new to the city, nobody knew me, nor did I know anyone. Therefore, I could neither count on the men, nor provide for matters as I might have done if I were familiar with the territory. The night was spent in this manner, and the messenger returned with the response that Signor Marcantonio had encouraged the locals to surrender for their own good, as they very much desired. As time proceeded, there was no appearance, nor would there be, of the reinforcements I had hoped for and expected. Despite the difficulties mentioned above, my resolve resulted from my confidence in the character of he who could provide aid.

As the morning turned to day, new messengers from Signor Marcantonio appeared, but they were not admitted. This seemed to me to be a sign of weakness on their part. Besides soliciting us with increasing appeals, it could be seen that they had not installed any artillery. Thus, I was reassured about what I thought to be the greatest danger. Hoping to persuade the city with this argument, I went before the elders, among whom I found a considerable number of the most important citizens, who began to press me to consent to surrender with greater insistence than ever. The fear caused by the lack of any appearance of reinforcements was more convincing than any arguments I could offer. Much discussion followed. However, I explained that I too would not want to face a danger as great as what they were imagining. Since Pope Leo, whom I represented, was dead, I had no certainty about who would be elected pope. It could easily be someone whose defeat might make me happy. I would not be harmed since I was not Parmesan, nor would I become subject to the French. However, defeat by arms would cause me great loss, because I would be forced to pay a heavy ransom. Finally, as their insistence and brashness increased, I told them in most clear terms and with vigorous retorts that unless I saw a greater level of danger, I would never consent and that they were seeking my consent as a justification because they could not do without it, because I did not have the means to stop them. Since I could do nothing more, against this affront, all I could offer was the threat that any agreement they made would never allow them any reprieve from being branded as traitors and rebels. During these discussions and altercations, a shot of artillery was heard from an enemy *falconetto* artillery piece. This artillery salvo caused an indescribable ruckus, from which it was clear that if the enemy had two cannons, no authority or reasoning would have been able to keep the locals from surrendering.

The sun was already high when one could hear the enemy setting themselves up into formation. I was already in the main square providing for necessities. The only remaining recourse for the elders and other principals by various appeals was to insist to obtain my consent to send out a representative of mine, and one of theirs to observe the size of the enemy troops. Count Cristoforo Torello had sent out a messenger to make this offer, certifying that they numbered five thousand troops. The locals concluded that it would be impossible to defend against such a number, which was probably true. They spoke with Messer Ludovico da Fermo, who concurred with the evaluation. Given our reduced forces and the vacillation of the locals, it would be difficult to defend ourselves against five thousand troops because they would be able to attack in many places at once. While these controversies and disagreements grew hour after hour, I remained steadfast, clinging to various arguments. When they realized that the enemy was approaching the walls, discussions broke off as it became more necessary to think about defending ourselves than surrendering.

Signor Federico thrust his troops at the bastion of the road between Porta Nuova and Porta Santo Michele. A vigorous assault opened with intermittent fighting in many locations along the walls between the fortress and Porta Nuova. Afterward, there began another vigorous assault on Porta San Michele, with fighting along the walls between that gate and the fortress. They had many ladders and attempted to scale the walls. Francesco Salamone and his company, who were few in number, were guarding these areas. Many times, either locals or men from other companies would rush to reinforce wherever they were needed. There were outcries and noise and a call that the enemy had breached the perimeter and was penetrating as far as the square, where I remained to direct everything point by point, as required. In other parts of the city, there was no fighting, except for a small assault at the stone bridge, which was easily repelled. As the fighting dragged on, the locals gained courage and massed along the walls. By the end, even women were bringing barrels, stones, victuals, and other necessities in support of those fighting.

The battle started between seventeen and eighteen o'clock and continued for four hours. By the end, the enemy retreated after realizing that they could not succeed. They left many dead, wounded, and their ladders on the walls before regrouping at Codiponte. There were recriminations by the troops against Signor Federico, and an altercation between him and Signor Marcantonio followed. Signor Federico complained that Marcantonio had not taken the battle to Porta Bologna and Porta Santo Barnaba as planned. The other retorted that the entire enterprise had been in vain, that the battle had been underestimated, leading to the deaths of many worthy men who had been falsely persuaded by the French that the people would not take up arms. Thus, with little honor and less profit, the following morning they dismantled their encampments and retreated to the other side of the Po.

The event was quite dangerous, not only because it is difficult to conquer such a territory with ladders and hand-to-hand combat, which is truly quite difficult. Those on the inside could defend themselves risking very little. In fact, on our side, there were only two dead and about fifty wounded. The danger lay in the pusillanimity of the city, which had to be propped up by significant effort so that it would not surrender. In fact, I am certain that if they had not attacked on that day, the city would have come to terms because there were no reinforcements in sight, nor did they have any faith in my words, so low was their morale. In fact, I was later informed that they had already decided to surrender and that when the cry broke out that the enemy were massing along the walls, they had come to find me and tell me so, in no uncertain terms. Added to this were the difficulties posed by lack of money and ammunition for the troops. Not having ammunition is quite frightening. During the height of the battle we were without light powder, and the gunners had to be supplied with heavy powder. However, with the aid of God, I can truly say that the city remained under the dominion of the church owing to my efforts. This was significant, not only because it undid the French plans as described above, but also because of the example set for other peoples to take heart, such as the Milanese who valiantly resisted the French when they passed through Lombardy with a very powerful army.

LETTER TO FRANCESCO MARIA DELLA ROVERE

Carnaiola, May 10, 1527

As I wrote this morning to your most reverend lordship, we have received notice through various channels, although not before last night, that on the morning of Monday the sixth the enemy took the Borgo as I notified you before yesterday. Then continuing in victory, they took Trastevere on that same day. In the evening at the twenty-third hour, they entered Ponte Sisto and Rome, which they then sacked with infinite homicides and cruelty according to what has become known. On the same morning, our lord took refuge in Castel Sant'Angelo and was of the opinion to flee to Ostia. However, after having learned from a prisoner of the death of Borbone,[1] and reports that they were not going to take Rome, our poor lord allowed himself to be convinced not to depart. Most certainly, until the very last day we retained much hope of defending everything. On the fourth, they had written to Count Guido to send them only the four hundred light cavalry and five hundred infantry and for him to come with the rest and join us. Notwithstanding such confidence, your reverend lordship may see how vilely Rome was lost and how the world was ruined in a single day's close combat. Signor Renzo and Signor Orazio and many others, accompanied by the useful and the useless, entered the castle with the better part and perhaps all the nobility and, according to my understanding, with many supplies and munitions of every type. From Todi came news that his Holiness had retreated to

---

1. Charles III, Duke of Bourbon (1490–1527).

FIG. 5 | Maarten van Heemskerck, *Sack of Rome*, ca. 1555–56. Photo: Rijksmuseum, Amsterdam.

Civitavecchia, although I do not believe it, since I have no confirmation. I learned today that the viceroy has joined the army, but I do not know for sure, although I would desire it. Nor has it been learned from the troops of the realm,[2] nor from the Colonna until today, if after such disgrace there was any movement at all. I do not know how they will cope, nor do I know his Holiness's plans. The latest news I have from them is of the loss of Borgo. Nor do I believe that they have had means to write afterward. His Holiness had previously desired and requested us not to enter Rome but to make contact so we would be in a position to impede enemy supplies. If we were to arrive in time, he figured that they could be reduced to a sorry state. Thus, according to this plan, we would then continue from here to the Tiber. On this assumption, we arrived at the

2. The "troops of the realm" would be from the Realm of Naples.

Castello della Pieve, hoping that the Duke of Urbino would follow the same route, especially since at Montevarchi, where we joined, he did not express any other opinion. On the day we left Cortona, he wrote for us to come to Castello della Pieve and that he would come to Pacciano. However, the following day he notified us that he had decided to march toward Perugia and then to Orte, intending to arrive there by the road to Orvieto and to cross the Tiber at Orte. We were concerned by the possibility of separation. However, we were much more upset after having heard the latest painful news since there are not enough of us to rescue the castle on our own, although the French are quite ready. Nor can we anticipate the mindset of the duke, whether he is still of the same mind and whether he will be able to join us without further delays. This is imperative, because any rescue must necessarily go by our route to the castle and not by his since the Tiber is between him and the castle. Today, I sent you the marquis, Signor Giangiorgio da Castiglione, and Lorenzo Cambi to arrange for a rescue, but I do not know how much hope to place in his resolve. The attempt was initially suspended as the enemy approached; however, there are now even more imposing reasons to act. Saving his Holiness's person is of such importance that it takes precedence over everything. Tomorrow, God willing, we will go to Orvieto, which we were prevented from doing today and yesterday by the elevated level of the Paglia. I believe that we will receive a response from the duke, who these lordships have decided to await, for they will not proceed unless he joins. Count Guido led the light cavalry and eight hundred harquebusiers on Monday evening to Ponte Solaria. However, upon learning of the loss of Rome, he retreated to Orticoli, where the rest of the infantry was. He wrote to me on the seventh, although I only received his message this morning. Due to doubts about the duke engaging, he wanted to go to Modena with the horse and infantry that he had led from Modena, a thought based upon his own interests without consideration for the danger faced by our wretched master or any memory of the countless benefits received from him. I wrote to him repeatedly to do nothing of the sort, and instead to come with all those troops with us from Orvieto. I do not know if he will do so, even if it would be dishonest to proceed in any other manner. This should not cause you to allow the troops you paid for to be taken to Modena.

I left your most reverend lordship a note regarding the infantry sent with Count Guido, the number of soldiers under every captain, and their payment schedules. There is no hope that the poor pope will be able to pay their wages. Yet, if we are to rescue his Holiness, these wages must be paid, and paid on time. Considering the present situation, we do not want to be left defenseless at the hour of greatest danger. I have no money, as he is well aware. However, the importance of such provisions must be recognized, and since it must be sent, then let it be accompanied by a detachment of light cavalry. If we have advance warning, then we will send an escort. I will write every day, although it is quite difficult to send letters because of the various detachments that are blocking the roads. I have no news of your lordship since we left Cortona despite having written almost every day by different routes. As for the rest, etc.

CONSOLATION

Composed September 1527 at Finocchietto[1] during the plague

Francesco, although I know you possess an unwavering and vigorous spirit, I am not surprised to find you overcome by great sadness. In a single period, too many misfortunes have converged to afflict you. It is not in wealth alone that you suffer, but in power, dignity, and what you value above all else, honor.[2] Because of the fall of a pontiff, you lost the Romagna presidency, a position that gave you considerable benefits and prestige that would have honored any great man born to a station above that of a commoner. You lost a pontiff who was uncommonly loyal to you. He held you in high esteem and always wanted you to advise him and negotiate important and secret affairs of state. During the war, he assigned you armies with so much authority that he reserved nothing higher even for himself. Therefore, besides having occupied yourself in honorable matters in which your character delights, you enjoyed great fame and esteem and would have retained this reputation with all the princes of Christendom. Throughout Italy, you were renowned and admired more than I believe you had ever hoped or dared imagine. From this position of power and reputation, legitimate and honorable wealth came to your hands that gave offense or displeasure to no one. I also know how much you valued seeing the way open for you to arrange the best and honorable marriages for your daughters. These losses, great in themselves, seem compounded by the way they occurred. For it was not the natural death

---

1. Guicciardini's villa near Florence, where he retired during the plague that broke out in Florence in 1527.
2. "Grandezza," literally "greatness," with the modern connotation of "power." For Guicciardini's ideas about the value of honor, see *ricordi* C15, C16.

of the pope, or some obstacle befalling you, nor some ordinary event that you could have anticipated that deprived you of so much status. Instead, atrocious and miserable circumstances caused that poor and wretched prince to become the unhappy prisoner of the Spaniards.[3] You must feel wounded not only by your own loss, for your personal interests, but also by the damage to Italy and to the entire world. You also feel compassion for that unhappy lord to whom you have so great an obligation for the benefits and the high honors that he gave you, and even more for the extraordinary faith that he placed in you. He often put his entire state into your hands, even though you were neither his relative nor had you served his family in challenging times, thus obligating him in any way.[4]

Besides the sorrow that you feel over his misery, I believe what troubles you is the notion that you were the one who recommended and urged the decision to start the war that gave rise to all his misfortunes. This impression that you caused these disastrous and ruinous events must vex you. However, I believe that you could bear this well enough if you had lost nothing more than the favors contingent upon the papacy. They were temporary and not yours by any natural right. Nevertheless, when I see that you have been stricken, one might say, personally, in your relationship with your native city, I believe that your grief has no limit. I also see that you have been maliciously and unjustly charged with a fine that your means cannot withstand.[5] If it is ever enforced, you must impoverish yourself to pay it. If you do not pay, you will lose your rights as a citizen, and perhaps even the right to reside in your homeland. Other inconveniences aside, it will become increasingly difficult to marry off your daughters, for whom you care so deeply. Those who requested your daughters in marriage in the past will refuse them should you now make the offer.

Because of the mood of the city, you are completely excluded from government with little hope that these upheavals, caused by error or malice, can be calmed as quickly as some may believe. So, after enjoying a position of the highest honor, reputation, momentous enterprise, and fame, you are suddenly hurled down to the opposite extreme of idleness:

---

3. After the Sack of Rome by the Spanish imperial troops on May 6, 1527, Clement VII took refuge in the fortress of Castel Sant'Angelo.

4. The Medici were expelled from Florence between 1494 and 1512.

5. Guicciardini writes how the Florentine republican government has singled out twenty wealthy citizens of questionable loyalty or reputation for forced loans to the republican government.

abject, alone, without dignity and without responsibility, lower in status in your city than a petty commoner. Thus, I believe that you are embarrassed when foreigners, passing through, who recall your past glory, learn how you have been reduced to such a base and unhappy station. Nor are your enemies a small concern. In return for having done what was necessary, and for having served your lord faithfully and honorably, you have made many powerful enemies throughout Italy.[6] They could harm you in many ways, especially if you go abroad where you will no longer have the protection of guards and men-of-arms as in the past. Of the power and the authority that you once enjoyed, you now retain only danger. Out of necessity, you must maintain a standard of living more expensive than someone of your present station and means can sustain.

All the troubles mentioned above are pressing, but I know how much importance you have always attached to honor. For its sake, you maintained your integrity and always respected the property of others. In all your work and activity, you strove to acquire a good name. I know how much you have always loved your native city and how much stock you place in keeping in its good graces with a solid reputation. For this reason, in all your great enterprises, you never strayed from the thoughts and behavior of a good citizen. Moreover, I am certain that these groundless accusations cause you to suffer deeply in your heart and are eating away at your soul. Without any foundation in truth, without any explanation, rumors have been spread everywhere that you avariciously and maliciously stole public monies during this war and allowed soldiers to rampage in the countryside. You are reputed to have the soul of a tyrant and to be an enemy of the city's freedom. This opinion has not only been expressed in words but more thoroughly by deed. In the decision to impose penalties, and in the selection of twenty persons to make forced loans, you are reduced to the same level as base, worthless persons, to usurpers with reputations for the worst sorts of corruption. You can no longer enjoy the good name and reputation as a friend of the people known for integrity and modesty, earned after so much toil and danger in foreign lands. Instead, in the homeland that was always in your thoughts, you are considered a dishonest, undignified, immoderate man who is a threat to public safety.

---

6. Guicciardini served as papal governor of Modena in 1516 and eventually as governor of the entire province of Romagna in 1523.

When I ponder these matters, and reflect on how much you have been wronged, and how little recognition your good work has received, God help me, I am in pain because of the love that I feel for you. I do not mean pain equal to yours, although I can imagine how I would feel if my affairs were in such a desperate state. If I could do anything to somehow alleviate your suffering, I would prove my sympathy by deed, even if it involved great sacrifice on my part. Powerless as I am, I can try only to console you with a soothing measure of words and speak to you as a friend.

Your afflictions are undoubtedly severe, and the reasons causing you to suffer are convincing. However, if you think carefully, ultimately are there not even more convincing arguments for you to take comfort and consolation? I speak of arguments easily within the grasp of man's understanding, and not outside our daily existence that is so delicate and cannot withstand overpowering remedies and medicines. You should accept and understand the words of philosophers or theologians on the subject, for far worse maladies than yours are easily curable. You should think of the life to come, in comparison to which this life exists only as an instant. God often sends tribulations not to punish men but to purify them. He who patiently bears trials for his love should consider it a blessing to be visited by him here, in this manner, because of the significant advantage in the beyond. Anyone who could bring these lessons to mind would find more pleasure in your discomfort than you have ever found in any happiness. He who takes a philosophical approach understands that the rewards of fortune are of no importance and should be treated as the vilest things. Whoever loses them loses a useless and burdensome load, rather than something of value. Happiness and the supreme good consist only in virtue and in the riches of the soul. Someone, I repeat, who remembers this, even having lost what you have lost, would not deem to have lost anything at all, but would feel lighter, unburdened, and ready to continue his way.

These things are quite true, and if we purified our souls, as we should, our infirmities would heal, and we would always be happy and content in this world. I believe that anyone willing for these reasons to reject the world and not care or worry about his own troubles is not merely praiseworthy but also quite admirable and even blessed. However, I can excuse someone prevented by human frailty from reaching so high and, with every adversity, remembering himself to be a man. As much as I want you to reach this level of perfection, I must confess it is alien to me. I do not want to imitate doctors who prescribe medicines that they would not take themselves. Therefore, let me speak to you on a lower level, more in accordance with the nature of men and the ways of the world.

I am convinced that the loss of the position you enjoyed with the church, such as the Romagna office and being a confidant of the pope, has caused you little harm. On this account, you need little consolation. This is not because those advantages were not as important and as worthy as stated above. Rather, I know that you are not so imprudent nor such a poor observer of the ways of the world to ever consider them as anything but alien and temporary and liable to be taken away or given at any moment. A change in the pope's mind, even though you seemed firmly established, could surely have arisen from the whims of his character, a change in court, or many other circumstances. He could have taken everything away from you at a moment's notice. In the end, his death, which you knew could come at any time, would eventually have deprived you of everything. You must remember that Leo's death occurred during the period of his greatest success and victory, and you had hopes of obtaining some reward for the travail that you had endured for him that summer.[7] If his end came suddenly and unexpectedly, you knew that the same could happen again to this pope. It does not matter how much you hoped his life and your good relations would continue because you knew that it could not last forever and your position could be lost at any time. Nevertheless, you still would not have lost anything that was your own by natural right but something purely contingent and temporary. Therefore, I am certain this does not vex or afflict you at all. If you had lost nothing more, in a few days, even after a few hours, you should have completely forgotten about it.

Of course, it is praiseworthy and pious of you to feel sorrow that the pope's affairs have come to such a miserable end. As you have told me many times, you never find yourself in a mood or thought happy enough not to change to the deepest melancholy by the mention of his captivity. This is out of consideration not for your own losses but for his lamentable misfortune. Nevertheless, this alone should not keep you in your present state of great and perpetual sorrow, in need of consolation from

---

7. Guicciardini first worked under Pope Leo X, who died December 1, 1521, suddenly leaving Guicciardini in charge of a garrison at Parma in the midst of a battle against French forces.

others and me. Since the matter did not principally concern you, this grief should eventually run its course after a few weeks. When unhappiness is born from compassion for someone else's suffering, there is no reason for such suffering to continue day after day. It should wane of its own accord. Therefore, let me state once again that the reason for your sorrow has a source other than this state of deprivation of those things that you know were not even naturally yours. They could not exist in perpetuity, since the moment to lose them could have arisen at any time.

The substance of your unhappiness lies in the infamy and hatred that you seem to have contracted among your fellow citizens. You have also been reduced in status, not in comparison to what you enjoyed in past years, but in comparison to your peers in your native city. You also feel wounded in an area that you value as much as life itself, in those things that seemed to be intrinsically yours forever. Therefore, the substance of my consolation consists in this: come what may, and whether what you are calling a calamity will continue or not, it must be enough for your peace of mind to realize that you have been falsely accused. You are completely innocent, and your conscience is clear. Your conduct in this war was beyond reproach. The truth is that you handled public and private funds with absolute integrity and what Thucydides wrote about Pericles may proudly be claimed about you.[8] He was without a doubt incorruptible in financial affairs. Indeed, there never was a man who worked with greater diligence, thriftiness, and passion against useless spending. You are to be doubly praised, because your tenure was long and extensive, and you enjoyed a free hand in your administration. Everything was under your control without any supervision. Therefore, more than for others the words of Paul befit you, "He could have done but did not, and he could have transgressed, but transgressed not."[9]

Nor is it true that you allowed the destruction in our territory. You are not to blame either in action or by negligence. To the contrary, you toiled and struggled to prevent it so adamantly that you made enemies and even put your life in danger. Therefore, let a clean conscience be the foundation and solid basis for your consolation. You are completely innocent of all the calumnies attributed to you. You can boldly say that

---

8. Pericles (ca. 495–429 BC) was an Athenian statesman. Thucydides (ca. 460–400 BC) was an Athenian general and historian.

9. From Ecclesiasticus 31:10, "qui potuit transgredi, et non est transgressus; facere mala, et non fecit."

you have never taken the money of others. I never permitted it. In fact, whenever I was able, no matter what, I always made sure that none of the citizens and subjects of my city or even outsiders and foreigners were ever injured or abused by anyone. Keeping this in mind, the false charges and rumors should not disturb you because it is vain and ridiculous to heighten one's outrage by claiming innocence and false accusation, as if suffering unjustly causes more pain than suffering with good reason.

I confess that in a certain sense someone who understands that they deserve to be punished should not lament at all. Anyone punished for an act they have committed is forced to recognize his own faults and declare, "I deserve this and worse." When considering the reasons for a sentence, someone who is innocent should not feel any pain or displeasure at all. The guilty feel greater torment, afflicted by their own conscience. They receive no relief because of the realization that they have no right to lament about their punishment. Those are the pains and the thorns, the worm that gnaws at the gut, the flame, born of itself that never allows repose. The guilty are forced to admit that they are the cause of the pain they suffer; it proceeds from their actions and deeds. It is like the boulder of Sisyphus that never stops or rests but keeps those who have sinned without punishment in a state of continual suffering and burning. Those who are guilty of a sin and receive no punishment suffer a continuous fire. Outward and formal sentencing is slight in comparison to being continuously afflicted and tormented by one's own conscience, which cannot be expelled without shame and displeasure. The more it is hidden and kept inside, the more it afflicts, gnaws, and burns.

Since you are innocent and blameless of these imputations, the main and principal part is lacking, or to put it better, the substance of any anxiety you may feel. You lack what is most difficult to console. What remains, if you choose to take heart and have a more positive outlook, requires no consolation. It is as if you were stranded in the countryside during a great downpour, but with the very sort of hat and clothing that water cannot penetrate. Not a single drop has touched your person or even the clothing close to your body. Once you arrive home, you find that only your outermost articles of clothing are wet. Once you remove them, your person and other clothing appear as if it had never rained. If you think about it, are not these false voices against you also purely exterior? You remain as true, honest, virtuous, as before. You have been stricken by a calamity that is not unique but frequent in antiquity and in our own times to men of virtue, prudence, generosity, and uncompromising modesty. In fact, it is normal for rare and excellent men to suffer the winds of envy. There are so many famous examples that it is inadequate to name just one. Those who live like saints and perform countless acts for the nation are always cut down by rumors and slander, lose their possessions, sent into exile, and even deprived of life by an ungrateful people and nation.

So how can you complain? You are neither the first nor the only one to suffer such unhappiness. It has happened to an infinite number of great and good men. Furthermore, up to now your pain is quite bearable. You have not been stripped of your possessions nor sent into exile. There is no sentence or mark of infamy against you. There has been only some rumoring. The matter of this groundless penalty and forced loan are just manifestations of the hatred and poor opinion that these slanders have generated in men, not the final results. How then can you complain if confronted with something that is not unusual, unheard of, but frequent and common? Many in equal circumstances have been abused much more than you have. To put it plainly, all you have is a wet hat, boots, and coat. Remember that you were born a man, subject to the ways of the world, to the whips of fortune like all men.

The great and perpetual happiness that you enjoyed until now should have made you realize that you were subject to human affairs. This should have been fixed into your consciousness, and made you wary of being at fault, considering the lives ruined before yours. Even children, or the illiterate, know that prosperity does not last, that fortunes change. You are no stranger to study; you have witnessed much and managed many great enterprises. How can you be surprised and feel oppressed by this situation? Can you not bear a brief period of unhappiness after so many years in which you felt honored and content? Believe me, this is a slight matter in comparison to what often does occur. Until now, there has just been some rumoring among the ignorant rabble, of which knowledgeable men take little account. You have always aspired to this calling and profession. Do you want your life to impart a lesson and meaning different from those who have preceded you?

You also cannot claim that you did not foresee this or other contingencies. Many times, during your period of prosperity, I heard you remark how wary you were of good fortune. You spoke of how fortune is liable to change, never stable for anyone. Even if I had never heard you say that, I know that you are not so ignorant of the ways of the world not to envision this possibility. It is normal for someone like you, who has managed and still handles great matters, to feel beaten down in this manner. Things do not always go according to plan. One must understand that rumors and public condemnation are just the fruits of envy. So why complain? You wanted to manage great and honorable affairs, and now you must suffer the consequences like everyone else. You should be pleased with yourself. Your career was much more successful and longer than is commonly the case. Nobody ever enjoys perpetual happiness. Very few have done better than you have, and an infinite number, either in the beginning of their efforts or of their troubles, suffered some obstacle from fortune. For you until now everything has gone very well, not trouble free, but there was never anything in your affairs to cause you real pain. Now adversity has paid you a visit, but in comparison to what the world can deliver and does inflict every day upon everyone, rather than complaining you should thank God for not sending anything worse. Instead of feeling that the situation is too harsh and severe, you should pray that he stops now and sends no greater woes.

What if this undertaking, that excited you so, had been as successful as first anticipated? You would have acquired more power, reputation, and honors than those you lost. There is such a difference between the two outcomes that you should even consider the possibility that fortune took pity on you. You knew from the outset that the enterprise was fated to go awry, and you would not come out unscathed. You are indebted to fortune since your losses have been bearable. Rather than insisting on being unhappy because the enterprise went badly, you must understand that it was not your affair, but rather that of many princes. You were not involved as a prime player but as their instrument. Winning or losing did not depend on your good or bad luck, but on the luck of the pope, emperors, kings, and the world whose course and revolutions do not consider the fortunes of you and your peers. Therefore, you cannot complain about the cause of your suffering. Instead, you should realize that this disaster was due to the bad luck of others, not you. In fact, you suffered comparatively little and could have easily expected to suffer much more.

Consider the suffering of others, the miserable predicament of those who held the same rank with the same prince as you. In this affair and undertaking, they played the same part as you, yet in comparison, your fate has been mild. You have saved your person, liberty, rights, and your conscience is clear. As for your honor, in reality and substance, nothing has changed. It may seem besmirched in the opinion of commoners and the ignorant. However, this has given you an opportunity to understand the maliciousness of envy.

Nor should you be disturbed by what I stated at the outset. The recollection that you were among those who supported the war, the source of all this ruin, may gnaw at your conscience. Here you must bear some of the blame. However, this only strengthens the argument for your consolation. There was little if any consultation after the final decision to undertake the war even after it was discovered that the king of France did not plan to honor the terms of surrender he made with the emperor at Madrid.[10] Your conscience should be troubled if you gave poor advice out of ambition or malice. However, you should not vex or disturb yourself for a mere error in judgment. In instances of such importance and uncertainty, this often occurs to men wiser and more expert than you. A conscience is reproachable only when guilt is willful and deliberate.

You and the others who shared your opinion are freely absolved from guilt because of the nature of circumstances, as anyone who carefully considers the facts of the case must admit. The pope had been mistreated. The path for a monarchy under Caesar in Italy appeared to be open. The pope had an excellent chance to ally himself with the king of France, the Venetians, and even the king of England.[11] The imperials were weak, had few followers in Italy, and were out of money. They had made enemies of the citizens of Milan, who did not take up arms out of ambition but to protect themselves. Anyone who considers these facts will be forced to admit that rarely did a prince undertake something so just and necessary, and with greater hopes for victory. Everyone, including men of knowledge, cried out against the timidity and indecision of the pope. He seemed to be moving slower than necessary toward a decision. Of course, events went differently from expectations. Yet one cannot blame those who argued in favor of the war, because facts had persuaded even the wisest men to support it. How can a prince's counselor be expected

---

10. After the 1525 Battle of Pavia, King Francis I of France was imprisoned by the victorious forces of the Holy Roman Emperor Charles V in the tower at Pizzighettone in the Po Valley.

11. The pope here is Clement VII. Caesar as the Holy Roman Emperor is Charles V. The king of France is Francis I. The king of England is Henry VIII.

to advise not only on human affairs but also astrologers' readings, spirit conjuring, and the prophecies of friars?[12]

You are not to blame if your advice about the war did not correspond exactly with the outcome. You deserve praise for doing as much as possible for events to unfold as expected in theory. The outcome may have been different if others with roles in the war had behaved as well as you did, or if the pope, after having entered this sea, had navigated according to your counsel. Therefore, your advice, which was always reasonable, is not to blame. Nor are you to blame in the action itself since you never failed when you were in charge. You should be pleased with yourself and realize how innocent and blameless you appear. Rest assured, the spread of rumors about your honesty and the damage by the soldiers will also be cleared up promptly. The truth will be revealed, for you as for others falsely accused. Time alone, without other help, will clear the imputations against you that have no truth in them at all.

Sometimes charges are proven false, but if they have some hint or appearance of truth, even the wisest people may reasonably believe them. Further clarifications and time are needed for these charges to be cleared. However, your case is so plain and simple that everyone understands how senseless it would have been for you to allow our country to be pillaged to acquire hate and infamy, and gain nothing for yourself. It is well known and documented that the money spent in this war did not pass through your hands. If you ordered that the money be spent, others can confirm whether payments were made or not. Those who handled the money are still alive. The pope hired them, so the accounting they render will in no way diminish or enhance your reputation.

You must realize how little weight this charge carries. How can you doubt that you will soon be free from these difficulties? The long memory of your honesty, known and celebrated in foreign lands, has not faded. Your former reputation still resounds in this city, even if somewhat tarnished by these latest rumors. But as the charges weaken, your good name will return and, along with the truth, will extinguish this groundless charge even further. I am also convinced that more people have said

---

12. A reference to Girolamo Savonarola (1452–1498), who briefly conditioned Florentine politics before he was excommunicated by the Borgia pope Alexander VI and was later tried and executed by the Florentine Republic on May 23, 1498. Savonarola predicted that Italy would suffer devine wrath as retribution for moral laxity. In 1528, Guicciardini collected the *Estratti savonaroliani* excerpts of Savonarola's prophecies.

such things than believe them. With these recent troubles, men not used to suffering said the first thing that came to mind. Others who had also not suffered were incited by envy. Although many believed, the matter will be cleared up easily. Prudent and impassioned men did not behave in this manner because it was like the overcoat that I mentioned before. From afar, it might have seemed that you were soaked by something besides water. However, anyone who was nearby would realize that the truth, your coat, would be dry within a few days. Eventually it made no difference whether one had observed from near or from afar since there would be no spots, as it was only water. In this manner, the multitude that considers things superficially heard that it was oil and not water and that is what they believed. Wise men who examined more carefully were not so easily fooled. However, since the incident is not recent, everyone now recognizes that it was water, and the mantle of your reputation will once again be clean, immaculate. I have insisted on this point to persuade you that this infamy will pass, and you should pay little heed since your conscience is clear. Yet I know how profoundly some men value honor and would never imagine allowing their reputation to be questioned, even among the ignorant.

I do not want to insist just to persuade you that the people's suspicions about your relations with the Medici will pass. However, the time will come, perhaps sooner than you think, when you will again enjoy a solid reputation. Yet this manner of consoling you when everything is so evident seems too effeminate. If you are blessed with a greatness of spirit and virility, as I believe you are, and if no greater harm is done to you than to be on the receiving end of some unfair treatment, then you will handle this unpleasantness without difficulty. I also believe, in fact I am certain, that if the city remains steadfast and does not drown in this great approaching storm, before long you will no longer be rejected. Even in these strange times, men will eventually realize that they lost something by not appreciating your virtue and experience, qualities that cannot go unnoticed under the present shortage of men. I also believe that because of the way you have lived and the memory of the past, men will come to realize that you are not against freedom. You have always supported governments that benefited and served the city. You never favored or encouraged anyone who sought a revolution. I believe this; however, I want to put it aside because as I said, you should be satisfied without recurring to such arguments. All the books and histories that you have studied, the enterprises that you have managed, must have trained your spirit to remain steadfast and resolute. In fact, the memory of your achievements, like the rule of law and truth, will carry more weight than vain rumors.

I will readily admit that many praise a life of leisure and tranquility. However, few ever had the opportunity to serve with honor, and therefore do not embrace the active life as readily as retirement. Every day one can see that those reduced to a quiet and secluded life are upset at having left their work and ambitions behind. As soon as they perceive an opening at power, they throw themselves at it without any embarrassment about abandoning the peace they praised so much. Such men did not choose a quiet life out of a love for God, or weariness of the ways of the world and fortune, or out of any true or real choice, but out of necessity, anger, or poor health. However, I will repeat that you could learn to be content with such a life even if you do not find it as attractive as your former existence.

You should not be upset to the point that finding yourself excluded would seem like a disaster or calamity. In my opinion, one must not reproach but rather encourage the ambition of those who never undertook any great deeds. For they also want to demonstrate their ingenuity, virtue, and the talent given to them by nature, or which they acquired accidentally. If such men do not do something at least once, they will spend life as useless persons born to benefit only themselves.

This sentiment does not apply to you because you managed important events with success. You proved your worth in great enterprises on a stage more suited for someone of a higher station or of a different profession. However, if you wanted to be known as incorruptible, that money, friendships, prayers, and respect of the powerful were not enough to turn you from the straight and narrow path, you have proven this so publicly that you could desire nothing further. If it was dear to you to be known as courageous and virile, ready to face travails and great dangers in the field, or the siege of a city, this is known and believed even too readily. Ask anywhere you were stationed, the people you governed, the armies under your authority, all will state that you are a man of ability, resolute at trials, adept at decision making, and expedient in action. They will also give an account of your defects, because nobody is born perfect. However, they will celebrate you in the main points. Therefore, the reputation you bring from abroad is alive and well among us even if you were abroad working for the church rather than directly involved in the affairs of the city. You have no need to prove yourself in any way, and you should avoid further duties, negotiate the waves of the storm, and guide your boat into port, loaded with goodwill and rare praise from men.

On the other hand, the desire to work is praiseworthy. A man who is aware of his good qualities may persuade himself because of the times or other reasons to serve his country or abroad. Alternatively, he may be driven by a sense of duty and the desire to act. I do not believe that this is what bothers you, even if you presume more of yourself than from others. Life in Florence is not such that a citizen may perform great deeds alone. Yet when possible, you followed your instincts and were prepared when the occasion presented itself and your country called. Nor should you be displeased at all, if having performed such deeds was a loss for the country and those who would have directly benefited, when they did not value or want your help.

Those who desire an active life have other motivations. They may have an appetite for honors because they dread going through life without having ever held important offices. This is not as praiseworthy as the reasons mentioned above, but it is not damnable either. I do not mean just a desire for a good reputation and glory. This is also not your case, since you were active from a very young age. It has probably been hundreds of years since our country has produced a citizen more honored than you. Others may desire enterprises just to turn a profit. Besides being a lowly calling, I do not believe that this concerns you either because if God preserves your means, at your station, you will have more than enough to live comfortably. I also remember having heard you say many times that the goal of all your efforts and travails was not wealth. You knew that no matter how much you earned there would always be citizens in Florence, without your virtue or rare qualities, richer than you. Therefore, you were more interested in honor, where you could hope to be without peer, for others could match you only by being more virtuous.

There are men of another type who do not desire enterprises for the trappings that come with them, but simply because they take pleasure and find sustenance in work. I think this better describes your situation. For you, having a goal is pleasing in itself, a trait bestowed by nature. It follows, therefore, that if nature gives men a certain inclination, to force someone not to act according to their nature would be wrong. Here let me state that enterprises of the type we are considering, in statecraft and government, have many difficulties, displeasures, and dangers. Anyone who becomes involved only to satisfy an idle whim will doubtlessly find more trouble than satisfaction. Or perhaps there will be not much difference, for finding oneself excluded can also cause anxiety. Consider the following carefully and you will realize that anyone who undertakes such enterprises without understanding why such activity is desirable will remain amateurish in their efforts. The work would be routine, cut and dry, and so stark that he would not miss it upon retirement.

There remains the last objective that appeals more than all others to generous souls of noble talent, and this is ambition itself. I mean the desire to be held in esteem and honored by men, to maintain a powerful reputation, and to be well known, pointed out by others. Demosthenes as he walked in the street was flattered to hear an old woman returning from the water fountain say in a low voice to her neighbors, "That one there, that is Demosthenes."[13] Managing affairs of state and having power makes you, in a manner of speaking, an object of adoration for others. This appetite is excusable, for admittedly, to be held in reverence among men is a beautiful and blessed thing. In nothing else does it seem that we more resemble God.[14] However, this sentiment should not dominate you, especially if you consider how much effort, how many travails, suspicions, and dangers there are in such a life compared to the ease, rest, security, and contentment of the soul in a leisurely and tranquil existence. The latter may seem preferable, or at least without so much difference between the two to justify denying a role assigned by fate. Those who strive for superficial and vain goals are uneducated or inexperienced, without vision in these matters. They allow themselves to be blinded by the splendor of the trappings of power. However, you are experienced in the ways of the world because of everything you have read and seen. You understand how fortune may vary. Your experienced hand knows that the only good thing about power is its outward appearance. Beneath that cover, it is full of danger, insult, exhaustion, and trouble. You must not be concerned with the vanities that drive others, but only by true reasoning based upon a solid foundation.

Many times, I have heard you, like most men, desire honor and service. By the grace of God and good fate, you came out many times head of your expectations. Nevertheless, you never found any of the satisfaction you imagined at the outset. The lesson, as you often say, if anyone were

---

13. Athenian statesman and orator, 384–322 BC.
14. Guicciardini's *ricordo* C16.

to consider these matters carefully, is that it would be enough to extinguish this thirst. However, if that life is not as satisfying as the ignorant believe, why is it such an object of desire? I admit that to be esteemed and well reputed by others is a beautiful thing. Your words and ideas are celebrated, and you interact with the major power brokers in your country. Upon careful consideration, a life free from greed is also pleasing. You rely on yourself rather than the opinion of others. You may organize your time as you like, even rest should you have the inclination, without being subject, or at least less subject, to changes in fortune. You are not as concerned should others profit. You can enjoy the city or your villa as you please, to the contentment of your mind. All of these things are absent from the workings of an ambitious life. Because of the adoration it inspires, honor does have a similarity to godliness. This is also true about a life with a measure of security and calm, content, tranquil, above the pains, vain concerns, and perturbations of men.

You could certainly disagree with my words and opinions. If you were a person whose status and qualities were unremarkable, worthy only of an abject and humble station, then the quiet life would be enough for you. This sort of life allows a clear conscience, tranquil mind, and an untroubled soul. Yet, I do not feel this perfection in myself, nor do I seek it in you. However, I do say that your case is quite different because of the great enterprises in which you struggled in the past, and because of your reputation. I will not recount common opinion of your good qualities, for I do not wish to seem like a flatterer. However, you still seem attracted by the active life, unable to do without esteem and honor. You are surrounded by honored relatives, who like you will always command respect in the minds of men. Therefore, the marrying of your daughters or other affairs considered above will not cause any difficulty. You will not have a mundane retirement. Considering the letters and the news of affairs that you receive, you will be able to account and dispense with your time with honor. You will have leisure with dignity, a life that in the judgment of ancient writers is as desirable as the active life but without the danger. This is preferable to being active and living with the dangers that have marked your life until now.

You will be able to live in leisure with dignity, with memories of achievements and the reputation attained through long and perilous service. You can spend time in the city or at the villa, alone or in conversation full of the thoughts, works, and memories worthy of your past. Either I am fooling myself, or your situation will be desirable, tranquil, secure, and honorable. It would not be any less praiseworthy to accept this condition than to insist on a more active existence. In fact, it would enhance your reputation. Since you gave a good account of yourself by working and acquiring a reputation in that life, now you have an opportunity to give a similar account of yourself in leisure and demonstrate your ability to organize yourself as well in action as in retirement.

Some wise men say that life is like a comedy, in which praise for the actors does not depend on the part assigned, but rather on how well everyone plays their role. Since everyone must play an assigned part, the only thing that is really yours is the way in which you do so. The character that we play in the world is the one assigned to us by fortune, but what is praiseworthy is the way we live given our station and fate. If playing a part well in a comedy is praiseworthy, then someone who plays two parts should be praised even more, especially if the parts are different! Therefore, if you consider carefully, your reputation is not diminished because you passed from activity to leisure. Actually, if you perform well, your reputation will be doubly enhanced. If the role that you have played until now earned you rare praise, then it will be even more notable for you to have performed well in two roles.

You must have read about Scipio Africanus, who went into exile so he would not have to bear the spectacle of an ungrateful nation.[15] He was so respected that even thieves went to see him and pay him homage. Leisure does not extinguish the memory of virtues past nor does it obscure the praise men attain. Did you know that once Diocletian abandoned the empire, he found contentment in his garden, in agriculture?[16] When recalled by the empire, he did not want to return to a life that had been so miserable and unhappy in comparison to the quiet he had been able to enjoy. Books are full of praise for tranquility and honest leisure. I do not mean leisure as idleness, but without the obligation to ambition or enterprise, able to respond to letters at will, to work in the fields, converse and reason profitably with friends. Nor is it an alienation from civil life, but a chance to live freely, securely, and with dignity, a lot certainly preferable to that of kings. I will not belabor the point by praising leisure with the grandiloquent terms

---

15. Scipio Africanus (236–183 BC), Roman general who defeated the Carthaginian general Hannibal.
16. Diocletian (244–311), Roman emperor.

common to many writings, because if the results do not please you thus far, if in these few weeks you have not yet begun to enjoy yourself, then to try to convince you otherwise with these words would be pointless.

In my judgment, you should consider yourself blessed to be afforded a chance to live like this. Although if your soul is not so disposed, at least this type of life should seem better to you than the previous one. You may become dissatisfied, because the world has a way of never being completely perfect in every aspect. Every life is lacking in some manner. The best are those that lack fewer important things, and yours seems to be one of these. External splendor is more vanity than anything else, without anything that really matters or is missing from life. I used to notice that you did lack some things in your previous affairs, that perhaps were not evident, but which did exist. It may appear that you are lacking on the other side, but that is not the case. Considering the station of your birth, how could you ever have hoped to achieve half of what you achieved? You have enjoyed more success than you ever hoped, so how can you call yourself unhappy? If you complain, you would be an ingrate. If your numerous honors had not come over the course of a lifetime but in a space of ten or twelve years, your life would still be considered a success. If you had received those honors earlier, accumulated them one after another, would that have been good or bad? You will certainly reply that it was a great blessing, and you could not do otherwise. Nor could you lament that everything ended too quickly, because what came early would have seemed enough had it taken your entire life to achieve. It would be as if a worker who has an entire day to finish a project complained about finishing at noon, because the rest of the day would seem empty. Or a merchant who wanted to earn in thirty years, God willing, thirty thousand ducats, and good fate had him earn the sum in only ten years.

You must not concern yourself with this undue infamy currently afflicting you. Since you are completely innocent, there is no reason to be upset. Given the nature of the matter, you may rest assured that everything will be quickly resolved and you will regain that measure of integrity and virtue that your actions and labors merit. You should also not be concerned about having counseled in favor of the war that ended so badly. After the liberation of the king, everything was decided without your input.[17] If you made an error, it was an error in judgment and not purpose. The advice was good

---

17. Another reference to Francis I (1494–1547), king of France, imprisoned in the tower of Pizzighettone after the Spanish defeat of the French at the battle of Pavia in 1525.

given the situation, for advice cannot promise results. In addition, you did more than your share, and if others had acted similarly, everything would have gone differently. Nor should you torment yourself over what you lost with the church. Those things were extraneous, and you knew that you could lose them any day. In fact, you should be thankful they lasted more than you had reason to hope at the outset. Nor should exclusion from positions in the Florentine government cause unhappiness, for you know how those things go, such a situation cannot last forever. For someone who has prospered so much, you must realize that those positions do not provide satisfaction and contentment of the soul, as many believe. You have earned enough from all this that if God conserves your means, you will be able to live honestly according to the customs of your people. In those positions, you earned something of inestimable value—a good name and a reputation for honesty and virtue, truly a glorious legacy.

The ambition to be esteemed and honored, placed among those who govern, is not that enviable but replete with struggles, displeasures, and dangers and should not be valued more highly than a life of repose. Contentment and security of the soul lie in the tranquility of honest leisure. This is especially true in your case, for you have the company of letters, news of the world, and a reputation owing to the good opinion resulting from memory of your accomplishments. So now, you will have leisure with dignity. Furthermore, you have relatives and other advantages in this country. Your life will not be abject and anonymous, buried away and neglected. If you are not to be directly involved in the action, you will have wind of it, be in the news and memory of men, a part of civil conversation, but without the obligation of direct involvement. If you are still dissatisfied, you will be acting like someone liberated from bondage who longs for his former life. Such an attitude is unreasonable; rather, it is a consequence of the habit of being in service.

The arguments I have made seem more than sufficient to me. They are in tune with the nature of our frailties. I will not repeat philosophical authorities who never gave much credence to the rewards of fortune because it changes too easily. Even when it does last, there is no tranquility and quiet of the soul, which is the main form of happiness. There is also the memory of Christian law reminding us that we all must die. In comparison to the next life, this one lasts only an instant. Our happiness or unhappiness must be measured according to the consequences our labors will reap in the life beyond. In fact, tribulations of the world are often desirable because they are a message from God. Those who receive them with a resolute spirit have a means of acquiring eternal happiness. Therefore, if you consider this situation as a Christian, a philosopher, and a man of the world, you will find either that this new life is quite desirable or at least not so bad as to deserve more complaint than due and proper. You still have the honor and reputation that you need and deserve. In addition, you do not seem like someone who was born yesterday, untested in the ways of the world. Everyone will recognize you as a person of the highest learning and virtue, with a soul forged by experience.

ACCUSATION

Your honors, God could not be asked to grant anything more propitious for the republic.[1] The new law promulgated with such ardor by the defenders of our liberty grants us a new opportunity that will serve as a notable and fortuitous confirmation of a new beginning for our republic.[2] There can be no doubt that divine will itself allowed us such an opportunity, not some human counsel or agency. The efforts of the grand citizens who opposed us and wanted to subjugate everyone by blocking enactment of the law despite acceptance by the entire city are evident to everyone. They are seeking to hinder its implementation through the machinations of influence and threats, so that nobody powerful will ever be convicted. They are trying to obtain by the collusion of a few what they were unable to obtain directly with the consent of the multitude.

I am ardently opposed to their actions, for I cannot think of anything more pernicious or nefarious for the republic. In fact, to be honest with you, omnipotent and supreme God, the declared protector of our city, inspired me to convene a trial to the benefit of the people. This is not the case of an obscure citizen accused of light infractions, something so unimportant that the republic would hardly benefit from his punishment or suffer damage by his acquittal. No, we have before us Francesco Guicciardini, thief of public monies, ravager of our county, a man who detests private life and favors the reinstallation of the Medici. He is a friend of

---

1. Guicciardini imagines himself as the defendant at his own trial during the short-lived restoration of the Florentine Republic after the Sack of Rome and the defeat of the Holy League against the imperial forces of Charles V.
2. The final Florentine republic came into being after the Medici were expelled following the Sack of Rome in 1527.

tyrants, the occupier of your city hall, and a determined enemy of common liberty.[3] He is full of such grave, notorious, hateful sins that his acquittal would be inconceivable. Yet he still holds enough power that his conviction, the clearing and eradication of a scourge from our republic, will be a great service. Also, if we set an example now, we will make it understood finally that these new trials place more weight in truth, religion, and the severity of the judges than in outside interests or corruption.

Rest assured, Your Honors, that what motivates me is my love for the republic and an overwhelming desire to see our liberty secured. I know that one of the best possible foundations for liberty is the terror and deterrence of the law. This is what drives me. I have no particular quarrel with him. In fact, as youngsters, we often spoke and were on good terms. Nor am I so well positioned that I can ignore the enemies that I will make after having prosecuted this case. My nature, as everyone knows, is not to offend or take pleasure from the suffering of others. Nor will I gain any great praise upon his conviction, because the facts of this trial will prove themselves, without any prosecutor's tricks. His sins are as enormous, dangerous, and evident as the criticism I would receive were he to be absolved. Men are more apt to recall a memory that does them harm than one that gave them pleasure. When enterprises go awry, the outcome receives more attention than its preparation.

However, I will not allow the nature of the case to intimidate me. What if Mr. Francesco Guicciardini's only sins were his ambition and the threat he poses to our liberty, but the rest of his life were unstained by serious crime? Alternatively, what if his morals were corrupt but his spirit and present condition did not pose a threat to the republic? I doubt that the integrity of his habits could defend him from the charge of ambition. Can the fact that he does not presently constitute a threat excuse his other sins and outweigh the demands of justice, especially given the immodest favoritism and extraordinary means you see employed by his friends and relatives? It is hard to tell which should motivate us, hatred for his character or fear of the consequences of his actions. However, the outcome of the trial cannot be in doubt. Everybody considered him as good as convicted the very day he was called to stand trial. After the

---

3. The prosecutor of Guicciardini's imagination is referring to Guicciardini's actions on St. Mark's feast day in 1527, when Guicciardini countered a popular uprising from taking control of the city government.

presentation of his crimes of avarice, theft, and the pillaging of the county before these judges and the people, the city will no longer have to tolerate his evil pestilence. What if the people had run in a fury to his home, to his property, to his daughters, to force him to suffer what he so unjustly inflicted upon so many? I hereby declare that in this war, Mr. Francesco Guicciardini stole an infinite sum of money from our community. To steal, he allowed our soldiers to live at the discretion of our city, which means he allowed them to rob and pillage as if they were our worst enemies. The authority he received to defend and preserve our state put it to plunder. I believe that similar things occurred in the lands of the church. However, I will not present injuries done to others, since our sufferings have been pain enough. Nor will I speak with malice or bias, because there are too many witnesses and evidence for the matter, which cannot be hidden or avoided. These charges do not come from a single individual, or a couple of witnesses. These charges are from people who are neither suspect nor hostile, or who might have something to gain by making a false accusation. These charges come from hundreds, even thousands of men, from an entire army under your command, an army you supported and that now hesitates to accuse you falsely. These charges come from entire provinces: the part of the Romagna subject to us; the people in the Mugello, Casentino, Val di Pesa, Valdarno, Arezzo, Cortona; from everyone who lives in these cities, in our villas and villages. If the birds, the rocks, the trees could talk, if our walls and towers were not mute, they would echo the cries of our peasants and the screams of our unfortunate maidens.

You will hear testimony from your fellow citizens about how when the army heard that there would be no pay and they would have license to live by discretion. These charges come from people worthy of trust who heard such statements not once or twice, but an infinite number of times in different places. Of course, he will produce his book of monthly accounts to prove otherwise. However, the Cortonesi, the Romagnoli, the Aretini, and an infinite number of your subjects confirm the same charges made by city dwellers. The Piacentini, the Bolognese, and the entire Romagna region under the control of the church make a similar report. In these places, as in our countryside, the crimes were infinite: with homicides, rapes of women of every age and type, old, young, girls, married, widows, virgins. Many of your castles and towers were sacked with a cruelty that would not have been expected of an enemy.

I beg the people patiently listening, hearing so many indignities, so many iniquities, so much pain, not to succumb to fury, do not stone this sick individual! Restrain yourselves because the judges must handle this case. It may have been more beneficial, more befitting the dignity of this city, and a better warning to others, if before the indictment, he had been exterminated or burned in his house in accordance with the fury of the people and the demands of posterity. Or, he could have been cut into pieces here, at the feet of Judith, at the doors of this building whose authority he violated in so many ways.[4] Thus, upon the same spot we could honor the memory of someone who saved their country and punish another who oppressed it. Now that the case is underway, and the trial has begun, it might set a poor example to kill him. Therefore, while the accusations are being read and the matter is before the judges, I ask you to allow justice to take its course. Your judges are prudent, virile, and honest men who are dedicated in their responsibility to our freedom. They are aware of the importance of his conviction. They have no fear of vain threats. They will not allow corruption by appeals or other means. They know your will. There is no danger of a compromise of justice, or disregard for the common good. As the judges rely on the prosecutor, you and the republic can rely on the judges.

Let me state once again that because of the unparalleled avarice of Mr. Francesco, your country and many provinces have been destroyed, replete with every crime imaginable: fires, homicides, rapes of women and virgins. Your own soldiers pillaged your castles with more savagery than would have been expected of an enemy. The towns of Barberino, Borgo, San Lorenzo, and Decomano, Pontasieve, San Casciano stand as witnesses to what occurred. The same report comes from those rich, beautiful and almost city-like castles at Valdarno, Figline, San Giovanni, and Montevarchi. They suffered such impiety and cruelty that our citizens envied Laterina, Quarata, Chiassa, and other places occupied by the Spaniards. Those we called our soldiers, to whom every month we doled out the pay through Mr. Francesco, treated our subjects a hundred

---

4. Donatello's statue of the biblical figure Judith outside the doors of the Palace of the Signoria in Florence, like Michelangelo's statue of David, was an emblem of republican independence. Judith was the young and wealthy widow of Bethulia who went to the encampments of Holofernes, general of the Assyrian king Nebuchadnezzar. After plying the general with wine, she cut off his head and brought it to the besieged Hebrews, thus inspiring them to victory.

times worse than they treated our enemies. I am not even broaching the subject of the grains and fodder they consumed. Nor will I speak of the wine spilled from barrels and canteens, the lakes formed owing to military drunkenness. Nor will I speak of livestock; whatever they could not eat they took away for sale in other provinces. They abandoned and left countless animals lifeless in the fields for the wolves. I will not speak nor lament about these things.

This is not a case of mere military excess. A country at the mercy of a supporting army must expect that army to feed itself, but not to ruin everything that is comestible. Everything was in the hands of Mr. Francesco: the furniture, fitting stores, houses, villas and buildings, the merchandise overflowing in places like Valdarno. Everything was subject to the same discretion, with the result that nothing remained intact in our houses and storerooms. Nothing remained that could be taken away. They claimed to be taking things as a form of payment. However, they not only took what they could carry. They destroyed, broke, and ruined the beautiful ornaments of our buildings. How many fires did they set all over the country! The houses burned, accompanied by the sound of breaking and shattering. There was fighting at the strongholds, estates and castles that did not want to open to them and experienced every sort of avarice, libido, and cruelty with no difficulty, since nobody had fled. Everyone or at least the most part awaited them as friends. Should they have expected otherwise from our own army, led by one of our citizens? Who would ever have thought that a son of Piero Guicciardini would harbor such a den of iniquity, that such a good, well-behaved, Catholic father produced such a pestilent weed? How many women were overpowered? How many men were clubbed and wounded? How many killed? Everywhere your peasants, your subjects, your stewards were taken and forced to buy back their freedom, to pay a ransom on themselves.

Should I lament the fate of peasants and subjects? If only God had willed the cruelty to end there and go no further. Our citizens were imprisoned, ransomed, and then tortured—those same citizens who had given whatever they could, who had taken food out of their own mouths to pay the levies and the taxes so that the soldiers would have money. Our citizens were accustomed to good treatment because our soldiers were housed, cared for, and honored by all. The same soldiers you had paid, retained, and lodged now tied, stripped, tortured, and murdered you. Ask the soldiers why they consumed your grain, wine, and livestock.

They will answer that they had not been paid and had to live on whatever they could find. Ask them why they pillaged, sold the furnishings and merchandise, and took hostages. They will tell you that even a soldier needs more than just food. They will claim that they had received permission from Mr. Francesco. Ask them why they forced themselves on the women? Why they burned so many houses? Why they killed so many men? Why they destroyed and ruined so much beautiful handiwork? Why they committed so many crimes without any benefit to themselves? They will tell you in a unified chorus that they saw that Mr. Francesco did not have any respect, humanity, or pity for his homeland and fellow citizens. They thought he hated them and treated them like enemies. Therefore, the soldiers concluded that the worse their actions, the more it would please him.

Oh ribaldry! Oh unparalleled wickedness! Oh gullibility, patience, and sweetness of the Florentine people! You have done so much evil, offended everybody public and private so atrociously, done worse to us than any enemy, put us to pillage and stole our money, killed us and murdered us with our own arms, the very arms that we gave you for our defense. Now you have the gall to show your face in the city hall, in public, in broad daylight. When the court called, did you dare to appear and hope for acquittal without being torn apart by this kind, good, and patient people? I cannot believe that you would dare show your face in Montevarchi and Figgine. Yet here you are, every day at the city hall and in the square, before the judges with a countenance of such impudence. You act as if you were a regular citizen and not the cruelest enemy of this city. As if you were a defender of the homeland and not a wicked vulture and pirate, as if you were a defender of liberty instead of a soiled and pestilent tyrant.

But it is no surprise, judges, that with such evil there is no embarrassment, shame, no hint of modesty. In fact, it would be astonishing if it were to the contrary, because there can be no respect or shame where there is such a receptacle, such a den of enormous and damnable sins. Wise men say that it is difficult to have one virtue without having many. Similarly, a vice is usually not alone. The greater the sin, the less likely for it to be without many dangerous companions. It is certain, judges, that when I consider how many atrocious crimes come together in a single deed, I do not know how to find words to express myself, or imagine a sentence that would be enough to punish it. His crime is not limited to his actions, nor to what he caused or permitted, because so much occurred under his order and authority.

All can agree that stealing the salary money was a criminal offense. What about the armed robberies the soldiers perpetrated in public, the rape of so many women, and the homicides? Was this just avarice? What about the lust, cruelty, and sacrilege, the churches and houses of worship plundered like everywhere else? Like the poets say of Cerberus, his sin has three heads: lust, avarice, and cruelty. In addition, his betrayal took the form of the cruel, wicked pillaging of the entire country. Many of our citizens were murdered on his authority with the arms entrusted to him for their defense. Should we accuse him of parricide?[5] The suffering was not just in his homeland, but in everything public and private, all subjects, friends and neighbors. So how should we define it? Not even Demosthenes or Cicero would know what to call his crime. His crimes have more heads than the Hydra; one is disease, another fire, all one hell. It is a sin that one hundred axes, one hundred gallows, all the punishments in existence would suffice as punishment. Yet you dare defend yourself, and what is more, have the effrontery to seek an acquittal? You would do better to remove yourself from trial and refrain from appearing here, for your very presence reopens so many bitter wounds. If you carried out the sentence on yourself, you would demonstrate that you are no longer completely blind and still have some vestige of shame, some inkling of conscience. Since you cannot reduce your punishment, at least you could try to quell our outrage and incite no further hatred.

So, I ask you now, why and with what hope have you come to defend yourself? What are you counting on, your eloquence? Your wickedness is greater than can be excused or denied. Do you hope to benefit from some past service you performed for the city? You are an example of all the evil a citizen can bring to his homeland. Are you relying on our good nature, on the gentleness of the people and the judges? The injuries you committed universally and particularly are too recent, too immense, to be forgotten. It would be too dangerous and damaging to pardon you. There is no one among the judges or in this multitude not atrociously offended by you or because of you. Some had their goods pillaged and their houses burned. Some were imprisoned and tortured. Those who suffered less have paid so much in robberies and taxes that they are in dire

---

5. *Parricidio* in Italian also has the meaning of killing one's homeland or country.

need. Either they lacked necessities and were compelled to consume the capital designated for the dowries of their daughters, or they must now provide for themselves by relying on their reputation to obtain credit. Yet here you are boldly stating how secure you are in wealth and means? I know well enough that you have stolen enough to corrupt ten judges, two entire cities. Yet, there are judges who are good, honest, and devoted to liberty. They know something you have never understood, that honor is worth more than money.

Do you hope to frighten or to scare them? I see your face full of audacity, pride, and anger. It is as if your army was still with you to intimidate us with the threat of pillage. I know what you are after, but now your time has come. Now you must live like any private citizen. You are hated by all, without protection, authority, or standing. You are a monster, as welcome as a snake. Even under these circumstances, the judges are strong willed and virile enough not to hesitate, for to act contrarily would label them with eternal infamy. Perhaps you are relying on the influence and the reputation of your relatives, the help of your many friends, in the wallowing that the Medici partisans have done on your behalf? Do you not realize that the time has passed for money spent like that to have any effect? The city is free, no longer subject to tyrants. Now the law and justice rule, not the appetites of private citizens. By lobbying for you, the pro-Medici party is not helping your cause, for they cannot erase the terrible memory of those times. You have committed so many atrocious crimes and have earned such universal hatred that your relatives can do nothing for you. Even if all the judges were Guicciardinis and Salviatis, they would be compelled to convict you. So where for the love of God can you place any hope? We can only await your learned defense.

In your defense, you will probably claim that the money spent in this war passed through the hands of Alessandro del Caccia. Alessandro's books will confirm that the funds were indeed spent on soldier's pay and other requirements.[6] How can books and scribbles be more believable than the sworn declarations of so many men? Should not the firsthand experience of witnesses carry more weight? Such a defense is a testament to your impudence. If there were no other avenues to the truth, I would be forced to admit the validity of those books, not because they are credible but merely because we would be left with no choice. How-

---

6. Alessandro del Caccia was the papal treasurer.

ever, when the truth is so manifest, and the evidence is so clear and irrefutable, there is no need to waste time on such arguments. I hereby declare that Mr. Francesco stole our money, and I give you the testimony of not one, not two, not ten, or a hundred, but thousands upon thousands of witnesses of every type, origin, and nationality, all without any outside interest in this case. It may be more in their interests to keep quiet. On the other side, I see only one witness, Alessandro del Caccia. Who received our money? Alessandro del Caccia. Who says that our money was well spent? Alessandro del Caccia. Who says that Mr. Francesco did not have the money? Alessandro del Caccia. Who wrote everything in those blessed books? Alessandro del Caccia.

This entire game is as predictable as a baited hunt.[7] In individual cases of less importance, one witness is not enough to establish a finding unless there is no opposing evidence. So how can we rely on a single witness in a case of such public importance, especially when there are thousands of opposing witnesses? If the quantity of witnesses is the deciding factor, how can we compare an entire army to one man? If the quality of the witnesses is what matters, an entire army of nobleman, lords, and captains surely contains witnesses of higher station than Alessandro del Caccia. Even if all the evidence were in his favor, he is still suspect because it is not believable that he allowed someone to steal without taking part in the plunder himself. Is a witness believable who by excusing Mr. Francesco also excuses himself, and by implicating, must implicate himself? How can the scribbles of a partner in crime be credible? Also, surely, someone who did not suffer any shame, fear, or conscience for his murderous acts could be expected to have the nerve to keep false accounts!

Tell me now, Alessandro del Caccia, as a merchant you are used to managing money and you must understand just how important this is. Does it seem reasonable that the management of an almost infinite sum of money, hundreds of thousands of ducats, was so sober, so careful, that you were the only person in charge? Why did it not require any written receipt of those who had received monies or some form of oversight by a third party? Was your word alone enough to allow no room for doubt? Was it somehow more convenient for you to handle large sums differently from the way a cautious merchant would handle a couple hundred ducats? Did

---

7. A rare joke by Guicciardini, who seems to be making a play on the double meaning of *caccia*, which means "hunt."

it seem unnecessary for you to manage the affairs of the country in the same way that you would manage the affairs of Iacopo Salviati?[8] Were you both so blinded by avarice and sin to think that a crime that is so immense and involved so many people would never come to light? Did you believe our city so incompetent to allow such questionable accounts? You certainly must have enough respect for us to realize that you might have to explain yourselves before this court. Perhaps you should have been more careful when committing such evil and more creative in covering it up. However, of course the war was waged in the name of the pope. As his ministers in the field you might have only expected to give an account in Rome, where things are laxer, and everyone is corruptible. Where the pope, as in the past, would be as liberal with other peoples' money as he has been careful with his own. Mr. Francesco would have had enough power to keep everyone's mouth shut, and Iacopo Salviati's influence would have protected Alessandro. Who knows, perhaps Iacopo is a party to this fraud, because the takings are so large that it is difficult to believe that Mr. Francesco could collect everything in a single sweep and keep everything for himself, even if he has a big belly.[9] Nor could he have satisfied Alessandro by giving him ten *soldi* on the lire. It is more likely that they had plotted together to form a league of two against the pope. Iacopo had been instrumental in getting Francesco to Rome, so once Francesco was ensconced, the two of them played the game together. Partners in ambition became partners in plunder.

Observe judges, how everything is becoming clearer and clearer. The investigation of one crime reveals another. Search for one thief and you find many. With theft, we now can understand that the books were cooked. With Mr. Francesco, thief number one, comes Alessandro del Caccia, thief number two, who acted under the shadow of a certain Iacopo Salviati. We are at a point where the truth will come to the light, as it does for divine justice. You may consider a demand for restitution from Mr. Francesco. He was in charge and had the authority to dispense

---

8. Iacopo Salviati (1461–1533) married Lucrezia, daughter of Lorenzo de' Medici. Besides being Guicciardini's father-in-law, Iacopo Salviati was also father-in-law to Ludovico de' Medici (1498–1526), also known as Giovanni dalle Bande Nere (John of the Black Bands) for the insignia worn by his troops. His son Cosimo de' Medici established the Medici ducal line, which ended the Florentine Republic. The prosecutor is implying that Guicciardini owed his career as a papal governor to the pro-Medici connections of his father-in-law.

9. The prosecutor is referring to Guicciardini's corpulence.

the money, pay the soldiers, and authorize expenditures. Observe that now he will not want to pay for something owed by someone else, and that is why he will reveal his secret book and his accomplices, and implore you to fine everyone according to their take. He will likely add that while he was governor of the territory held by the church, his honesty was well known and it is untenable to believe that if he valued a good name in foreign lands, he would want a bad name at home. To this effect, he will produce witnesses, testimonials, and letters from those communities in the hope that we will believe in something that is far away, separated by mountains, instead of what is before our very eyes.

I have no idea how you behaved while abroad, nor will I attempt to find out. I do know and will clearly declare that you performed quite miserably here. It is no miracle that you continued to be so evil, because anyone accustomed to such behavior inevitably worsens. When you were a youngster, you behaved well enough here in Florence, so you have no excuse and deserve even more hatred. You did not go bad at an early age owing to poverty, or factors that might merit some compassion. You were rich, earning immense sums by the time you were forty. Therefore, it is impossible to have pity or forgive you. If you turned bad at that age, with all your experience, you would have no concern over losing your good name and, surely, your wickedness would continue if allowed! So, remove your Lombard and Romagnolo witnesses, and the papers you cajoled from other communities. I will not accept them or make the effort to find fault in any of them. I know how life is in cities where men have never enjoyed liberty or empire. They only understand their personal interests and how to curry favor to those more powerful than themselves. They lack seriousness and have no concept of right and wrong. They are as servile in spirit as in need. They would perform a thousand false sacraments every day just to receive a letter of recommendation from a count in Lombardy, a request from a governor in Romagna, or a note from a bishop or a cardinal. Everyone is aware how people act in those places. Why would they do anything on someone else's behalf, in a forum where they have nothing to lose? I have never been to Lombardy or the Romagna, but I am not so poor in friends, nor is the truth so defenseless for letters and witnesses with little relevance to decide this case. The words raging inside me come out with a sense of shame that you went through such expense and effort to bring so many sealed letters here.

Therefore, he clearly is a thief, although the quantity, order, and measure of his crimes are still uncertain. It appears he stole as much as he pleased, beyond our imagination, and I am not speaking arbitrarily. How to settle such a debt? The amount he cannot prove was legitimately spent must be reimbursed. Anyone who owes must pay their debt. That is how honest, good men behave. Negligence should harm those who practice it, especially if it is someone who has acted wickedly. If this manner of proceeding does not please you, judges, then the laws have provided an alternative. They require that whenever the amount of damages owed is not certain, the amount awarded depends on the statements of the plaintiff. Anyone who causes such rulings to be reached owing to their irresponsibility cannot complain when such measures become necessary. Your Honors, you still have not heard the crimes of his greed, which are infinite and impossible to bring forth. You have heard only those that I have been able to present. You must also consider how his sin of ambition will endanger our freedom if we do not respond appropriately.

I declare that in this city no citizen received as many benefits from the Medici as he. Nobody lost as much from their fall and nobody has as much to gain from their return. There is nobody who would be as unhappy to remain a private citizen, and nobody who received more from the Medici who was not a blood relative, or gained rewards, services, or favors done during the period of their difficulties. Should we allow those who received money or favors to retain everything? In this manner, they will not have lost anything owing to the Medici's fall, nor will they gain should they return. They did not earn whatever they gained because they performed an act for the good of the republic. However, he has no blood ties to the Medici, no special relationship. A long time ago, he did acquire a house from them, but after so many years and events, this has almost been forgotten. Nevertheless, for eleven years he held administrative and judicial positions of great honor and prestige. From these he received countless earnings, benefits, and power. It has been many years, even ages, since a citizen came out of Florence more honored abroad than he was. These positions were not to be his for a set period, although he was certain to retain them during the lifetime of the pontiff,[10] who respected him greatly. He became substitute governor in a province as important as the

---

10. Clement VII.

Romagna. During the war, he oversaw the pope's armies. In peacetime, the pope chose him to be near to advise and to manage the pope's most important affairs. These are positions of power and profit with earnings of not just a few thousand ducats per year, but a potentially infinite amount. The prestige in such a position is also noteworthy. Anyone so empowered by a pope is renown throughout Italy, adored by the entire Papal State, with power and reputation among the foremost princes of the world. He obtained this influence from a pope who usurped the government of this city, which is the position of power and authority in the city that Mr. Francesco wants for himself. Mr. Francesco could then take care of his friends, relatives, and anyone he desired with all possible honors and benefits. For how could the pope deny someone who knew the secrets of his state? And what about his lackeys? The city suffered such indignity under Medici rule that I must use that word. How could they refuse anything to someone who had the esteem and the ear of the prince on whom their every hope depended?

Mr. Francesco has lost these useful, great, and honorable things owing to the fall of the Medici. He might hope to recover everything and perhaps more if they were to regain power. However, if they are defeated, as all good men should desire, he wil have no income, power, and authority. He has been absent from the thoughts and considerations of princes, equal to any one of us whom he would have previously assumed to command, or even disdained to engage in conversation. For eleven years, he inhabited and dominated a noble and magnificent city, protected by a great army and obeyed by the greatest lords and gentlemen of Italy. The expense of his court was not that of a private citizen, but a prince. Now he lacks income and authority and finds himself subject to the laws and opinions of men. It must be bitter for him, whether in public or in private, to live as a regular citizen, as abjectly as each of us.

Judges, do not believe that the cities he governed are as poor and weak as those in your dominion. Do not believe that someone who governs for the church has the modest court and retinue or the limited authority of your rectors, who have a meager salary and are obligated to live by your laws, close to the city, so that every day the subjects may have access to them. In fact and appearance, they could be said to be no more than private citizens. However, imagine great, abundant, rich cities with noblemen, counts, and barons, where the governors have a regular salary and huge expense accounts. They have immense authority, not subject to any law or rule. Everything happens according to their will. Since the pope lives far away and is preoccupied with more important matters, his subjects have no recourse without great expense and difficulty and to little avail. Therefore, the subjects bear the injuries done to them by their governors rather than waste time and money seeking a remedy that could further provoke those who caused their injuries. In practice, the governor in one of those cities is its lord.

Judges, some of you certainly must have seen Mr. Francesco in Romagna in a house full of tapestries, silver, and servants with the run of the entire province.[11] The pope was far away and remanded everything to him so that he was not accountable to any superior. He had a bodyguard of one hundred German *Landsknechts* and halberdiers and went about the city in the company of mounted guards surrounded by a retinue of hundreds, never without an escort of at least one hundred or one hundred and fifty horses. He was swimming in titles, by the "your lordships." You would not have recognized him as your fellow citizen. Considering the importance of the enterprises, and his unlimited authority in the government of an extended dominion with all the pomp and circumstance thereof, you would have thought him a duke or a prince. With those armies, he was not like one of your commissars, even if our encampments and the authority of our city are in no way inferior. Our commissars may seem powerful to the eyes of some, but they are not supreme. He was not like that at all. He found himself in a situation where he had the authority of a prince as great as the pope, who always headed great alliances and the largest armies, in places with many great captains, gentlemen, noblemen, and lords from all over Italy. He had the ability to confer largesse and prestige to an extent that he was not just honored but also almost adored.

Everything was subject to his authority: the letters of ambassadors, of princes and dukes, even from the king of France, decisions for hiring, purchasing, everything. In his bearing, attitude, and desires, he no longer seemed like a private citizen. His words and manner exuded a will to be obeyed and understood by a nod of the head. He acted like someone who had lived the life of a prince and expected such a life until death. The title of commissioner struck him as being an inadequate indicator of his position, and so he had himself called lieutenant, which literally means

---

11. Guicciardini was first appointed governor of Modena in 1516.

someone who holds the same position as the pope.[12] How can we possibly believe that someone who has lost so much is not crestfallen over the fall of the Medici? Someone who could hope to regain so much would desire to regain power night and day. Is someone who lived like a lord for so many years ready for private life, ready to bow his head to the likes of us? When anyone leaves this building, the Signoria, it takes a month to readjust to former life, even if our appointments are only for two months and we take office aware how soon we must leave. Our authority is also limited and under supervision to the point that we are like aristocracy in name only. Can we believe that someone who enjoyed eleven uninterrupted years of benefits, reputation, power, pomp, and honors, someone who hoped to perpetuate that status rather than see it end, would patiently endure a return to private life, stripped of everything that set him apart? How can he bear for mediocre citizens like us to treat him as an equal, permitted to speak with him as it were a common occurrence? How can he endure the shame of having us as his colleagues in the courts? How can he tolerate being observed, judged, and eventually convicted by the likes of you?

No, Your Honors, such a situation cannot possibly endure. Not only are all his thoughts and plans focused on regaining what he lost, but even his dreams at night are filled with bodyguards, couriers, government, armies, lords, and tyrants. I am usually more inclined to think the best of my fellow man rather than the worst. If I had not witnessed the open affectations and avarice over the course of his life, then I too might be persuaded that his spirit could be tamed. If only he had been able to modestly enjoy the years of his good fortune, now he would be able to accept what will follow as any sensible man. Rather than pondering his personal interests or his obligations to tyrants, he should work to ensure the prosperity and liberty of his homeland. However, when I recall his past life, I have come to realize that wickedness is an integral part of his character. Reason convinces and demands me to admit, even if I would rather not do so, that the only thing he thinks about and desires is to satisfy his greed and return to the life where he thinks happiness lies.

When he was a young man, I knew him, and we were on speaking terms. You would not believe how restless he was, how driven to dominate his peers. He always had to be first in everything and was a troublemaker, sowing discord and scandal. I will establish that these charges are

---

12. Guicciardini became lieutenant general of the papal Holy League army in 1526.

not mere inventions, Your Honors, because many of our classmates who are worthy of belief are still among us. If questioned I am certain they will not deny the truth. Furthermore, they will reveal that because of his restlessness and ambition some of us called him Alcibiades, in recognition of his covetous, restless, and unsettled spirit, which was accurate and prophetic, since he has caused as much damage to Florence as Alcibiades did to Athens. When someone demonstrates this sort of character at such a tender age, what can be expected later in life? Is there not a proverb that states you can tell a good day by morning? Adults know how to mask their feelings and dissimulate but the young cannot and reveal everything in their hearts without hesitation. If he was like that at such a tender age, when it would be uncanny for someone so young to have a drive for the thirst for power and honor, just imagine what sort of person he became afterward and is today. He chose a way of life and enjoyed enough good fortune to stir ambition in someone whose spirit would not be excited by such impulses, so what effect could it have had on someone like him whose soul is aflame with ambition?

Judges, it is difficult to deny one's nature, difficult to reject the habits fused in our bones since the cradle. Anyone who by necessity or some contingency lives contrary to their nature can bury those natural inclinations only after a long struggle. Someone who takes up a life in accordance with his nature will find it rewarded and nourished every day. So, if someone is ambitious by the grace of God, he will become even more ambitious if events foster his natural tendency. Remember that Caesar displayed the seeds that would be the ruin of his country when he was only a boy. I do not have much information about the years after he left Florence to study, but given his beginnings, it is reasonable to assume that he behaved no differently during his absence. In nature, early years always correspond and correlate to the years of maturity.

After he returned from his studies and went to Spain, he practiced law, from which he hoped to gain benefits and honor.[13] He gave some indication of his restless spirit, although one closely observes how he positioned himself in the issues contested between the *gonfalonier* and the city's most important citizens, who criticized the *gonfalonier* for having assumed too much power; even if the real dispute was their unwillingness to accept

---

13. Guicciardini went to Spain in 1512 as Florentine ambassador to the court of King Ferdinand of Aragon.

popular rule.¹⁴ Like those dissatisfied with Soderini, he gave some outward indication of his dissatisfaction, which was noticeable only upon close inspection. At the time, he was not well known except to those who had the occasion to speak with him directly. Because of his age, he could not participate in the courts or in public deliberations, and his lifestyle appeared to be serious and modest. Even though he was not wealthy, he chose a wife without a great dowry against the wishes of his father.¹⁵ She was the daughter of Alamanno Salviati, who at the time opposed the *gonfalonier* more vigorously than most. The only reason he chose such a marriage was to be able to consort with seditious elements and earn the approval of the pro-Medici faction. His attitude would have been revealed if it had not been for the influence of his father. Oh, if only God had made the son more like the father, a man who never became embroiled in such affairs! He advised his son to proceed with greater discretion than he would have done otherwise. Therefore, after three or four years, a very brief period considering his age, he excelled in the legal profession and benefited from the good counsel and reputation of his father and his many relatives. His overall appearance was one of such prudence and goodwill that he gained election as ambassador to Spain by the eighty at the age of twenty-eight.¹⁶ He won more honors than had ever been received by any young man in our city. Because of his ambitious nature, about which very few were aware, he took full credit immediately for this event, since he is well endowed in the qualities needed for such enterprises. You should not think that he would ever have been elevated to such position so young if he were not well qualified. His thirst for power is more dangerous, for if he had just displayed a hint of incompetence or lack of drive, he might be saved and we would have no cause for fear. However, since he is so capable, it would be foolhardy not to take this case seriously.

The fact that he held the ambassadorship of Spain when the Medici returned caused much discussion. If I were prosecuting this trial for personal reasons rather than my love for the republic, I would use this opportunity more ruthlessly. For prosecuting not only magnifies proven facts but also heightens doubts, foments suspicions, and never leaves anything

---

14. Piero Soderini served as *gonfalonier*, city leader, of the Florentine Republic from 1502 to 1512.

15. In 1508, Guicciardini married Maria Salviati, daughter of Alamanno Salviati.

16. Guicciardini was elected by the council of eighty as ambassador to Spain in January 1512. Soderini's republican government fell to the Medici in August 1512.

untried that could increase the predicament of the accused. But my goal is different from those of a normal prosecutor, since I am interested in the public good rather than an ordinary victory. I am not interested in seeing him convicted for crimes he did not commit. Therefore, I will present this case in a more straightforward and simple style and not attempt to prove anything about which I am not certain, or mislead the judges into believing anything other than the truth.

Your Honors, many believe that although the republic sent him to Spain to safeguard our city's freedom, his activities with that king favored the return of the Medici. He is why the king sent an army to reinstall the Medici. There are many theories about possible plots, because there is so little certainty in such matters. When the news arrived in that court that the Medici had regained power, the king congratulated him in public as a friend of the Medici, as will be confirmed by witnesses. Since the republic sent him as ambassador, he should have behaved differently, unless the king knew he supported the Medici. In fact, after the Medici returned they allowed him to remain in that post for nearly a year. This seems odd since he had no prior connection to them. Once he finally returned from Spain, before he had even seen any of the Medici or done anything for them, they courted him and honored him in public. They could not have made a greater demonstration of goodwill to anyone they knew to be on their side. This line of reasoning seems convincing, but I will not force the issue since I do not want these charges to carry more weight than can be supported by the evidence.

If these charges are true, in all deference to your wisdom and prudence, no speech could adequately convey its wickedness. No punishment no matter how severe could equal a crime of such unnatural treachery. For there is no greater crime men can commit than depriving their homeland of liberty. Such an act has more evil ramifications than can be imagined or expressed. It is even worse considering the circumstances, since the city had trusted him and accepted him as her representative. He perniciously used the name and authority that the republic confidently and honorably invested in him for her ruin! I will not call this betrayal, murder, or parricide, because these terms are too weak to convey the enormity of what he did.

Come what may, I will not be able to think of his unexplainable ingratitude without exasperation. I am simply amazed at the corrupt nature of his actions. At such a young age, with the consent of those who had the required legal authority, he received more honors than previously bestowed upon one so young by a free city. He held a position usually reserved to honor our elders. From this beginning, he could be sure to reach the highest offices and authority that a citizen may earn in the republic. However, this demonstration of goodwill and trust did not move him. Instead, he became the friend and representative of tyranny, an instrument to keep the boot on the neck of the homeland to which he owed more than just that normal measure of respect common to all citizens. He owed the republic more because of the honors that he had been granted. Yet he placed more stock in the favors a tyrant could grant him in Florence. This decision must have troubled his conscience. He did not value the honors and authority of a free city, which are secure, glorious, and give infinite satisfaction to anyone whose stomach and soul is not corrupt.

I am unable to think about it without anger because I despise your vices and I fear the danger you represent. However, I still wish you no harm. I remind myself that we are all men and citizens of the same country. When I recall the conversations we shared years ago, the memory pains me. I feel compassion for the degree that your character and wickedness control you. You used your considerable talents in letters and rhetoric for evil. You had the potential to become the pride of the city, honored by all. You would have enjoyed an almost unheard-of level of respect and goodwill among your fellow citizens. Instead, because of your harmful appetites, you have become an instrument of offense to your homeland, an enemy to all citizens, hateful even to yourself, ultimately detested in the memory of men. Let us go directly to the facts in his case.

Upon returning from Spain he was received by Lorenzo de' Medici, whom he had never met before.[17] When he arrived, he was received with such kindness, honor, and confidence as to increase the suspicions of those who had thought that he sold and betrayed our liberty while serving as ambassador. He was quickly made a member of the seventeen, who were their most intimate and honored friends. He gained the highest rank possible for someone his age. He received invitations to attend closed meetings where only very few are welcome and where everyone else was at least twelve or fifteen years his senior. He obtained everything he desired for his brothers, relatives, and friends. What his life was like and

---

17. Lorenzo di Piero de' Medici, Duke of Urbino from 1512 to 1516, to whom Machiavelli dedicated *The Prince*.

how he ingratiated himself toward the tyrant cannot be known in detail. Records of those times are not public, since they always acted in private, but what they did can be understood from the results. They did not accept him with such confidence upon his return from Spain because they had somehow been able to deceive him, for they continued to honor him with increasing demonstrations of their love and goodwill. This clearly means that they considered him a friend who was useful to their tyranny, which is the only thing that a tyrant notices. A tyrant tries to see clearly into the souls of men, to raise and use those he can trust and who favor his rule. They must have found such qualities in him. The honors they bestowed upon him were not limited to Florence and your attention. Shortly thereafter, without his even asking, he was appointed governor to Modena, a position highly sought after in Florence and Rome.[18] Of course, he showed his gratitude to all, but especially to Madonna Alfonsina, that singularly greedy and ambitious woman.[19] She was the one who nominated him, for which he was always grateful. Remember, people tend to favor those who resemble them, which is further proof of how affected he was by ambition and avarice, of which that woman was a paradigm.

From these beginnings, his political career flourished. Every day he gained the favor and confidence of the tyrants and soon thereafter obtained the governorship of Reggio and Parma.[20] He was then appointed commissar general with supreme authority in the war against the French. He then obtained the presidency of the Romagna, until the pope finally called him to Rome as his close advisor and secretary. In Rome, he was appointed lieutenant in this pestiferous war, endowed with such power and rank that he was no mere functionary or minister of the pope but more of a comrade, a brother, a facsimile of the pope himself. These occurrences were so sweeping and unusual that it is hard to believe that they gave him everything so suddenly and then increased his rank as he proved himself. They took him into their confidence and recognized that he is tyrannical just like them. If just one of them had favored him, then one might conclude that it was a mistake, a misunderstanding, a similarity of nature, or a convergence of stars. However, he was accepted, liked, and trusted by every one of them: Leo, Clement, Giuliano, and Lorenzo, even

---

18. Guicciardini was appointed by Pope Leo X in 1516.
19. Alfonsina de' Medici (1472–1520) ruled Florence as regent from 1515 to 1519.
20. Guicciardini obtained this governorship in 1517.

by Madonna Alfonsina, that possessive and inhumane woman. I cannot believe that they were all somehow deceived. That they all had an inclination like his or that each was under the influence of the same stars. Explanations about conformity of character or stellar convergence are less tenable than the simple fact that they recognized him to be a friend of tyranny and an enemy of the liberty of his homeland. This was the tie; this was the conjunction, the way to gain their acceptance and goodwill. If you lack this attribute, you lack what a tyrant desires and seeks most in men. If you did not have what they want and value, they never would have been so pleased and taken by you to have allowed you to become one of them.

Your Honors, I expect he will try to make arguments to obfuscate something that is very clear. Perhaps they were searching for a tyrannical appetite in those that they hired in Florence, but he served abroad in the affairs of the church, which they held as princes and not as tyrants. He will describe his honesty, trustworthiness, his diligence, and the dangers he faced. He will try to bring praise and honor to something eternally stained and shameful.

I confess to you, judges, that this defense would frighten me, it would make my soul tremble, because prima facie, at first glance, it seems so true and magnificent. However, I find comfort in your prudence and the knowledge of events you possess. You are too experienced to ever allow deception by unrelated matters. You will want to penetrate to the marrow. There is nobody so ignorant of the ways of the world, with so little experience, that he does not know, as I stated earlier, that the first thing a tyrant rewards and searches for in a citizen is admiration and trust in his regime. He tries with every manner and avenue to discover if a subject feels this way or not. This is quite reasonable, since a tyrant's first aim, his primary objective, is the retention of power. That is always his first thought and interest. That renown and most serious author, Cornelius Tacitus, wrote how in his last hours on the day of his death when age and infirmity had consumed his body and soul, Augustus left a message about whom to trust to Tiberius his successor.[21] Therefore, it would have been impossible for him to favor or honor a citizen of questionable loyalty who did not desire the continuation of his tyranny. As Solomon said to the student in the story, love and the opinion of being loved are reciprocal. A tyrant will never favor someone who is not his friend, or is unreliable and may

---

21. Cornelius Tacitus was a Roman historian (ca. AD 55–120) who lived under Nero.

turn on him because in a city used to freedom, one cannot rely on half measures. Everyone either loves liberty or loves the tyrant, and he who loves one must hate the other.

Nor is it useful to make a distinction between the interests of Florence and the church in this case. If you were willing to support their power in Florence, you also would have favored their rule in the pontificate. If you favored one, then by necessity you also loved the other, for they are interrelated and connected. One could not fall without the fall of the other. If they were in any way unsure of your feelings, they would have kept you in Florence like your peers. How can you explain why else they would have employed you to such an extent, especially since you are married and are a layman? The positions they gave to you are usually reserved for the clergy. You may retort that their decision was due to the scarcity of virtuous and capable men, certainly a modest defense in a field so competitive. Perhaps our youngsters will learn from your example to speak with the modesty appropriate for a citizen. However, we must realize that arrogance goes hand in hand with ambition. We should not be surprised or amazed that someone with so many shortcomings would also be guilty of pride. If pride is the mother of ambition, as it truly seems to be in this case, then it is fitting that we should see mother and daughter together.

I admit and reaffirm that your qualities are rare indeed. You have the talent to manage great enterprises, and if the pope had to elect his ministers from only one city, perhaps your explanations would be tenable. However, even if you are capable, you are no miracle worker. The pope has the resources to select his ministers from every nation and there are always an infinite number of candidates vying for such appointments. You presume that you are so high in our esteem to think that we will believe that he ignored the pleas and the ambitions of everyone at court to drag someone like you away from the cases in your legal studio. Besides, you had other concerns at the time and had no experience in the government or affairs of the church. Therefore, I beg you to stop such a vain and arrogant defense because, rather than providing any reason to reduce our suspicions, it only reveals your true character and the immoderate opinion that you have of yourself.

Why am I spending so much time on this, with endless and needless speculation, when it is possible to introduce so many hard facts about irrefutable events? As is commonly known, after the death of Lorenzo, the cardinal Medici wanted you to remain in Florence so that the government of Florence would be in your hands and you could replace your brother Luigi.²² He did not call for you idly as an excuse to keep you busy in the affairs of the church and the papacy. He wanted you to represent his interests here and maintain his power as someone he could trust with the secrets of tyranny. His conclusion about you is well known, even though your instructions remained secret. Now it has been revealed that he planned a marriage between your families. If this never happened, it is not because anything I have said is untrue. To the contrary, when the war broke out, he wanted to have you where you could best serve his regime. Then when the pope died, he lost control of the situation until the election of the next pope, which changed everything to his favor.²³ So why do you not just admit that from your quarters in Rome, you could eventually control everything in Florence as well as abroad? Remember that nothing of any importance was ever decided here, all decisions, even the most minor laws were referred to Rome. How can you deny that the pope relied on you completely to handle the affairs of Florence and elsewhere? Should we now believe that he did not have thousands of opportunities to know you down to the soles of your feet after you managed his affairs for so many years? He chose you to be the most trusted instrument of his tyranny, because after a thousand tests he had observed well enough to know you for what you are.

Let us come finally to what everyone, the entire city, has witnessed with tears in our eyes, despair in our souls, and now must recall with deep desire for revenge. Who prevented us from entering our city hall on that St. Mark's Day?²⁴ Who stripped us of the liberty we sought to regain? That fateful day will forever be remembered with tears! The memory of his misdeed must endure as an example in the stones and the name of this city! Oh Citizen, if you even deserve this title, for you are more detestable, more pernicious to our republic than Alcibiades ever was to Athens, or Sulla or Caesar to Rome!²⁵ They oppressed a liberty that was old and dying, you oppressed ours on the very day it was reborn and

---

22. Lorenzo de' Medici is the then Duke of Urbino. Giulio de' Medici is the future pope Clement VII. Luigi Guicciardini is Francesco's brother.

23. The pope who died is Leo X. Clement VII was elected pope after the brief reign of Hadrian VI.

24. On St. Mark's Day 1527, there was a popular uprising in Florence that Guicciardini diffused by speaking to the mob at the entrance of the Palazzo della Signoria.

25. L. Cornelius Sulla (138–79 BC) was a Roman general who established a temporary monarchy.

revived. They were driven by a sense of personal injury, or danger, or the disdain of their enemies to make themselves masters of their cities. Nobody harmed you. In fact, everyone honored and respected you. Yet you sold everyone, the entire country including yourself, into bondage. A faction of wicked citizens who sought to oppress other citizens supported them. You alone put the yoke of bondage on everyone's neck.

There was not a man in the city of any station or age who did not run to the city hall on that fateful day, even the closest and most intimate supporters of the Medici. Your brother, who was serving as *gonfalonier*, had them declared as rebels through legitimate city protocol.[26] Either your bother and the Medici supporters did not want to appear out of step with the majority, or they did not have the courage to form an opposition. Everyone was joyfully congratulating one another. The elderly cried, the young jumped, nobody restrained themselves. Everybody spoke excitedly about how we had regained our liberty and soul. We are no longer in bondage, no longer slaves. We have come out of the darkness. Out of Egypt.[27] Oh happy day, oh joy, oh day of eternal memory, when God finally delivered his people!

Amid all the noise, confusion, and general jubilation, all the soldiers dispersed and the Medici were fleeing on horseback. The Marquis of Saluzzo and the Duke of Urbino were ready to allow events to run their course.[28] You, alone, prevented the ruin of the Medici and resuscitated tyranny. You restrained the soldiers and those lords. When they returned to the square, you were their leader, to everybody's ruin. How could our people, innocent and unarmed, more used to commerce and peace than combat, how could they oppose such impetus, resist such fury, and fight against armed men, military personnel? You drove the people from the square and made the Medici our masters once again. Your wickedness did not end there. You immediately reclaimed the city hall, the majesty of this city, the bulwark of the law, the holder of all public councils, the defense and foundation of our liberty and glory, the city hall before which every citizen must obey and be humble no matter how grand or proud. Men are accustomed to kneeling before its voice, to trembling before its stones. If you were a citizen and a man rather than a beast and monster, then

---

26. The brother is Luigi Guicciardini.
27. A biblical citation from Psalm 114.
28. Michele Antonio de Vasto and Francesco Maria della Rovere.

you would also kneel and tremble in reverence. But you are harder than stone, fiercer than a tiger, more envious than Lucifer himself. It was not enough for you to overwhelm with your wicked thoughts, conspiracies. Your betrayal kept liberty out of our grasp.

Do you all remember when he came to speak with us, accompanied by Signor Federigo?[29] He warned us that the city was in imminent danger from many men of arms, artillery, and infantry. Some of the people retreated, others were ready to take up arms. Then he came out with the most terrific threats face afire, eyes full of arrogance, with words full of fury, his spirit aflame. We believed that he acted out of concern for the city, to protect us from danger. We believed that he remembered he was a Florentine just like his brothers, in-laws, relatives, and all the nobles in the city. After the riot calmed, we wrote him letters begging him to come to the aid of his homeland, to lead the armies in our pay for our protection. We did not know that behind this effigy of a man there was such malice and poison. We believed that his body had a soul, not the spirit of a devil. We never trusted Signor Federigo, for how could a foreigner love our country if he did not love his own? We believed in you. We trusted you. We believed your sweet words and promises. You persuaded us to believe that here were dangers when in fact there were none. That the obstacles were great when in fact they were minimal. The people were tired and in revolt, and wanted nothing more than for night to fall so they could return to normal. Your broken promises convinced us to abandon the city hall, to put the yoke back on our neck and disperse forever. Then miraculously God once again granted us back our freedom. What have you gained in this war? You are the worst enemy of your homeland because of the unpardonable atrocities that even your father would not forgive, were he alive.

So how can it still be a matter for debate that you are a friend of the tyrant? The proof is overwhelming and not even worth discussing. All your actions have unmasked your immoderate ambition. It is clearer than the sun that you could never accept a return to private life. Your single desire is to reacquire what you lost, and you would stop at nothing. This appetite of yours for power would bother only me slightly if it could be satisfied without the return of the Medici to Florence. As Neri di Gino said to Count Pioppi when they came to terms at the Arno bridge and

---

29. Federigo Gonzaga da Bozzolo (1480–1527), Italian *condottiero* military leader.

Count Pioppi left the country, "I would like you to be a great lord, but in Magna." Your earnings, reputation, and haughty air would not concern me if you were lord or president of the Romagna and you advised and governed all the popes now until the end of time, as long as it does not mean our enslavement. However, Pope Clement will never become great enough to recover the fragmented and broken dominions of the church without returning to the state of Florence for the money to wage his wars. If he cannot have one without the other, neither can you. You can be sure that this city is reasonably jealous of its liberty and has learned from the past how to behave in the future. Never again will she allow a citizen of your ilk to serve her. Nor will she ever agree to do business with someone who day and night thinks of nothing but putting back the yoke that he and his predecessors used to oppress the good citizens over the years. Therefore, you will be unable to achieve the result that would benefit you the most. Even if you can no longer make use of us, can there be any doubt that you will still try to implement your schemes?

Furthermore, Your Honors, let me state that his identification with the interests and hopes of the papacy means there can be no doubt that he would love to see the Medici return to Florence. We have observed this inclination in him before he went into government. He is unaccustomed to equality and civility. He feeds on tyrannical thoughts and actions. He has no love for liberty, or for the reputation that a citizen may have in a free city. He does not understand how fulfilling and how fruitful private life can be with tranquility of the spirit, and love and benevolence of fellow citizens.

Someone may remark, or perhaps it may occur to you, Your Honors, that all these things seem to be true. One must admit that someone whose tastes are depraved will never enjoy flavors and foods different from the ones that gave him nourishment and sustenance. Yet such an individual without the backing of significant resources cannot do much harm. Nor are his wicked intentions of much account since he no longer has the means to put them into action. Despite what he has been in the past, now he is a lone individual, subject to our laws like the humblest citizen. He no longer has any authority over soldiers, governments, or peoples. So how can he pose a threat to our liberty? His immoderate ambition and desire for power will cause him perpetual torment and agony. The present state of affairs is more of a punishment for him than a danger for us. If only this were God's will and all my efforts, preoccupations, and enmity were unneeded! However, anyone who believes this is fooling themselves. He is so capable that he needs constant surveillance, for one can never be sure of what he may do.

As you know, he has many friends and relatives in the city and is well regarded in the countryside. He enjoys a solid reputation abroad and has many friends owing to the great enterprises that he has managed over such an extended period. He is known in princely courts as someone with a great deal of experience in government. He has such remarkable qualities in oratory, spirit, and intelligence that were he a normal citizen he would be of much use to his country. Because of his nature, these same talents pose a danger. Since our freedom is so recent and the city still not completely united, many citizens are still doubtful. The government, as is often the case initially, is more confused and unpredictable, which raises suspicions. We do not have to fear tyranny from a private citizen, but from a pope, who could resurge at any hour even if he seems defeated at present. The state of Italy is in more flux and uncertainty than any period in the last thousand years. To assume that the world will maintain its present course is unwise because contingencies could rise at a moment's notice, which would greatly increase the troubles, difficulties, suspicions, and dangers we face. In this state of uncertainty, it would be unwise not to realize the danger posed by an enemy at home who enjoys a following and reputation abroad. He is certainly capable of fomenting political upheaval since he is so intelligent, and his pen and voice are so persuasive. He has the spirit to attempt new things and the ingenuity to use his tongue and pen to persuade. Night and day, he thinks of nothing but how to restore tyranny and suffocate liberty.

In the group that expelled the *gonfalonier* in 1512, there was nobody whose abilities were comparable to those of Mr. Francesco.[30] The tyrants seemed exhausted, the city was enjoying its freedom just as it does now, and everything was much more orderly and solid than now. The affairs of Italy were more settled and secure. Nevertheless, if those inexpert and poorly reputed youngsters could overthrow the government so easily in 1512, if such a small, poorly tended seed could produce such a pestilent fruit, what could he do, given his present abilities, standing, courage, and opportunity? What could this deep-rooted tree of a man do now with his

---

30. Piero Soderini (1452–1522), *gonfalonier* for life, unsuccessful in preventing Medici restoration in 1512.

great spread of branches? At the time, it certainly did not seem our liberties were at risk since its foundation appeared so solid. The *gonfalonier* for life was an honest man who was a friend of the people. The Grand Council had endured for years.[31] The government was widely supported and certainly not feared, and by its very age had erased all memory of political instability.

If the danger had been recognized at the outset and some remedy taken, perhaps not everything would have been taken away, lost. Too much security and abundance made us negligent and more timid than we ought to have been. Your Honors, Piero Soderini had many qualities, many excellent virtues worthy of respect: prudence, intelligence, eloquence, and great experience. He was as honest and correct as could be desired. His great modesty allowed no insult to others or to himself. He was particularly diligent in the care of public monies. He loved liberty and the people as his very self. He was humane, patient, and Catholic. Before becoming *gonfalonier*, he had already served our nation and was known and worked hard for the homeland. He was known throughout Italy and well regarded in France, where we do so much business. He came from a noble and honored house. His father and brothers were a great resource for this city. He had a charming and pleasing presence, was childless, and had remained above the fray of discord and sedition that marked those times.

Since he had so many admirable qualities, he was elected *gonfalonier* with universal acclaim and great expectation. He would have been up to the task, if to his many qualities just one had been added. He should have been more suspicious and less trustful of our more wicked citizens. When he suspected anyone, he should have acted more resolutely to be sure of their intentions. However, he thought that his sense of propriety was shared by others. He did not think it proper to have people accused without foundation. Perhaps he thought it was not fitting for the city, or privately he thought that it would be dangerous to mistreat any citizens. Thus, plots were never discovered until they could no longer be dissimulated. He did not act at the outset to defuse situations when resolution would have been simple. He allowed them to protract until it was too late. Because of his negligence or patience or pusillanimity, he died in

---

31. The Grand Council was the most directly representative body in the Florentine Republic.

exile, and we have suffered fifteen years of cruel, insolent, and damnable bondage. Had he properly handled the contingencies that arose during his tenure, our perpetual liberty would have been assured. The reason to suppress a potential troublemaker is not only to remove a danger, but also to set an example so that anyone else considering a plot against the state would fear the consequences.

I recall what happened to my good friend Filippo Strozzi, whose name I mention not out of any sense of malice, for I think it is well known that I owe him a great deal. When Filippo Strozzi was a young man he married Clarice, the daughter of Piero de' Medici.[32] The popular faction in our city was enraged, claiming it set a dangerous precedent for citizens to enter a relationship without public consent with the rebels who aspired to tyranny. Such a union between noble and respected families would encourage others to become closer with the Medici. As this boy developed a closer personal and business relationship with the Medici, it raised the suspicion that he sought to prepare the way for their restoration.

Taking his age into account, he could not have been thinking so far ahead. There was also no law that prohibited such unions, other than an ancient statute that called for a small fine. There was no hint of a plot, no activity against the state, just a marriage like many others done for frivolity or avarice, officiated by friars and other officials and no civic authorities. To claim that it was fomented by others as part of a greater conspiracy, one would have to be a soothsayer or a slanderer to make such a charge without any proof, which is inappropriate in matters of such importance. Criminal activity must be judged by the evidence, not mere speculation. There was no crime against the state, only the transgression of an obscure statute that was far from clear in its wording and could be easily disputed. When a decision is taken in doubt, some leniency is required. Even if more severity were warranted, Filippo could be held accountable only according to that old law. To break apart that marriage would have been an act of tyranny, detestable in a free city where men are supposed to live in liberty and magistrates are supposed to rule according to the law. What more can I say? Inexpert men were deceived by sweet sounding words and the *gonfalonier* was deceived by his nature.

---

32. Filippo Strozzi the Younger (1489–1538), Florentine banker to Clement VII and the Papal States, joined the Florentine exiles after the death of Clement VII in 1534. The army Strozzi raised against Cosimo I was defeated at the Battle of Montemurlo in 1537. Strozzi was captured and died, possibly killed in prison the following year.

So, Filippo Strozzi received a nominal punishment and in a few months, he was restored to his previous station. If it had been an affair of state, the punishment would have discouraged any others. Instead his impunity gave rise to license, and what could have been a foundation of our liberty became a source of our ruin.

Everyone remembers Bernardo Rucellai, a citizen well known for his literary talent, intelligence, experience, and knowledge of events. But he was also more ambitious and restless than appropriate for a citizen in a free city.[33] For many years he was an enemy of the Medici, since he and his sons had been harassed and even sent into exile. Then owing to a quarrel he had with Piero Soderini before he became *gonfalonier* and his inability to accept the level of equality in a post-Medici Florence, he began to favor their return. He became a supporter of malcontents, a corrupter of the young, who are easily deceived by evil things that have the outward appearance of goodness. His garden became a sort of academy. Many scholars and young people came to discuss literary topics and aesthetics. He became a siren for the discontented even though he was not particularly brilliant or eloquent. From outward appearances, it did not seem that he was doing anything shameful or ill-advised. Nevertheless, given the man's character, reputation, and his influence over so many malcontents and youths, his activities would have concerned anyone who took a closer look. Many wise men wanted something to be done, adding that it was ill-advised to tolerate the actions of such an influential, powerful, ambitious malcontent. In matters of state, plots must be thwarted early, especially if they are led by men of substance. It is not that easy to prove or to reveal such things, nor safe to wait until they become general knowledge, so the repression of a few can ensure the general welfare.

On the other hand, it may seem extreme to take such harsh measures unless corroborated by hard evidence. It serves no purpose to antagonize leading citizens and incite a backlash by spilling blood or needlessly sending people into exile. Suspicion and supposition alone are insufficient without evidence that is readily understandable, otherwise taking any action will alienate rather than reassure. Even those against any change in the city, whether out of goodwill or a reluctance to endanger themselves, will turn against you out of necessity or fear. This manner of handling

---

33. Bernardo Rucellai was a Florentine aristocrat who hosted literary and cultural gatherings at his gardens, which became known as the Orti Oricellari.

such affairs was approved either owing to general indifference or the disinterest of the *gonfalonier* himself. If Bernardo had been sent into exile, the plant that produced the poison that killed our liberty would have been destroyed. Tolerating him allowed the malcontents to consolidate their position and to corrupt the minds of the young. That garden, like a Trojan horse, produced the plots for the return of the Medici and the fire that destroyed this city. By the time everything became common knowledge, it was too late.

Your Honors, in cases like this I often hear the defense attempt the following tactic. They will ask you to believe in Mr. Francesco and those who will speak for him. Allow him to confess that he plotted the return of the Medici, but also let him appeal to your clemency for a pardon. For such generosity, he and his relatives will be indebted to you. By setting an example of mercy, goodwill, and kindness, many who now fear your wrath will become eternally obligated to you. These arguments are inadmissible because they are more fitting for a father than a judge. Then they will ask you to consider his present station as a mere private citizen, without any flourish of activity that might arouse suspicion, as low and as abject as possible. They will ask why we insist on believing in evil when we can just as easily believe in goodness. He has worked so hard, faced so many dangers, that he now craves peace, security, and wants to enjoy what he has earned with so much effort. One must be wary of desiring someone for an enemy, when they could just as easily be a friend. For if he is condemned on suspicion alone, many other friends of the Medici will fear the same end. The nobility would despair, and we would endanger the state by fostering hatred rather than goodwill.

They will try these arguments and many others besides, for anyone defending evil must by necessity be more inventive than someone supporting a just cause. Your Honors, when such arguments are made they appear pleasing, sweet, beautiful, useful, and safe, but in reality, they are ugly, bitter, insidious, dangerous, and poisonous. Your charge is to remember, to always keep in mind, how excessively Mr. Francesco has benefited from the Medici. He has always been their instrument and minister. Now he is absolutely dissatisfied and can desire only their return because above all he is ambitious and, because of their fall, has lost the great honor and power that he can recover only by their resurgence. It would be impossible for him to reaccustom himself to private life, an equal to those he used to dominate. Besides, he has committed serious offenses against the people when he deprived us of our city hall and did not allow us to regain our freedom. Either he doubts that he will ever be punished or despairs at the prospect of having to live in a free society. His thoughts, plans, actions, works have always been so inexcusable and unjustifiable that he will always oppose liberty whether overtly or covertly. This is his pain, his infamy, and his enslavement.

Your Honors, I urge you to remain vigilant. For the more convincing the arguments, praises, prayers, persuasions, and exclamations and threats, the more you must harden your hearts, thoughts, and souls. You must also remember that a trial of a conspiracy and plot against the state does not proceed like a normal trial. Other crimes are accepted only after they are exposed, and result in punishment only after a conviction. Guilt may not be determined solely on intent without the actual commission of a crime. Because of its seriousness, this is the only crime where charges can be pressed before the act is committed. In this case, punishment is not only for those who have acted or tried, but also those who desire or consent to act and or even those who just had some prior knowledge of events.

Our forefathers had Mr. Donato Barbadori beheaded because he knew about a plot but did not expose it.[34] In my day, Bernardo del Nero was beheaded for the same crime.[35] This law exists in the statutes as well as in the common laws established by the founding fathers of the republic. They were more vigilant about the prevention of a crime than in exacting revenge afterward. They included this law because of many clear examples of punishments and investigations from the past, and they were driven by a desire to be vigilant and enforce the law to deter what is principally a crime against the state to which we are bound by an obligation greater than that which ties us to our relatives, our fathers, even our very selves. If the law demands a horrible execution for anyone who kills his father, then someone who kills his homeland deserves something worse, because we have a greater tie to our country. By damaging our country, we hurt many people, not just one. It is not taking the life from someone who only had a few years to live, but from something that could live in perpetuity! Other crimes can be easily punished once they are committed, because the administration of justice would not be destroyed. But once

---

34. Donato Barbadori was executed following the Ciompi riots of 1378.

35. A self-made man without the advantage of birth, Bernardo del Nero (1424–1497) is Guicciardini's spokesman in the *Dialogue on the Government of Florence*. He was executed for not revealing the plot to restore Piero de' Medici in 1497.

the state changes, and freedom is oppressed, he who makes revolution no longer fears punishment for the evil that he commits and may even have the authority to offend those who least deserve it. Other crimes are particular, since they affect only the individual, this one is universal and affects everyone. As with other crimes, punishment cannot amend the harm, but it can provide a sense of satisfaction that equals the offense. What is taking the life of a single wicked man who plots to usurp liberty in comparison to the numerous evils and destruction caused by the ruin of an entire country? To level a charge for this particular offence, there is no need for great quantities of evidence. For a sentence to be carried out a crime does not even have to be completed. To ensure punishment it is enough that he desired and knew about it. All that is needed is the suspicion that he had motive and means to act.

There are some nations, greater and wiser than us, that have always acted in this manner. We should admire their virtue and at the very least add to their fame by referring to them. After the Romans expelled the Tarquinians and their kings, they also confiscated their goods and put to death a clique of noble youths plotting their return. After the Romans established their liberty on a firm foundation of good laws, they did not think it sufficient merely to have punished the guilty; they removed anything that might raise suspicions, even by example. The Romans thought it necessary to remove any vestige of authority that might cast a shadow on liberty. They thought it better to be accused of excessive diligence than to allow any room for negligence. Therefore, they sent Lucius Tarquinius, the consort of the king, into exile even though he was one of the main enemies of the conspirators.[36] The violent act for which the Tarquinians were expelled had been committed against Lucius's wife. Lucius then helped Brutus to reveal the plot and was even elected as coconsul with Brutus. The Romans' main interest was the health of the republic. To purge every memory of tyranny from the city, they committed an injustice against a citizen who had been one of the founders of their liberty. This is reasonable because more care must be taken to ensure the safety of everyone than the well-being of any single individual.

The Athenians taught humanity, religion, and many arts not only to all of Greece but also to many foreign nations. Besides always being

---

36. Lucius Tarquinius was the last Etruscan king of Rome (534–510 BC). Lucius Iunius Brutus is a traditional founder of the Roman republic.

quick and vehement against anyone who plotted against liberty, they were wary of any citizens who surpassed all others in nobility, relatives, wealth, reputation, or deed. They decided, as is quite true, that the true friends of liberty are mediocre citizens of lesser standing. Those who leave mediocrity behind for greatness will sooner have reason, cause, and occasion to try to oppress others rather than to favor equality. The security of the republic depends not only on an absence of opposition but also on an absence of anyone with the ability to oppress it. Therefore, every ten years they called a council of the entire citizenry to see if a majority thought that some should be sent into exile. Those exiled did not always have a poor reputation, nor were they guilty of having plotted against the republic—for such cases they had the regular courts. They chose someone who was more talented, better respected than anyone else, and who had acquired their renown through virtue, hard work, and even endangering themselves for the good of the country. Wise rulers of republics understand that liberty faces many dangers and may count on fewer defenders than enemies. To preserve a republic, extreme diligence and vigilance are necessary. Potential malefactors cannot be allowed to thrive and gain confidence. Action against them must be taken early to eliminate any plant that casts a shadow over all others. Provisions must be taken against anything that arouses suspicion. Everyone's well-being must not be compromised by taking care of a single person. But why seek foreign examples when we have our own? During the days of our forefathers, Mr. Corso Donati was a citizen of great virtue and reputation who had done more than anyone else in support of the government in power at the time.[37] His wife was the daughter of Uguccione della Faggiuola, a foreigner who led a powerful faction. This marriage raised suspicions that Corso planned to usurp our freedoms, so the wise and virile of days gone by, men of old, took appropriate action. They did not merely note his comings and goings, search for proof and witnesses, or try to discover whether his marriage was a normal union or an act whose ulterior motive was to threaten the city. They realized how difficult it is to understand someone's intentions, but they also realized that any delay could be dangerous. In a private matter, as opposed to those with a wider range, suspicion may at times acquire the force of proof. So, the very day

---

37. Florentine politician (d. 1308) known for his temper. Appears in Dante, *Purgatorio*, XXIV, 82.

in which their fears arose, they accused, indicted, and condemned him. What is more, without delay, the people, with arms in hand, went to his house to carry out the execution. They did not feel that their liberty was secure until they saw him cut to pieces on the street.

If only we had the prudence of such wise republics or the character and will of our grandfathers and great grandfathers. If only we were as jealous of our bride as we should be, as reason and experience should have taught us to be. Perhaps then we would not be embroiled in such a sordid, atrocious, horrid affair and set such a poor example by proceeding so slowly. There would be no fuss about evidence and witnesses. The people would not be here at their leisure, as if the case involved somebody else, to hear speeches and await the outcome of this trial. Someone who has always been an enemy of the law would not be allowed to use the law to defend himself. Mr. Francesco, you would not be allowed to speak, for you have always spoken only to deny our right of be heard. You should not be allowed to defend yourself in the very square where you expelled the people under threat of arms. You should not even be allowed to look at the city hall that you stole from the citizens with a thousand frauds and deceptions.

The day after the expulsion of the Medici, when you insolently turned against the opinion of all in this city, on that day, that very hour, the people should have run to your house in a rage to tear you to a thousand pieces, to carry out a sentence you deserved for years. A sentence, I say, as plain as the nose on your face or emblazoned on your forehead which in the eyes of the honest citizenry would seem to be the most just, desired, and eagerly anticipated spectacle that this city has ever witnessed. Your blood would have served as a sacrificial offering befitting our country and liberty. But instead you forgot all about what you had done just a few days prior and you impudently and spitefully entered the city hall. The Signoria should have made you jump out of one of the windows instead of allowing you to return by the stairs that you climbed so vigorously to strip us of our recently recovered liberty. That is how republics must be solidified, with examples that endure for ages in the memories of men.

When I was young, Francesco Valori was a good citizen with great authority. When the people rioted because of the events with the friar, he went to take control of the city hall from his house in Palagio on order of the signory and was killed in the streets by the relatives of Niccolò Ridolfi and others he had helped punish earlier for plotting the return of Piero de' Medici.[38] How come the entire country now hesitates before acting to ensure its safety against an evildoer, when in the past a few private individuals had the will to act against such a good and noble citizen like Valori? Then we are surprised that someone is always attempting to suppress our freedom with the effrontery of endless plots and conspiracies. Now someone who openly and cruelly took our liberty from us is somehow allowed to enjoy the benefits of citizenship and legality just like those who founded our republic. Since we have come to this point, we can only imagine how he will continue to use our civility to his benefit.

He or someone else may remind you, claiming to be a friend of the republic, about how unwise it is to send citizens into exile, to create expatriates, for there are many examples when such people have damaged the city and started trouble. He will say that the citizenry will flourish with good treatment and suffer under punishment. It is more useful to have them within the city as friends than abroad as enemies. If he is convicted, many will despair; every day they will fear the same end for themselves. His acquittal will reassure everyone and calm the undecided. Finally, if he cannot convince you using rational arguments, he will appeal for mercy and compassion. He will lament about how much he has suffered and been persecuted. He will present a thousand precedents of your liberality and beg you not to take up a new attitude now. He will say that you act according to your true nature, and like God who is the ultimate example and source of mercy. These arguments might be permissible if there were any hope he could change his ways, or if compassion on your part would not ruin this city. For his sins are infinite and surpass the crimes committed by citizens in this town for the last hundred years. Someone who has exceeded every limit of wickedness should receive no mercy. Mr. Francesco, if you were not so incorrigible I would be no less fervent in defending you than I have been in accusing you. I would second your own arguments, and those of your relatives, and speak about the merits of your father. But such gentleness and compassion would bring ruin to our homeland. Everyone must understand that we cannot destroy ourselves just to foster your well-being.

The events of the past that we bore with such suffering must have prepared us to face the future. Whatever we did not learn by reason, we must learn by experience. By now we should understand the difference

---

38. The friar is Girolamo Savonarola (1452–1498).

between goodwill and ineptitude and not be so confused at the real meaning of such arguments. One preserves the good and the other excuses the wicked. In 1494, our fathers showed mercy to the followers of the Medici, pardoning all past affairs and exalting all to honors without any reservations. But they never changed their attitudes. In fact, it encouraged others to stir up trouble because they hoped to enjoy the same impunity. What followed was the loss of our liberty. The outcome of showing mercy was our oppression, and once again we found ourselves in the mouth of Pharaoh. If the same policy is repeated now, the same results will follow to our shame. Happy is he who learns at other's expense, for it is foolish to learn from one's own. What do these examples do but encourage the wicked to plot and ensure a following for tyrants? Who would not want to be the tyrant's friend in Florence when it leads to status and power? Whenever the tyrants are exiled, there are no real consequences for their followers besides a few dozen ducats in fines or extra taxes. Other cities are run in a manner that discourages the restoration of tyranny, or if the tyrant is already present within the city, citizens are prevented from becoming their followers and coconspirators. But we do everything so that when they are abroad, someone inside opens the door for their return. When they are inside, we lock them in, so they cannot leave. This is not mercy or kindness but anarchy, chaos, self-inflicted cruelty. When we lose our liberty, we think of nothing else but how to regain it. When we have liberty, we lose all memory of how to preserve it.

Remember, Your Honors, how long and what a burden the last period of bondage seemed to us. Remember the speeches, tears, oaths we swore to restore our liberty. Remember above all that God himself miraculously restored us; we cannot claim any credit owing to our virtue or efforts. When we took up arms to reclaim our freedoms, our enemies fell back as soon as we acted. When it seemed like we were oppressed and under the yoke again, God, I declare, once again miraculously restored our liberty. He did not act so that we could let it slip away. He has entrusted us with the capacity to preserve and protect our freedom and not lose it because of incompetence. Let us not tempt the Almighty and give him cause to turn his eyes away from us. He rarely performs such miracles and rather expects men to fend for themselves. I will try to understand if you pardon Mr. Francesco because you are not convinced that his nature will make him as pernicious as before, although an act of mercy will probably make him even more inclined to evil. You may consider paying him some deference so that the pro-Medici faction does not despair or become too frightened. What you have not understood is that they are incorrigible, and that it is madness to convince through kindness those who must be bound with severity. A good doctor unsuccessful at prescribing cold cures will try the opposite path and administer hot remedies. We have tried so many times to heal the city with gentleness and clemency, but the result is that the sickness has spread, and all we reap is hardship and bitterness. It is better to frighten the Medici faction than to encourage it. It is better to have them despair than to give them reason to hope. It is better and safer to keep someone abroad who will pose a threat once they are back in the city. I wish that everyone could live in the city, but not at the cost of endangering the public. It is better to choose the lesser of two evils. An enemy abroad is a cause for fear, but an enemy inside will result in evil.

You have now been able to hear the inauspicious, unusual, and unexpected sins of Mr. Francesco, which must seem unimaginable without a certain effort. If you are horrified now, how will you react when you have heard everything? For I will reveal the source and origin of his misdeeds, which surpasses any limit of ambition and avarice.

As the president of the Romagna he carried enough weight to be able to hire his own brother as his vice president.[39] He often conferred with the pope on matters of state, affairs so vast in the range of a pontificate that their scope is difficult to understand and even more difficult to explain. He found himself with more reputation, authority, and income than he could ever have hoped for, more than he could have ever even dared to desire. The truth is that his rank surpassed any sense of his origins as a Florentine citizen. His position was more suited for a cardinal, a man of some station, than for a regular citizen. Nevertheless, even the honors, benefits, and power that would have seemed excessive even for a cardinal, were not enough to satiate this fountain of all greed in his corrupt soul. He had led armies in triumph in Lombardy, paraded in excelsis in front of all the people he governed over the years. He had to be the one who decided in war and peace because of his singular access to the pope. I also believe that he had the opportunity to steal immense amounts from the treasury. For any of these things or for all of them together, because a single sin this enormous must have more than one origin, he spoke, argued, exclaimed, and made all others his subordinate. He convinced

---

39. Iacopo Guicciardini was Francesco's brother.

the pope to take up arms in this pernicious war, lighting the fire that has already burned half of Italy and may eventually burn it all.

The pope did not have to make that decision, for he faced no immediate danger or pressing enemy. The war was a conflict between the emperor and the king of France and did not directly involve him. Each of them respected and honored him, and they were no longer fighting in Italy but elsewhere. The pope would have retained his status and authority had he remained neutral. His place was to negotiate peace between them and to promote war against the infidels in Hungary, which at the time was so close to the fire that would consume it just a few months later.[40] Such a role would have better suited his character, as has been borne out by the results. In fact, it was common knowledge that he was ill-suited to such difficulties and disputed. Mr. Francesco's boundless ambition and avarice, his restless nature and immoderate appetite steered the pope into a decision that was so shameful, dangerous, and costly that it came to directly involve our city.

The pope's rank, forces, abilities, and capabilities were ill-suited to play a part in a war between two great princes. He should have sided with the winner the way our fathers always did, according to occasion and necessity. It was not our place to mix in the affairs of the greatest Christian kings, to put order in all of Italy, and to be masters and arbiters of who should stay and who should go. We need to be on good terms with everyone so our merchandise, on which our livelihood depends, can be exported everywhere in safety. We did not need to offend a great prince unless we were forced to do so. Or at least we could have done it so that the offense taken would not outweigh practical considerations, with an apology accompanying the damage caused. We do not need to spend our money for other peoples' wars. We must save to defend ourselves from the victors instead of harassing them and endangering the life of the city. We could have leisurely sat by and observed the war as it progressed with the idea of buying peace after hostilities at a much lower price. Instead on the first day we bought war and ruin. We had a thousand ways to save ourselves, now we have none. If the emperor wins, we will be sacked. If the king of France and the Venetians win, we will be hunted and enslaved. One king hates us, the other disdains us. We have wasted so much treasure that all sources, public and private, have been dissipated.

40. Hungary was invaded and conquered by the Turks in 1526.

The armies of friend and foe have both been in our country, and both treated us with extreme cruelty. We have lived in fear that this poor city would be sacked, burned, or worse, and we remain in a state of constant alarm. Our expenses and instability grow every hour. We cannot throw off this burden, and if we remain under it we will crack.

These things have the same source and origin. Mr. Francesco drove them. Mr. Francesco organized them. Mr. Francesco incited them. Mr. Francesco fed them. You complain that the monte di pietà is not earning and your daughters cannot get married.[41] Mr. Francesco is the cause. The merchants complain that they cannot do business. Mr. Francesco is the cause. The poorer citizens have exhausted their savings, are in debt and dire straits because of the damages they have suffered and because of the extra taxes they have been forced to pay. Look at him, he is the reason why. The entire city fears being sacked; here is the source. But why should I cry only for the troubles of this city? The calamity and ruin of the entire world comes from you alone. Because of you the holy name of peace has been exiled. The entire world is at war, under arms, aflame. Because of you, Hungary has been abandoned to plunder by the infidels. Because of you Rome was sacked with such cruelty to the private and collective ruin of so many of our citizens.[42] Because of you heretics dominate holy sites and relics have been thrown to the dogs. You are the scourge, the ruin, and the fire of the entire world. So how can we be surprised that you live as the enemy of God, that all men, all lands foreign and domestic, everything is subject to disease, famine, and plague?

Do you all want this disease to go away? Do you all want abundance to return? Would you like to send these terrors to the heretics and infidels? Then exile Mr. Francesco to Constantinople or to Pagania, or better yet to hell.[43] This country would be happy once again, the air serene, even the stones would laugh. For fear, evil, and all devilry will follow him wherever he goes. Given these facts, Your Honors, you must realize that we are not dealing with minor or obscure crimes, or petty matters. What is at stake is our liberty, our well-being, our very lives. We will not be punishing one citizen or one man, but a disease, a monster, a fury.

---

41. As a public debt, charitable pawnbroking institution, the monte di pietà also facilitated the provision of dowries.

42. The Sack of Rome by the troops of Emperor Charles V took place on May 6, 1527.

43. Pagania seems to be a name that Guicciardini invented to indicate a place inhabited by pagans.

To me personally, the outcome of this trial no longer matters. What matters are the people, the city, our well-being, and our children's futures. I am satisfied that after my presentation of the evidence, he will have been so thoroughly prosecuted that everyone will expect him to be found guilty and condemned accordingly. The rest is up to you, Your Honors. I am a humble citizen who voluntarily took it upon myself to accuse him, so let any repercussion fall on me. My country did not expect this from me, nor did I act under any obligation. I would not have suffered any consequences had I not made the accusation against him. Now as respected and honored citizens, you may wonder what is expected of you. The people have demonstrated their faith by electing you to this court. They have put the entire republic into your hands. Strength in numbers will protect you from any backlash. Not to act accordingly would be a demonstration of the worst sort of wickedness. Everyone understands that their very lives and their children's futures depend on the outcome of this trail. Were he to be absolved, this law, which is the foundation of our liberty, would be rendered meaningless. There would no longer be any respect or fear of the law. All crimes, insolence, and plots will go unpunished. There would be no more need for laws, magistrates, or trials. With his acquittal, these things will be killed. With his conviction, they will exist in perpetuity. Your decision is liberty or tyranny, health or ruin for all.

It also is a matter of your personal health, Your Honors, and the health of the impudent ones who helped this wicked man. If he is rescued from your hands, he will not survive the wrath of the people. If your arms do not kill him, the stones and the arms of this multitude will kill him. If the people begin to reason for themselves, who can tell where their justifiable disdain and desperation will lead? Let them be satisfied with the blood of this monster, lest they take revenge against those who defended him and sheathed the naked sword of justice against heaven and hell. There is always someone ready to incite the people, and if the others hesitate, I will be their instigator, their ringleader. What else are we supposed to do? What is the point of living in freedom if our liberty is always threatened and taken away? Let everything decay into total confusion, everything be ruined, chaos rule, rather than bear witness to any more of these indignities. I state again, if need be, that I will be the ringleader, the instigator, the first to pick up a stone for the people and freedom.

But it will never reach this point; all we must do is let him act without further prodding. For by now, Your Honors, you must understand the degree to which this situation has impassioned and inflamed everyone. Don't you realize how difficult it is for the people to restrain themselves? Don't you see their gestures and motions? Can't you hear their comments and murmuring? Even now there is the danger that their patience could turn to anger and action. The clouds and storm of their fury will be vented not only against the authors of wickedness but also against its helpers and seconds, against anyone who knew about it, against anyone who could have acted to stop it. They are held in check only by the promise of your verdict. If they are denied, all bets are off, everything will be in flux, and the entire people will be in a fury. There are those who pray God to be free from such wrath, so take care, Your Honors, not to incite them. Your Honors, you must provide for us with acts of prudence by performing what you must with faith, goodwill, and wisdom. Everyone quite deservedly expects you to be on the side of good, liberty, and the health of the nation. Do not shirk from your duty, from yourselves and what is expected of you. Do not give rise to what could be an extremely dangerous scandal and the cause of infamy and danger for you, and infinite damage to this city. To put this fire out now, all that is needed is a little water; otherwise all the water in the Arno, the Tiber, and even the sea will not suffice.

DEFENSE AGAINST THE PRECEDING

Your Honors, I am aware that it is inappropriate for someone who is innocent, with a conscience clean, to fear or be perturbed by false accusations. He should be confident that God, as the highest judge, would be his protector and defender and not allow truth to be suffocated by slander. Nevertheless, the unusual events before my eyes are affecting my spirit. I find myself here before a multitude that observes me and is witness to my troubles. I am the first, almost as an example, to be called to trial and examined by so many under this new law, this new manner of deciding a case with public hearings where everything that a citizen has or can have is at stake. A few months earlier I was so happy that my friends envied me. Now I am so afflicted that I appear miserable even to my enemies. However, I have faith that God almighty will not allow someone to be wrongfully oppressed. Judges, your generosity and wisdom comfort and sustain me, make me confident of my acquittal. How else would an innocent man react in the presence of judges such as yourselves? In fact, I feel that being called to trial could even be considered a blessing.

Of course, I would be better off had these groundless charges and rumors, which have now become fixed in people's minds, never been so unjustly leveled against me. However, since their arrival I could desire nothing more than for the chance for my innocence to be clearly recognized by everyone, so I may finally go out in public as in the past. Everything will eventually be settled, for as the proverb says, time is the father of truth. In the long run, it is impossible for the truth not to come to light. After so many contradictions and disputes, when the truth is known it will be blinding, complete, and splendid. If my accuser is driven to prosecute by his zeal for the republic, as he himself has stated, then as a citizen, I cannot hold anything against him for his efforts. However, if he has been induced by ambition, as many believed before, and now that he has been heard many more believe, I am grateful for his impudence. Does he not realize that I will be defended and relieved by the very weapons he thought would offend and oppress me? Let me speak about his motives later.

The entire basis of my innocence depends upon God and the judges. Therefore, let me first pray with all my heart to the Almighty that the outcome of this trial will be decided on the merits of the actions I committed. If I am infected by the sins as charged, then I will not challenge a deserved punishment, and I will serve as a fitting example of the severity of Your Honors. However, if I am innocent, allow me the opportunity to demonstrate why and to illuminate the minds of the judges. Let the authority, bestowed on you by the people, be used to punish the wicked, but not to destroy the good.

Judges, I do not ask for mercy or compassion, or that you recall the generosity that I have shown many of you in the past. I ask only one thing: that everyone make a decision that is reasonable and honest. Do not come here with your minds already made up. Arrive at a decision that is formed here, in front of this tribunal, not plucked from the rumors and opinions of the commoners, or from the slander of the malicious. Let a decision derive from the arguments, witnesses, and evidence presented here at trial. Suppress any preconceptions, restrain your spirit and prejudices as if you were hearing something today that you had never heard spoken of before. Be resolved not to decide according to what many have vainly believed, but by laying your own hands on this open wound. Do so in accordance with your wisdom, with the understanding that it is better to acquit according to the demands of justice than to convict without cause or due process. You must realize that for the good of the republic, an innocent man must not be convicted on mere slander and rumors. This is also the will of the people whose only care is that the truth be known, even if they believed prior or believe now that crimes were committed. It would be unacceptable for me to be punished without first being allowed to speak in my own defense. Nor should I face the judgment of ignorant and superficial men, but persons of prudence, goodwill, and seriousness who demand the truth.

Certainly judges, if you have the forbearance and spirit that I expect, then once this veil, this fog of false charges and rumors is removed, you will realize that the voices against me are groundless and unfounded. Never has anyone been called to trial with weaker, more superficial slanders. No one will ever be absolved with more open, solid, and just cause. I am certain that upon hearing my side of the story you will be moved to have compassion for me. I have been unfairly subjected to the tongues of the malicious, unjustly attacked by everyone without cause. You should consider my case to be your own, for it is potentially everyone's situation. For if this can happen to me without any reason or cause, then it can also happen to anyone, even to you.

Thus, envy and malice can implicate the innocent, as has been done to me against all truth. It has been within the power of error and ignorance to make people vainly believe about other cases what is now believed about mine. In fact, many are more susceptible to this danger than I am. Over the years, I have earned certain notoriety. These were not the experiences of one day, but many. Over the years my honesty and other qualities have resonated in this city. In all modesty neither my family nor I have ever had any cause for shame. So, it seems unbelievable that such rumors against me would surface so easily. Nor did it seem possible for such a confirmed and well-established reputation to be so easily erased. Yet it took the slander of a single day for everything to be forgotten, and just an hour to believe the contrary of everything that had been believed for so many years. Anybody who until now has not had the chance to demonstrate their worth will have reason to be apprehensive, especially if virtue is something hinted at rather than proven by experience. If one false rumor that lasted only four days cannot be counterbalanced by the memory of my past works and actions, nothing will be able to stop it from becoming even more ensconced and ever more difficult to extinguish and eradicate. My own situation and predicament could become the situation and predicament of many others. What has happened to me could happen to anyone, and more easily to many more than just to me. Therefore, judges, in this trial I rely on your goodwill and prudence. You must be aware that the consideration that you give to me may be useful to you all. Any wrong you do to me could by its example someday damage you and everyone.

Therefore, let my defense rely on what is true and just and allows no retort or objection. This trial must be decided according to the truth without relying on charges, rumors, or outcry. The witnesses must be examined with diligence, the proof weighed, the circumstances carefully considered. If I am allowed this, which nobody can deny me, then I am already absolved. I am already a free man. Your Honors, I will not make a motion for an immediate ruling regarding the evident falsehood of these rumors. I will not make such a motion; however, were I to do so, I would not be asking anything unreasonable or unjust. On one side of the scale would be all the things that I have done in the past, everything that everyone has known and believed about me over the years. On the other side, nothing except a strange report, an uncertain rumor without origin, author, or merit. Would it be an injustice, I say, if certain and studied reasons caused a vain, unfounded charge to be rejected? However, this is not what I am asking. I do not want my affairs to depend only on the recognition of all the hardships, sweat, and dangers that I endured for so many years. I will be well satisfied and content if your decision is impartial and neutral. You should believe the charges if they are clearly demonstrated by the evidence, not hearsay. You must be ready to believe that the charges are groundless if truth and reason demonstrate them to be false.

This will form the basis of my defense instead of other possible strategies. If I did not have complete faith in your judgment, I would put forward a greater effort in writing, adding more evidence so that everyone, even those who believed the slander against me, would understand how falsely I have been accused. In every period, in this very city as in others, this has happened to an infinite number of men of the greatest virtue and goodwill, who were the pride of their countries. In fact, it seems such troubles, perhaps owing to envy or misfortune, frequently and insidiously strike those who deserve it least. So, what so many have undergone before is now befalling me, and in the future, could easily happen to anyone.

Let me state that Rome never had a more useful or wiser citizen than Fabius Maximus. His prudence and ability to improvise slowed Hannibal's victories.[1] When it was useful to the republic, he was given such powers to save the city that the people came to believe that he was in league with Hannibal. He became so infamous that as dictator he was given a colleague, something that the Romans never tried again. However, as the truth of his actions became known, his merits were recognized and everyone admitted that the city had been saved because of him alone.

---

1. Fabius Maximus (ca. 280–203 BC) was a Roman general criticized for losing battles against Hannibal (247–183 BC), the Carthaginian prince and general, during the Second Punic War.

I dare state that in that wise and famous city of Athens, or in any other republic since, there has never been a worthier and more glorious citizen than Pericles. He governed a free city for thirty years not through force, factions, or corruption but by relying on the authority of his reputation for virtue. Nevertheless, during the war against the Spartans, a war that he favored, some protests occurred, and the people removed him from government under a cloud of severe charges and rumoring. Later, after they realized their mistake, he was reappointed with greater prestige than before.

There are similar examples from the past of our own city, even examples from within my family. Mr. Giovanni Guicciardini was the commissar of our camp in the siege of Lucca.[2] When our troops were forced to retreat, he was groundlessly accused of having taken money from the Lucchese and put on trial before the rectors of the city. The whole matter was pushed through by Cosimo de' Medici, who was then aspiring to power.[3] However, Giovanni's innocence was proven, and he was most honorably absolved by the judges. I remember that when I was still a child similar charges were leveled against Piero Soderini to the point that insults were painted on the door of his house.[4] The charges against him dissipated after a few weeks because they had no foundation, and before a year had passed, he became *gonfalonier* for life with great celebration.

To these I could add an infinite number of examples. But it is superfluous, judges, for your wisdom is quite capable of distinguishing between slander and the truth. One has a clearly definable beginning and a certain author, with details in time and method. Its origin, progress, and methods can be seen and not hidden or denied out of existence. The more time passes, the more it becomes solid and firm. The other has no head, no beginning, its source is unseen and its author unknown. It is varied and confused and there is no distinction in the time or method of its propagation. In this case, the slander is limited to a vague charge of theft but without any details about what, how, and when. It is a slander that is as ignorant as somebody coming from Egypt, and the more it is investigated,

---

2. Giovanni Guicciardini (1385–1435).

3. Cosimo de' Medici (1389–1464) was a banker with papal connections who gradually assumed control of the government of Florence to the point of assuming the moniker of *pater patriae*, the father of the country.

4. Piero Soderini (1452–1522), *gonfalonier* for life; he was unsuccessful in preventing the return of the Medici in 1512.

the less truth it reveals. The more it is researched, the less truth is found. The more one wants to discover, the more uncertain it becomes. Time by itself can consume and reduce it so much that in the end whoever believed it will be ashamed of themselves. Let us now see what type of accusation we have before us, Your Honors, so you may decide if I deserve contempt or compassion.

The first charge in the accusation is that I stole an infinite sum of money, and to steal, I allowed our soldiers to sack this country. This sin is so great, enormous, and horrible, that all the art of the prosecutor's speech, all the vehement exclamations he made would not be enough to demonstrate a minimum part of its seriousness. But one cannot determine guilt without defining the crime and the possible accessories to that crime in terms that would not allow a false accusation. Everyone understands that a valid accusation supports itself without relying on the ingenuity of an orator's tongue. Our country should learn to place a greater value on prudence and goodwill than vain artifice in speech. For despite all the study of Cicero and the philosophers, what the country needs are good, serious, and peace-loving citizens rather than flowery speakers who are never useful and always damaging if they do not combine prudence and seriousness with eloquence. Should the mark of a skillful prosecutor just be an ability to convict someone whose could be acquitted with difficulty, or convict someone who should never have been charged? Or is there more to be said for basing a prosecution on what is solid, weighted, and certain and true, rather than on idle argumentation that seems slight from afar and can go up in smoke under a little pressure?

When he called an entire army as a witness, I expected to see this square full of men-at-arms and horses. I admit some apprehension on my part now that I am so reduced in station, so abandoned by fortune. I would have trouble defending myself against a single man let alone an entire army, wherever it is now. However, if only God had created all armies in the image of this one, for then we would never have to fear any war or enemy, for this is an army that cannot be seen, heard, does no harm, and provokes fear in no one. It is an army fit for these slanders. If someone hears about it, they may believe in its existence. However, anyone who takes the trouble to examine for himself will see that there is nothing and nobody here at all. Thousands of men, entire legions have been reduced to four, maybe six witnesses who upon cross examination admit that they are not sure what they are talking about. I will not move to disqualify them as I justifiably could. As they have stated themselves, they suffered serious damages in the transit and the lodging of those troops. However, since they will never be able to claim damages against those who injured them, they are here now seeking a solution to their difficulties as the only available option.

Anyone knows how fragile witnesses can be at trials. They must never give the appearance of impassioned feeling, or even a scintilla of bias. Something as important as a man's conviction hangs on their statements. Perhaps the law should not be so dependent on the words of men, knowing how easily they can be corrupted. Even in cases where there appears to be no corruption, there is always some doubt that some form of corruption may have influenced the outcome in secret. However, owing to the practical difficulty of proceeding otherwise, relying on witnesses in trials is a necessity. The law must be workable, but without ignoring potential doubts and suspicions. The result is that a witness may be excluded when it can be alleged that they have a bias in the matter at hand, no matter how slight.

Therefore, if I made a motion that these witnesses who claim to have suffered serious damages are not credible and no account should be taken of their statements, the judges could not deny it. Nor would this multitude be surprised, or would you know what to say in rebuttal. Yet, look how calmly I am proceeding, how much I trust the truth. Because the evidence supporting my innocence is so solid that I will not object to these witnesses of yours, or any others who could be removed. I will not contest them. I shall afford them the same level of trust as you do. In fact, I place them at an even higher level. Where you have produced them as soldiers, I will be content if the judges accept their word as gospel. For I have no idea whether their statements are true or false, but I am certain that they cannot harm me. Perhaps you think that I have allowed you a great advantage, but to me it seems that I have allowed you nothing at all.

What exactly do these blessed witnesses have to say anyway? They claim that when the damage was done, they heard some infantrymen caught in the act of stealing attempt to explain their actions by claiming they had not been paid. These infantrymen (if only they included a captain or at least some men-at-arms!) also allegedly remarked that Mr. Francesco was the one who had given them license to steal. This reduced scene is the meat of all their testimony. Oh, what devastating testimony, what conclusive proof, what awe-inspiring witnesses! They are not even sure who these soldiers were and what companies they came from. Were they regular soldiers or just adventurers who had mixed among the troops, as occurs with all armies? How can we accept them as witnesses and rely on their testimony in a case of such importance and interest?

The law demands that in every case, even the humblest, all witnesses' names be known, as well as their country, origin, profession, and social status. This is so that they may be interrogated, and so that it may be determined if they have any prejudices, and so his disposition may be understood. Anyone who has a poor reputation, or leads a bad life, is not to be trusted. Furthermore, anyone who is circumspect in their actions is likely to act similarly while giving testimony. Even when they appear to be completely honest in every way, they must tell everything they know, every detail they ever understood, observed, heard, every who, what, where, when, and how. They must give every possible detail so that the matter may come into the light and be thoroughly examined. How can we believe anonymous witnesses, or witnesses of poor condition, swordsmen, ruffians, witnesses more used to profanity than proper speech, witnesses who themselves were thieves, caught in the act of stealing?

Didn't your own witnesses, to whom I afforded my full trust without making any objection, didn't they testify that they heard these soldiers speak after they were caught in the act of stealing? If we were to allow the testimony of people who steal and then speak to cover themselves after being caught red-handed, no thief would ever be hung. What did you expect them to say? We stole because we have faulty characters, because we are thieves, or because we never exercised any other profession? What wife is not able to invent some excuse when someone is found on top of her? What thief free in the square ever confesses before being imprisoned and put before the noose? What other excuse could they have come up with? Should we now expect soldiers to rob in friendly territory? Because there is no law, reason, or military practice that permits such behavior except not having been paid.

They do not state that Mr. Francesco told them in person, or that they took their orders directly from him. There is nothing to suggest that they had firsthand knowledge of him ever giving such an order or ever allowing such license. If the first and best men of this city were to testify in this manner, even the meekest judge would find it ridiculous. Any prosecutor or attorney who tried to introduce such testimony would realize that it would be a waste of time and money. So, why am I spending so many words on something so obvious? Why should I annoy when what I really need is your complete attention? If these witnesses are ridiculous, worthless, and prove nothing, then what is to be made of the arguments or external documents supposed to support their statements?

With strong witnesses, anyone presenting a case may strengthen their arguments with documentation or other sources, even theories. It is one thing to rely on witnesses who are not convincing, and another to have no witnesses at all. So where are the witnesses in this case? Not only are there no witnesses, but none has even been alleged, or even thought of yet. Maybe they will claim that this is due to the inexperience of the prosecutor, which would not be surprising because it is one thing to read Priscian or Aristotle, and another to try a case.[5] However, that is not it either, judges. He is surely learned enough to manage a common case, and believe me, he has not lacked teachers, consultants, and others in my profession whom I will not name because I have more respect for them than they have for me.

So, I am not so wretched as to lack those who would persecute me. Nor do I lack those who would be pleased to see me reduced in status to the point of needing the help of those who usually require assistance from me. What they really want is my blood, my ultimate downfall, my vulnerability to every possible calamity and misery. Woe is me, what did I ever do to them to have offended or provoked them to this point? If it is envy, I am surely so reduced in rank that by now they could show some compassion. As my fortunes have changed so should the attitudes of such men against me; yet this has not been the case. They have the same thirst to destroy and eradicate me that they had previously to debase me. In any event the prosecutor has certainly not lacked advice, counsel, or consultations.

If they could prove that I had spent large sums on money for myself, which might make the charges of theft credible, or that I condoned the larceny, you must believe they would have presented it by now. If there were other possible theories, clues, or statements, they have not been negligent to find them nor lack the effort to interpret them. If they had found evidence of robberies, crimes, or avarice in my past they would have introduced it. They would have tried to use the past to cast a shadow over the present, and rightly so, for whatever someone was in the past, so

---

5. Priscus (5th century AD) and Aristotle (384–322 BC) wrote texts adopted for the professional preparation of orators.

DEFENSE AGAINST THE PRECEDING   175

are they in the present. How can anyone believe that someone who has always been good would begin suddenly to turn evil, or that someone with an evil nature would abstain from wrongdoing when presented with an occasion? These arguments have not been made because they do not exist and cannot be supported. There are no witnesses, documents, no evidence, no source at all, just flimsy, whimsical conjectures. Everything is based upon the rumors and the outcry that you already rejected, which you ruled is not credible. I am confident in my defense that the robbery that brought the charges against me has not been established with any certainty. Anyone knows that, not only in criminal cases but even in a dispute over a few coins, when the prosecution has no proof, then the judge has no choice but to acquit.

Let me address the other charges made by the prosecution. Of the defenses for anyone called to stand trial, none is easier, more solid and expeditious, and shuts a prosecutor's mouth more effectively than the inability to establish a motive. The first day that I was called to stand trial, in fact the very day the names of the jury were made public, I saw that they were of such quality that an innocent person could desire none better because in my heart I expected to be acquitted and delivered from the wrath of my enemies. If I were not declared to be a thoroughly good man, at least I would not be declared evil and I would be content and would expect nothing further. However, since that day I have hoped to be absolved so that the entire city and everyone who believed the worst would accept the truth. Then I would regain the esteem and good reputation that I previously enjoyed among the people. So, what has been done here so far is not enough. I want to go further and prove to all of you what the prosecutor should have done. I want to prove not only that I did not steal your monies but never even could have done so. If I cannot prove this I will allow myself to be condemned, as should be the case if my adversary had been able to prove the contrary. This may seem like an unusual proposal, so severe that either you will think I am mad or you will begin to understand that I am an innocent man. Nor would it be enough if I were afflicted with some lesser form of madness, like someone who throws bread instead of stones, because if I were not to be acquitted I would be putting myself in danger senselessly. What is more, not only will I prove my innocence, but I will do so by limiting myself to the type of evidence admissible in trial, with solid arguments, witnesses, all clearly documented. If I do this, my fellow citizens, I will ask for nothing more, require no other favor, only that the negative opinion that you have had of me in these months be erased. Let the truth be known and the charges and the envy against me turn into compassion. Let us get down to specifics.

I am convinced, Your Honors, that these citizens either believe I allowed the soldiers to sack the county or that I wanted to steal the payroll myself and needed to compensate the soldiers somehow. If I did not steal your money, then it must follow that I did not have the country sacked. One act is caused by and depends upon the other. By proving to you that I did not steal, you must admit and then agree that I did not have anything sacked. Did you not say so yourselves? Why should I question you since your seriousness and prudence is not in question? Did not the prosecutor himself state that according to the soldiers I gave them my permission as way of payment? He made this charge because men do evil only for their own benefit or pleasure. As for me, if I paid the soldiers so they would not steal, what advantage would there be in making them steal, what contentment, what satisfaction of the soul? In fact, to the contrary it has brought all the harassment, arguments, rumors, charges, and trouble you see now. Usually when others steal they try to pass the blame on to someone else. Why would I seek blame for a theft committed by others? When others do evil deeds, they do everything possible to appear good. Since I am innocent, why would I do everything to appear guilty? So, we must all agree that if I did not steal the payroll, then I did not have the county sacked. So, let us determine if I did steal the payrolls.

Your Honors, citizens, and please let me now address the citizenry because what I seek, what I now work for, is the recovery of my good name, which I value more than anything else. What I sought from the judges was an acquittal, and I think that this I have already obtained. Because whenever someone is indicted, the first thing presented, before any proof or witnesses are heard, is a finding to determine whether the charges are credible or not. If they are, then that opens the door for more arguments to be supported by evidence. If on the other hand the opening arguments are weak, then the witnesses must give solid testimony for the supporting evidence to appear conclusive. In all cases, some doubt is natural no matter how well presented or reasonable the evidence. In criminal cases the casework requires great effort, especially where there are witnesses who can easily be biased or corrupted. If a well-argued case must rely on solid witnesses, then what should we make of the case before us where nothing has been proven at all? Of all the lines of argument one of the most reliable is the former life and habits of the accused, for it is very unlikely and hard to believe that someone will suddenly abandon their past behavior.

Your Honors, I understand this line of reasoning may not be easy to follow. It is natural for men to take a certain pleasure when they hear about the wrongdoings of others, just as it offends the ears to hear someone praise themselves. Since the prosecutor has decided to cast me as a thief, I am forced to say everything that demonstrates that I am not a thief. So, if any of this troubles you, do not blame me since I speak out of necessity. Instead you should blame the one who maliciously put me into such a position. Also, men are not praised just for having a trait whose absence would be a vice. Being honest is not more praiseworthy because dishonesty is a vice, for such behavior is considered to be reproachable. Would it be praiseworthy if I said that I was bright, prudent, and eloquent? For a person who does not have these qualities should not be blamed because these gifts of nature are not a part of their constitution.

Your Honors, I do not wish to recount what my life was like before I became governor of Modena. The prosecutor has already admitted that I was not undeserving to be elected by the eighty as ambassador to Spain at such an early age. I also hope that some of you may recall, even if my chosen profession leaves me subject to slander, that in terms of modesty and goodwill, I was never considered inferior to my father, whose habits and honesty have been targeted by the prosecutor several times. In fact, I thank him for making the reference. The mention of my father's merits can only help me, and were he alive he would certainly not regret having me as a son. However, I will not insist on this point because it could be retorted that I really did not have that many opportunities for wrongdoing because I was being observed by the entire citizenry and thus had to be careful. To act improperly would have been foolish and irrational. So, let me speak of the places I went so that I may answer the charges against me, although it must be said that in my profession Florence itself has not lacked disreputable practitioners.

When I was thirty-three I became the governor of the city of Modena. I had a level of authority that was greater than as related by the prosecutor. In my administration, there was never any oversight of accounts, or any appeal to my sentences. I found a city replete with factions, bad blood, completely shattered in every way. The power of my position and the condition of the city would have allowed me infinite opportunities to steal, especially since, as he has already stated, one does not live in these cities as one does here. There is no republic; no oversight of decisions taken. Nobody cares about anything but their own personal profit, for which they are ready and used to buy and sell anything. To the Modena position shortly thereafter was added the governorship of Reggio and then of Parma. I then served as commissar general with full powers in the campaign, after which I obtained the presidency of the entire Romagna region. Everyone understood that everything was remanded to my authority because for all practical purposes I had no superior.

You must believe that if it were in my nature to steal, I would have done so in these rich, faction-ridden cities that had been without courts for years. There was a ready acceptance of criminal activity, and infinite confiscations of property. I alone had the opportunity to convict, to exile, to pardon, to do anything I pleased. There was nothing to stop me; no penalty, no law. It would have been so easy that, God help me, I would have laughed at the tax collectors who are now my greatest worry. Many times, I was offered one, three, four, even five thousand ducats to save the life of someone who deserved death. But I was so driven to remain impartial, to keep my hands clean, that my superiors were competing to entrust me with one governorship after another without my even asking. Those who govern are subject to much slander, sometimes true but mostly false. Yet, with so much time and freedom to misbehave, nobody has ever dared to say that I took so much as a cent that was not mine.

Here are the dossiers from three pontiffs, including one from Hadrian,[6] which does me more honor than any of the others. There are also letters from the three communities of Parma, Reggio, and Modena. They wrote often quite effectively to petition Hadrian to appoint me as governor, claiming that the well-being of their cities depended on having me as their governor. Here are the delegations and the elections of ambassadors sent to make the same request. This was not some favor begged from the nobles, who were quite hostile to me because I did not allow them to oppress the people as had been their habit. These cities were living in times of utmost importance to their future and understood that their health or ruin depended entirely on the abilities of their governor. I served them for such an extended period that they came to know me

---

6. Hadrian VI, pope from January 9, 1522, to September 14, 1523.

well. Nobody believed that I would find favor with a new pontiff who had never even seen or heard of me. He should have cast me aside to appoint new representatives as is the common practice. Furthermore, I was aligned with his political foe, the Medici cardinal,[7] who was then in such disfavor that he did not dare stay in Rome.

After hearing the testimony of so many cities and the renowned and universal acclaim resounding in his ears, not only did he confirm me as governor of Parma, but he also restored me to Modena and Reggio, from whence the college and the insolent Mr. Alberto and Count Guido Rangoni had removed me.[8] I was not reappointed just because I was a former minister or a friend of tyranny, but in recognition of my honesty, the merit gained by governing those cities well. Here are all the documents, the honorable and magnificent words that I will not repeat out of modesty. These are my witnesses, not plunderers, or some anonymous and pathetic soldiers, blasphemers, and assassins. Your Honors, can you imagine the happiness when the briefs confirming my reappointment arrived in those three cities, the universal celebration, sounding of bells, fireworks and artillery? Everybody thought they had been reborn.

Here are witnesses, many your own citizens and merchants who passed through Lombardy and saw and heard these things. Listen to what they have to say and what others who have been in Romagna and still do business with the Romagnoli have to say. When you listen to what they say here today, you should also think of the testimony about my honesty and reputation in government service, and the great justices I performed. When these things came to my ears, even if I have by now heard them quite often, God as my witness, the knowledge that I earned a good reputation gives me more satisfaction than all the honors and benefits I gained while abroad. Yet, woe is me, what pain I suffer now that I am thought to be a public thief, murderer, plunderer, and the ruin of my country. Oh, vain hopes! Oh, uncertainty! Oh, plans that vanish like a mist! How many times did I think to myself I will return to Florence when these governorships are over, for I knew they would end one day? I may return with the means commensurate to my station, but I will be richer in reputation than in material wealth. The prestige of my goodwill

---

7. Giulio de' Medici, the future Pope Clement VII who succeeded Hadrian VI as pope November 18, 1523.

8. Alberto III Pio da Carpi and Guido Rangoni, Count of Spilimberto, were captains in the papal mercenary troops.

and honesty will never be extinguished. I will live happily with a clear conscience and a good reputation among men. This alone will make me happier than any other citizen in Florence.

Oh, how deceived I was! When my boat came in and the port was in sight, I thought I would finally be able to enjoy the fruit of so much hardship, danger, years of struggle and difficulties. God knows if I ever had a single day's rest. I envisioned a day when I could rest and take some consolation. Yet, everything was in vain, my hands were full of nothing but smoke. If I had lost all my belongings, my children, my homeland, I would not be suffering half the anguish. It seems too strange, unjust, and dishonest that when I was about to return home I should lose the good name for which I refused enough gold to outweigh the giant.[9] God as my witness, I am speaking the truth, for he knows the hearts of men, and from him nothing is hidden. Without this conviction, I believe I would regret all the good that I have done and all the evil that I could have done but did not. Yet, I still want to have faith in him. He must have had some purpose to allow all of this, perhaps so I would not be too proud and finally realize that everything good derives from him, not me. I am content[10] his will will be done. I beg with all my heart that the truth gets its due so that I may finally reacquire my good reputation. Let us continue with our discussion.

What about the good qualities that I brought to these governments, the honesty and good conduct I exhibited? If I behaved well in foreign cities, where I knew that I would not live for very long, and where having a good reputation did not matter, then what should be believed in my management of your affairs? Is it credible that I would seek a bad reputation in the place where I had to live, rather than somewhere where I had a thousand assurances of never being prosecuted for anything? To have a solid reputation is very important to me, and conversely to be held in poor regard could do me great damage. Would I have taken more account of those whom I would never see again, who could not harm or help me, instead of the people whose eyes I would meet every day, on whom I truly depended for everything, good or bad?

When I went to Lombardy I was young and poor. It was the first chance I had ever had to steal, but neither my age nor economic situation

---

9. The giant is the statue of David by Michelangelo in front of the Palazzo della Signoria in Florence.

10. The margin contains the note "vide an sit locus perorationis" (look at the end of the speech).

were enough to corrupt me. Now I am over forty and used to resisting temptation. I have enough means, although not as ample as some may think, just enough for a modest life in this city. So why should I have started to steal now when I could have done it before with far less risk, especially since I was inexperienced in these matters and I did not have a reputation for being incorruptible? Now I have acquired a good reputation, and I do not know what others may think, but to me it is worth more than any treasure. So, wouldn't I have made a better investment by trying to conserve it? Why would I have abstained in places where the governors are often so rapacious that illicit actions provoke little complaint? Why would I have stolen in a situation where even an insignificant theft, let alone a larger one, causes uproar? Why would I have been so careful not to steal from private citizens of subject cities, who had no recourse against me and whose protests would not be believed even if they made the effort? Why would I then pillage a republic as powerful as this one, which can examine everything and has the means to punish me?

Thievery in government at the expense of the oppressed gives satisfaction only for those who favor injustice. Why would I have refrained from stealing from a few to harm and steal from so many? If I had stolen, my reputation would have suffered, although nothing could ever have been proven because what is done in secret has no witnesses and leaves no trace. Would I have avoided that to commit a crime that would be obvious in a thousand ways and impossible to hide? If all of this is spoken about and believed now, even if it was never done, imagine what would have happened if something had been done. Finally, if I had wanted to steal, would I have wasted eleven years of chances?[11] Was it worthwhile to wait so long for an uncertain opportunity, subject to a thousand difficulties where I had to rely on the complicity of others to steal? In fact, even the prosecutor admits that in this case I needed help from Alessandro del Caccia.

Your Honors, the matter before us is so clear that is makes all other theories and reasoning fall apart. Consider your reaction if this case was presented here as an anonymous matter from some far-off province. If you were asked to give an opinion, you would conclude that it was not only improbable but impossible that someone so young and poor, who had been left unaccountable and with complete freedom in foreign lands, would abstain for so many years from stealing in a situation where he

---

11. Guicciardini was in the service of the church from 1516 to 1534.

could deny what he could not cover up, especially if the wrongdoing would displease nobody. Then at a later age, when he was better off, this same person would begin to steal from his own country, a place that had the capability to punish him and mark him with infamy without any hope of escape. If you find this unbelievable, then you must make a similar finding in my case. Of course, you may have been impressed more by the general uproar than the truth, and that may influence your decision. So, let me implore you once again to keep an open mind and refrain from believing anything that is not proven and demonstrated to your complete satisfaction. Why should I have been honest for so many years, abstaining from petty crimes, just to succumb to weakness? This is not according to the nature of things, nor can it be. As the proverb states, nobody turns bad suddenly. Those steps are taken one at a time. First one starts, then there is a pause, and later comes confirmation. If that is the way the world is for others, then you can be sure it is that way for me. Imagine me a thief as much as you like, as much as stated by the prosecutor. If that is the case, then I have a thief's nature and I would not behave differently from other thieves. Believe what is believable, but not what is contrary to common sense, custom, and the order and nature of things.

I ask you to consider a hypothesis that may raise more certainty than doubts. If I stole all that money, then either it is in my possession or I spent it. Here are the accounts of all my possessions from my books, which are not kept in the merchant's style but in a manner so that the truth is clear. Observe how these books have been kept by my brother Girolamo. Note how I was doing before the war, after the war, and now. Here is a note for the money paid in Venice that caused such uproar. Here are the letters and accounts Girolamo sent me from Venice. Judges, you know that all these documents were produced on the day of my indictment. The time at my disposition does not allow the slightest suspicion that they were composed as a response to my present predicament or were altered in the order in which they were kept. I am not the proprietor of some junkyard who keeps two sets of books as a matter of practice. Nor am I a fortuneteller who might be able to imagine what I would need for today's case two, three, even four years beforehand. So, what happened to the money? Remember how the proverb warns that lies have short legs, especially when faced with the power of truth and conscience. The prosecutor did not even expect me to produce my books, and could not have forced me to do so. It would be as if I brought my own set of weapons here to be used against me. There is a significant difference between not appearing or fleeing trial and subjecting oneself to prosecution, especially when not forced to do so. Perhaps no one in memory has done it before. If I were still in Spain, I would have come as soon as possible, with the mails. How could anyone be persuaded that I would give up my rights? If I am not fooling myself, Your Honors, I believe that I have been forthcoming beyond any expectation, but I will try not to be too insistent and offer much more than necessary.

From the beginning of this war until the fall of Rome[12] your troops and the pope's troops were paid every thirty days. Sometimes, because the money was not in order owing to a delay on the part of the treasurer, they had to wait an extra two or three days, but everything was eventually made good in terms of pay. The soldiers did not serve an hour without pay and had definitely been paid by the time they arrived in Tuscany. Who says so? Everyone, starting with the troops themselves. Here are the letters from different periods from Count Guido and Count Caiazzo, requesting provision for their captains, because soldiers were paid first. Here are the statements of captains and other witnesses declaring that in no other war in Italy were payments ever made so regularly. Here are letters from the pope's nuncio in Venice forwarding a request that the Venetians not make payments every thirty days even if their soldiers were becoming restless. If we had been able to satisfy them as well, then we would have done so without awaiting their requests. However, the infantry was under the command of leaders of the stature of captains such as Count Caiazzo, Count Guido Rangoni, and Signor Giovanni.[13] Therefore I could not manage everything as I pleased, and as will be explained later, this did cause some confusion. Is this enough proof? I believe that by now it is too much, and it is quite clear that I never stole anything. Let us examine one last piece of evidence that is so incontestable that it alone should suffice.

The money did not pass through me but through the hands of Alessandro del Caccia, the pope's deputy treasurer. Ask him to provide a reckoning of accounts, not me. There are no entries in my hand for provisions or for anything, not a single cent. So why am I being investigated

---

12. May 6, 1527.

13. This and following references to a Giovanni are for the soldier Giovanni de' Medici (1498–1526), known as Giovanni dalle Bende Nere because he required his troops to change their white insignia to black after the death of Leo X in 1521. Count Guido is Guido Rangoni, and Count Caiazzo is Roberto da Sanseverino.

for something that was done by others? I could have been called as a witness, but to claim that I was directly implicated as the main perpetrator is strange. I have never heard of anything so unreasonable. If you are suspicious or think that your money was stolen, ask Alessandro del Caccia, investigate him. If there was no theft and you absolve him, then you also absolve me. If there was a theft, I could not have stolen without him, but he certainly could have stolen without me. What kind of justice completely ignores someone who had to be involved and prosecutes someone who only might have been involved? A theft could have been committed without me, but not without Alessandro. So why am I the one being questioned instead of Alessandro? Is this the way you show the love and the respect you say you have for me, Iacopo?[14] Yet, let us leave our private affairs aside. Is it just republican zeal to require someone to give an account who might have been involved and ignore someone else without whom a crime could not have been committed? You are concentrating your efforts on someone who was not necessary for the commission of the crime and ignoring somebody else who had to be involved.

Do not claim to be driven by love for the republic or the general welfare because no city has ever profited by convicting an innocent citizen. In fact, sometimes it is more useful to turn a blind eye than to punish someone without cause. You can no longer deny that this entire matter has been driven by malice and anger. You thought to oppress me with all your talk, to incite the people against me and intimidate the judges into refusing me a fair trial. You planned to gain power by ruining me, to seem like a defender of the republic, ready to face any enemy. If you believed that I had a chance to be heard by judges who would proceed according to the truth and not rumors, in public, then you would not have undertaken this task. You never thought I would be able to prove my innocence. I am therefore indebted to both your malice and impudence, without which the truth may never have been revealed and a doubt would have always remained in the minds of men. Now because of your conduct I will come out of this affair stronger than ever.

Therefore, Alessandro must give an account, not me. I would like to cooperate with the prosecutor and act in accordance with his wishes. I will be satisfied if the accounts show that the money to be spent on the

---

14. Guicciardini gives the name Iacopo to his accuser and public prosecutor.

soldiers implicates him as well as me. I will also be grateful if he can prove that anything was actually stolen, that there was fraud. However, observe how well these books have been kept and ordered, all the dates coincide. Yesterday, you heard how Alessandro was able to justify everything. He produced the inspection reports, the captains' receipts, and the statements from many noblemen to whom anyone would rather remain a creditor than receive payment. So, what doubts can remain? What controversy? I strongly affirm that there was never any theft. I saw everything and know that if the payments were not made as noted by Alessandro, then I would have heard the soldiers grumble. They would have complained to me and demanded I make provisions. However, I never heard anything of the sort, and I made most of the payments myself. So, I am perfectly capable of making assurances for him without fear of retribution.

Let God be praised, for Your Honors, at this point I am happier than I have ever been before. Now it is evident that I am not a thief and the public know that I did not steal, and I have recovered my good name of old. My affairs are in better order than ever before. I did not steal, nor did I have the country sacked, because as we have seen one event could not have occurred without the other. However, about the source of so much damage and such disobedience, someone could still ask me, "if it was not your wrongdoing, then it must have been negligence or ineptitude?" I could answer by pointing out that I was indicted on charges of theft and malice, not incompetence. These judges are not empowered to rule or convict for charges other than those in the indictment. My goal is higher than just avoiding punishment. I am interested not only in a complete acquittal. I want to clear my name not only in terms of what has been thought and said, but even what could be thought or said. I am grateful for the opportunity to speak about this here and now, and I ask for your complete attention. Because I have clearly proven that I did not commit any sins, I will now further convince you that there is no cause to blame me at all. Nobody who suffered was as touched by their losses as I was. Their troubles have also been my troubles, for in this affair not only have I been targeted with enmity, but my very life was in danger.

Judges and good citizens do not believe that this was the only place to suffer, and the soldiers began to misbehave only at the end of the war. Every place we went suffered the same damages. This did not begin the first, second, or even the third month of the war, but on the first day, even the first hour. It was due to not only these soldiers but everyone, the

French, the Venetians, and even our own troops. When we arrived at the walls of Milan, the entire city received us as friends because of the poor treatment they had received from the Spaniards. They hoped to be liberated and treated well by the Holy League army. However, once they realized that things were going from bad to worse, they became openly hostile toward us. The same thing happened at Parma, Piacenza, and Bologna. By the time we reached Romagna, news of our reputation had spread, and we found the gates closed and those who did not do so regretted it later. You are well aware of what happened next. This process repeated itself in the territory of Rome, where the entire Orsini clan, which had eagerly awaited us, had lost faith. The same happened everywhere they went and even where they are now. Ask any town and you will hear how everyone suffered the same fate. This caused irreparable damage to our plans because it compromised the availability of supplies, guides, spies, and many other advantages that can be gained in friendly territory.

The root of this disorder and insolence is the character of soldiers, who are always inclined to thievery and evil. Such negative behavior is an ancient affliction and did not begin in our day. Remember the proverb states a soldier is paid to do bad and does worse. Soldiers have always been like that. Ask our elders if anyone remembers the war of 1478 and '79[15] and they will tell you how Valdesta and other places with garrisons were treated. These evil ways have worsened in our day, as far as can be understood, because of the poor example set by Spanish armies, who as you know are extremely violent and duplicitous. At least they have some justification or excuse since they are rarely paid and must live by extortion. They are so accustomed to dishonesty that they would rather be unrestrained without payment than be restrained because of payment. Their example has influenced others, for it is part of the nature of men to be inclined toward increasing levels of evil. Thus, even when they are paid they continue to behave in this manner. The conclusion to be drawn is that today's armies treat allies as badly as possible. The captains who have authority to control them have no incentive to do so. Nature also inclines them more toward acts of evil than goodness since they profit from the wrongdoings of others. Soldiers, who are allowed to do whatever they please, remain content and allow the captains to gain an ever-greater following. Here there are no exceptions; I was with Signor Prospero, the

---

15. Between Pope Sixtus IV and the king of Naples.

Marquis of Pescara, and the one from Mantua, and all the others in this latest war. All of them behaved identically.[16]

Such a situation is likely to exist in the army of a league like ours. Even if someone wants to provide for his own troops, he cannot provide for the others. And if one part acts badly, it is impossible to keep the others from doing worse. They incite each other and excuse their actions once an example for behavior is set. In an army with such diverse composition, the captains in the field never agree about whose troops should be restrained. This certainly causes never-ending troubles. For example, the French soldiers were poorly paid and had a leader incapable of commanding an army.[17] His troops did not obey him at all. They stole excessively, burned houses, and did immense harm. When the other soldiers saw this, they acted likewise. To be frank, the Venetians and our troops also caused trouble before they even came into the field, but not in comparison to what they did later. These were the overall causes of so much iniquity, although there was one other key factor.

The Black Bands caused havoc because they were accustomed to the license afforded to them by Signor Giovanni. When he died in the Mantua region,[18] their misdeeds increased because they remained leaderless for months, accountable only to themselves. After the German *Landsknechts*[19] crossed the Po, we were abandoned, without supplies, and forced to send the Black Bands into Piacenza, where they lodged at their own discretion. Since there was nothing to restrain them, they began to act even worse. Count Guido Rangoni went there later and offered them his services. I was at Parma, unable to depart and look after them. Because of the danger we faced, we were unable to do anything to stop them. The German *Landsknechts* were between Parma and Piacenza, and the Spaniards were preparing to leave Milan at any moment. We had already made the decision to head toward Florence. When we tried to assign the Black Bands with a leader, they refused and formed a sort of union among themselves. Since they were needed, we had to be patient

---

16. These are all Italian *condottieri*, or military men. Prospero is Propero Colonna (1452–1523). The Marquis of Pescara is Francesco Ferdinando d'Avalos (1489–1526). The "one from Mantua" is Federico Gonzaga.

17. Odet de Foix, Lord of Lautrec.

18. Giovanni dalle Bande Nere died in an ambush November 30, 1526.

19. *Landsknechts* were German mercenaries in the employ of the Spanish imperial army.

with them. There is no more headstrong or less reasonable creature than a soldier who knows his day has come.

Later when the German *Landsknechts* passed through Bologna and Romagna, we were short of men because we had to guard the entire territory after the Duke of Urbino[20] decided not to block their passage. Thus, the Black Bands were always far from where I was stationed, and it was impossible for me to remedy the situation. I was considering these events when the pope made his first agreement with the viceroy. Then later, in Florence, he tried to increase their pay. I tried to make sure there was no trouble with the money, and as always, I objected in my letters that such actions would cause more damage to our friends than to our enemies. Here are the letters that attest to these facts.

I knew that the Black Bands were insolent, and I observed the vile and reprehensible disposition of Count Caiazzo, a man who acted without reason, shame, or religion. I knew how permissive Count Guido was with his own troops. Our country was poor and short of supplies, and this brought out the worst in them. When the enemy headed toward Tuscany, I feared I would have to push these disorganized men into action. And I could not go with them because I did not dare to leave the Marquis of Saluzzo because so many important decisions were being made every day. Then new difficulties arose, independent of whether Lautrec advanced or not, that prevented them from helping us. As you must know by now, our well-being depended on his arrival. The league army was completely dependent upon him and everything else became secondary. The same situation arose when we were in Florence. I could not organize anything because I could not leave the Duke of Urbino, and the result was that the Black Bands remained leaderless. I had not even seen them after the death of Signor Giovanni except when they filed one time through a square in Bologna. Then Count Caiazzo was such a terrible and rapacious individual that his soldiers, so conditioned by his permissiveness, performed atrocities of every description that will not be soon forgotten. Because of these misfortunes, I could not go and take care of everything. Otherwise I may have been able to take care of some things, but this is not to say that I could have fixed everything,

---

20. Francesco Maria della Rovere, the leader of the Venetian troops. In his *History of Italy* Guicciardini assigns della Rovere with some blame for the defeat of the papal league army.

with such large contingents under the control of leaders whose abilities did not match their rank.

Count Caiazzo had two thousand infantrymen, and Count Guido another three thousand. These troops recognized them as their masters, not me. Since I could not control these soldiers, I had to approach their captains respectfully because we were in the thick of it. So, I tried everything possible. In Bologna, I spoke with the captains of the Black Bands, cajoling and begging them to behave themselves in Tuscany. To this end, I sent them the bishop of Casale as commissar, one of the most trusted and well-qualified servants of the pope. How many times did I entreat and beg Count Caiazzo in person and by letter! Here are his responses promising to behave, which proves that I did not allow the pillaging. I tried the same approach with Count Guido, but it was all in vain. Nevertheless, I did not fly into a fury since the Medici were already facing so many troubles. When I did finally had words with Count Caiazzo, the only result was to further compromise my safety. The entire army in Rome knows that when he realized the pope was doomed, he stopped me on the road one morning to kill me. The memory of that recent danger still horrifies me. But God, the friend of the innocent, helped me then just as he has before.

To conclude, I made every preparation and provision possible to avoid this chaos. Nobody else tried to keep abreast of the situation, endure the hardships and pains, and find some sort of solution to the problems at hand. I would have been perfectly willing to lead the troops myself, as often happened, especially since I was keenly aware of what they were capable of doing. We could not rely on the discretion of an enemy that surely would have done the same to Florence that they did to Rome had these troops not blocked their path. By now you must understand how events unfolded. You can be sure that all these evils occurred against my will since I could do nothing to prevent them. If my name had been as feared and respected in this affair as it was in Romagna and Lombardy, I may have been able to do more. After all, those suffering here were my friends and relatives, and I valued the respect I had earned among the citizens of Romagna and Lombardy. Why would I have sought to gain hatred from everyone to gain nothing for myself?

Your Honors, you must realize that I faced a thousand complaints and rumors every day. I knew how brutally my name was being bandied about. The thought of it is like a knife wound to the heart passing through my very soul. Out of love for others, duty, and honor, I would have spilled my own blood if that would have served any purpose. But I was reduced to a point where death would have been welcome. Yet one cannot do the impossible. So, I ask those who suffered and are angry with me out of passion or error to consider the evidence in this case and allow themselves to be governed by reason. Do not charge me with a crime that was beyond my power. Nor should they ever think that I was malicious enough to allow this injustice and madness without any personal gain, shaming myself and acquiring so many enemies. Nor am I so inept that I would not have prevented it if I could have done so. Whatever I lacked in ability would have been compensated by displeasure, disdain, and the incentive of the preservation of my honor.

I must now speak about the other part of the accusation, which, as he said, concerns my ambition. It seems that since he cannot disgrace me with actual sins and charges, he is trying to load me with suspicions and persuade you that I pose a threat to your liberty. Let me respond to the charges he thought strongest and leave other matters he mentioned aside because they are of such limited relevance that speaking of them could only annoy you. How should I respond to the charges he made about my childhood and about Alcibiades? His statements are totally false and were presented without any evidence, witnesses, or rationale. I am surprised that in a case of such importance, before such a multitude and jury, he could speak of infantile matters as if he were in the company of children. In all modesty, as he admitted, my character and the level of my studies as a youngster were of high quality. It is true that in my youth I behaved in a manner that seemed out of place for one of tender years. Because even then, I was not corrupt or irresponsible, nor did I waste my time. For these traits, I must thank my father, who was a fine and most diligent man. Anyway, if they had found my character repugnant, they should have just left it at that. But let us leave aside these trifles along with the discussion of the time before I went to Spain. The only thing he could come up with was that I married Alamanno Salviati's daughter against my father's wishes to embroil myself in the city's political discords. What of it? Should I have refrained from involving myself in such affairs just to avoid displeasing my father?

Observe, judges, how passionate and malicious men can be when they desire to slander. How it can blind them and blocks their common sense and intelligence. If there is one thing sons do in complete agreement with their father's wishes, it is choosing a wife, nor can they do otherwise. Because a son must depend upon a father's aid to sustain, organize, and support a household. Yet he insists that in taking a wife I did not respect my father because of my interest in the very things that would have kept me from acting against his wishes. This is so preposterous that I am ashamed to respond, especially since he spoke without any evidence and will have no chance here to respond. So, let us leave this nonsense aside and turn our attention to his other charges, which were also poorly supported but which would carry more weight if they were true.

In essence, the prosecutor has brought three charges against me. 1) In the mission to Spain, I plotted with the king for the return of the Medici.[21] 2) I took the square and the city hall from the people on St. Mark's Day. 3) I caused this war. The rest of his accusation consisted in an attempt to raise suspicions and persuade you that I should be punished even if I was innocent of the charges above. Since he has no witnesses, no evidence, nothing of substance, he had to rely on the unsupported presumption that I should be condemned because of some current rumors.

Let me respond to each of these charges carefully, Your Honors, and I ask you to listen with the same attention and kindness that you have shown until now. You will come to realize that I am sincere in my opinion about the liberty of the city and what happened to the monies in question. But you should not be surprised by the impudence and audacity of an adversary who has no compunctions about making false statements and relying on frivolous machinations to oppress and obfuscate the truth and innocence, and to trick the judges with vain exclamations and threats.

---

21. Ferdinand of Aragon. The Medici regained control of Florence with the support of Spanish troops in 1512.

SAVONAROLIAN EXCERPTS (SELECTIONS)

January 13, 1495

I am sure about what I have predicted, as sure as I am touching this wood. This illumination is more certain than the sense of touch. It has been fifteen and perhaps twenty years since I started to have these visions, although I began speaking about them ten years ago. I first said something in Brescia where I was preaching. Then God willed for me to come to Florence, the navel of Italy. Believe Florence. Do not think that the scourge has passed. For I see the sword turning around [*Charles was in the realm*].[1] The church must be renewed, as may be demonstrated by ten theses. For I tell you that the church must be renewed soon, the infidels must be converted, and that it is to be done soon.

[*Savonarola notes first the renovation and then the conversion of the infidels.*]

I saw a sword hanging over Italy, and many other things, which specify where that sword was pointed with the tip downward and a great storm and scourging to all, scourging everyone. I want to tell you, Florence, that the hanging sword is the king of France who is showing all Italy how the sword is not yet pointed downward, because God is awaiting repentance.

God calls for renewal.

---

1. Guicciardini's excerpts of Savonarola's sermons contain Guicciardini's own notes, which are separated by brackets in this volume. In this note, Guicciardini refers to the French king Charles VIII. Savonarola saw Charles VIII's 1494 invasion of Italy as divine retribution for Italy's sins. Savonarola's political prestige increased after he met with Charles VIII as part of a Florentine embassy and apparently convinced the French king not to sack the city.

FIG. 6 | Filippo Dolciati, *Execution of Savonarola*, 1498. Museum of San Marco, Florence. Photo: Wikimedia Commons.

Remember what was said. The king of France will come, or he will not come. I said God will go to the other side of the mountains, take him by the bridle, and lead him here despite and against every opinion. Remember, I told you that the greatest fortresses and most imposing walls will be useless. Your great knowledge will be worthless. Everything will be turned upside down, and you will not know what to do with yourselves. Remember the arrow in the cupola, on that very morning from my mouth came the words, *behold the sword of the lord will descend suddenly and quickly upon the earth.*[2] I told you that God had been moved to wrath. The sword has been readied. After many obstacles in preparing an ark, although not before it was readied, the flood came, and from that day everything is to be turned upside down by the French.

Florence, God has chosen you as his own. If you do not want to repent and convert, he will reproach you and choose others, as sure as I am standing up here.

---

2. Savonarola's Latin citations as reproduced by Guicciardini are in italics in this volume. Here Guicciardini's original note in Latin is *Ecce gladius Domini super terram, cito et velociter*. For Savonarola's writings, please see Girolamo Savonarola, *A Guide to Righteous Living and Other Works*, ed. and trans. Konrad Eisenbichler (Toronto: Centre for Reformation and Renaissance Studies, 2003).

Many years ago, I predicted the death of Lorenzo de' Medici, the death of Innocent, the revolution in this government, that there would be a revolution on the day that the king of France would be at Pisa.[3] I did not say this publicly, but to people present at this sermon.

The knife will come *quickly*, and this will be quick, as in the Apocalypse, but it could take hundreds of years. The exact period cannot be stated, because if I said that the tribulations will arrive in ten years, then men would not bother themselves to repent and they would say, I can wait to repent.

Italy is just now at the start of her tribulations.

The eighth of Annunciation on the . . . of April, 1495

I said to you, Oh people of Florence, that you were to make universal peace with the call of the six beans and the Great Council! Above all, that God wanted the city to be governed in this manner from now on.[4] Nobody should resist his will, because he could make the black beans turn white, that is, he could change the hearts of those who contradicted.

I procured the separation of the Lombard congregation, moved by that same light by which I have predicted the future.[5]

Florence pleasing the Lord.

The Virgin said: all the favors promised by God to the Florentines may still be revoked owing to their incredulity. Or, they could be restituted for Florence to become more glorious, more powerful, and richer than ever, extending her wings further than ever before, and more than many may think. She will retake everything that has been lost, and will not lose whatever she will gain, and acquire things that had never been

---

3. Lorenzo de' Medici and Pope Innocent VIII both died in 1492, with Savonarola purportedly denying Lorenzo absolution of sins in his last rites. French king Charles VIII invaded Italy and subsequently entered Pisa in 1494. Piero de' Medici (1472–1503) was the head of the Medici clan and de facto ruler of Florence following the death of his father, Lorenzo de' Medici. Piero fled to exile in November 1494, and a Florentine republican government was reinstituted, over which Savonarola, through his sermons, had considerable influence.

4. The fava bean voting method in Florence, in which voters dropped white or black beans into vats.

5. The controversy between Savonarola and the Lombard congregation of the Dominican Order was one of the opening disputes between Savonarola and religious authorities. Savonarola's biographer Roberto Ridolfi writes that Pope Alexander VI was unwittingly outmaneuvered into conceding Savonarola authority in the Lombard congregation, beginning a power struggle between the Vatican and Savonarola that ended in Savonarola's excommunication.

hers, and woe unto the subjects who rebel against her. It has already been four years under this illumination that I predicted to the Pisans that during these tribulations they would seek their freedom, which would be their downfall. The renewal of the church cannot come without great tribulation, especially in Italy, and even in Florence. Although of all cities to be scourged, Florence will suffer the least. For I beheld a ball that showed Italy completely upside down, with many cities completely upside down replete with great tribulation, which I will not name because it is not allowed for me to do so, and others that did not appear to be under tribulation, but were suffering on the inside. I beheld Florence under tribulation, although not as much as the others. I beheld another ball with the city of Florence blooming with lilies spreading out from the battlements beyond the walls far off in every direction, with angels all around, above the walls observing her. I said, Holy Mother, it seems favorable for the small lilies to join with the large ones, which in this time have begun to spread out, and the neighbors of Florence who rejoiced at her trouble will have more tribulations than Florence. This promise is absolute in every manner, but they will have fewer or greater tribulations according to whether they do more, or less good. When I asked *will these things occur?* The answer was *suddenly and quickly*. But tell them that just as you started to preach about the scourges upon Italy in Florence, which was five years ago, now, even though elsewhere it was ten, when you said *suddenly and quickly,* you added I cannot say the year, whether it will be in two years, four, or eight, never more than ten. Nevertheless, the scourge has come already and sooner than would have been believed. Therefore, speak thus, let me say *suddenly and quickly*, without being able to tell the month, whether April, July, September, a year, or two, or six, nor any other predetermined time, but *suddenly and quickly*, which will be sooner than many will believe.

After this sermon, which I preached and confirmed many times, whereby the king of France has been elected by God as the minister of his justice, and will be victorious and will prosper, even if the entire world is against him. In truth, as I told him in detail, that role may be retained only through humility. Yet if he does not redress any wrongs perpetuated by his subjects, he will suffer great tribulation, especially if he does not treat Florence well. God will make his people rebel, and will give him many difficulties, because God wills that he should be a friend and champion of the city of Florence, chosen by God to begin the reformation of Italy and of the church. If he does not want to be a friend to the Florentines out of love, God will not force him to be one by force. However, if he humbles himself and is recognizant, he will not be overwhelmed by tribulations. To the contrary, after he is humbled and purged, he will rise victorious, and when it seems that he is about to be eliminated, then he will resurge in victory. Through observance of what God has commanded him to say, he will acquire a great kingdom. If he does otherwise and does not follow the path that pleases God, then he could be rejected by God, just as occurred with Saul. In his stead, another shall be chosen as minister, just as David was chosen in Saul's place. The favors and promises made to him are conditional. Keeping with what we have said, he will doubtless be victorious and acquire a great kingdom. Otherwise he will run into great danger, and if the speeches of the just cannot help him, he will be rejected. Any citizen inside or outside who tries to place himself at the head of Florence or to remove the present government will be gravely punished by God, as will his house and followers, who will all end miserably. If the Florentines continue to follow the good life, the greater part of their tribulations will diminish, and a state of grace will soon arrive in which they may participate with their children, even more so for the children. If one were to mark all the believers and nonbelievers down in a book, you would see that seven-eighths of the tribulations will more surely descend on those who do not believe.

Tuesday after the first

[*Savonarola makes a long denunciation of the leaders of the church and then continues.*] I cannot yet, but if one day I had a little key for an opening, then I would do better and sing to the entire world. However, since the matter is becoming more constricted and must explode, then I will say and do what will amaze the entire world.

Kill me if you want. It does not matter to me. For *to die for Christ is to live*. Today let us have the vigil, tomorrow the feast, as would occur if I were dead.

These children will be the just citizens who will enjoy the good grace bestowed on Florence, and complete everything. Since their fathers do not want to do as they have been told, they will be rejected, and these children will be chosen.

Italy, Italy. Rome, Rome. The Lord will come, and will expel the wicked from his church. There will be such destruction, such murder, that you will want to abandon all benefits and say, "Oh, if only I were not living during these times."

Italy, Italy. Rome, Rome. Men will come without discretion, from a place that you do not even know.

Tuesday *post tertiam* [after the third]

Oh Italy, oh Rome! I will put you into the hands of people who will dissipate you to your foundations. I will bring such pestilence that few people will remain. I will lead beastly men into Italy and to Rome, cruel men as hungry as lions and bears. Many people will die to the amazement of all. Believe this friar. There will be no one left to bury the dead. Men will go into the street crying, "Bring out your dead!" But the people will be so reduced and so few will remain that grass will grow on the city streets.

The words of Amos will be fulfilled in this time, as I will relate to you. Today, I want you to know that what I related before in simple words, what I had told you by the words of Amos, is coming true in these times, just as I explain.

If Rome and Italy repent, these evils will not come to pass. But, I do not believe this will happen.

If I were dead or expelled, this illumination will not extinguish, because it has taken hold in many places and in all religions. You will see how it raises many people up against themselves and against their own orders, raising up in all of Italy and Rome. This fire has already been lit among bishops, priests, and cardinals. If you extinguish one, others will come more forcefully. I am here to defend this truth, which will either be done reasonably or by other means, natural or supernatural, which I do not want to tell you about now.

Saturday after the fourth

If the excommunication arrives, I will respond in a manner for you to marvel. Faces will turn pale all around, and it will seem quite good to you. We will send out one of those voices of Lazarus and you will see the excitement in the entire body. Remember the lists I told you about a year ago. They are lying in reserve. The Lord will give permission and will order them, and they will be eluded. Let the one who speaks ill of me in Rome, *idest*, or of our teacher Mariano[6] be forewarned that God has allotted a penalty whereby if does not correct himself, he will receive extreme punishment.

February 11, 1497 [1498] on Exodus

Have I not told you many times that when this affair seems extinguished, it will resurge more gloriously than ever before? See how everyone was saying, "He is done for, this movement is over." Yet, we are still here, wanting to fight and to win in any way. I say to you that there have never been times more glorious than these, nor times happier than these. For we want to perform acts that are glorious and great, and God will be the one to provide consolation to the just.

God permitted the excommunication to come to lend truth to what has been predicted and combatted with the dual power of knowledge and malice together, temporal and spiritual, to separate the good from the wicked, for it was not good for them to be together.

If a prince is not guided as an instrument of God, then he is at the same level as any of you, and may be tossed like an old tool. It can be declared that he is not being led by God. For he performs acts that are contrary to the common good and prosperity.

All theology, all laws, all the ceremonies of the church are ordained by charity. Therefore, he who rules against charity is anathema. Woe be unto him.

God has told me that the excommunication is invalid.

You will see that those who contradict this work are vicious. Those who believe, live well.

Those of you who have qualms, or have had them, you have acted against God, because if everyone were like you, the city and its good life would be ruined.

He who contradicts this work, contradicts Christ.

February 18

This time, war must be waged with weapons that are unsullied, for everything must be revealed.

---

6. Mariano da Genazzano (1412–1498), prior general of the Augustinian Order, preached against Savonarola.

The first brief I received from the pope[7] related an understanding that my preaching had been very fruitful, and many new things had been said in favor of God. He desired to speak with me and *by the power of holy obedience*, he ordered me to go there. This brief arrived at the end of July. I answered by requesting to be excused since I was ill at that time, as could be confirmed by the doctor. Therefore, I could not go down there without endangering my life. Also, my residence here was necessary for the peace of the city. This was during a period of much dissension among the citizens. He accepted this excuse quite well.

Then toward the end of September, another brief arrived replete with slander containing no fewer than eighteen errors. It was addressed to Santa Croce *regarding Geronimo Savonarola* as if they did not know who I was and filled with other trifles that for honor's sake I will not cite here. The first brief related how many positive things had been reported about me from many sources. The second then stated that much wickedness had been reported from many sources. Then another brief arrived, stating that I had spread doctrines causing discord in all peaceful peoples, and many other falsehoods, and thereby suspended me from preaching, even though the entire world is aware that I have brought peace to this city. I responded that the matters had already been settled, but my explanations were not heard. Therefore, I continued to preach freely. That was the period when I said I was not sent to preach by any man of this world, nor by any lord, but by God. Then another brief arrived calling for all the convents of Tuscany to become one congregation, whereas before in their brief they wanted us to enter the one from Lombardy, from which they had first separated us. Another brief came that *you preached false and perverse doctrine* and had not entered the congregation of Tuscany.

Those who wanted to do away with this preaching intended to damage the welfare of this city. They wanted to introduce tyranny here. They are not acting against me, but against you, hiding behind a friar's tunic. Come now! This battle must be waged with unsullied arms.

All my writings and weapons are in order. We must fight with unsullied arms and will win in any event. Behold, if one point is released, we will still amaze the entire world.

---

7. Rodrigo Borgia, Pope Alexander VI (1431–1503).

You may fear that they will not allow you confession owing to the excommunication. You will not lack confessors. You say that they will not want to bury you. As for me, I care not what happens after I am dead. Put a rope on one foot and throw me into the Arno.[8]

February 25

During Lent, we will expound the book of Exodus and have no doubt that we want to cross the Red Sea, and Pharaoh will not be able to do anything.

Oh, Rome! Oh, priests of Rome! I warn you not to ruin this movement, for she is what is bringing you to ruin, although the walls are not yet destroyed. Oh, wicked! Oh, faint of heart! You will be destroyed by this weight. When you think you have extinguished this thing, it will resurge with more life than ever, and the walls will come down upon you.

The morning of carnival, I will place the sacrament in my hand. Everyone shall pray. For this matter comes because of me. If I am a deceiver, then let Christ bring a fire from the sky down on me and cast me into hell. However, since it comes from God, then let it accelerate quickly. Let the prayers go to the ministers and write to Rome so that they all may do the same. Then, I will sing the verses, "*Stir up, O Lord, thy power, and come!*"

Last of February 1497 [1498] *Lent on Exodus*

Joseph's prophecy took fourteen years to fulfill. Moses took more than forty years. The things of the Lord do not come quickly.

Florence, the cup runneth over. Await. Await a great scourge. For no longer can prayers hold back this tide of destruction. We can pray that at the very least it may turn into pestilence. I do not know if this request will be granted.

In yesterday's procession, the wicked acted in defiance of God, worse than the Turks or pagans. You will therefore receive a great scourge.

Florence, remember at carnival they would have the friars parade in masks. I told you that you had placed your hand on the honor of the Lord. Yet, you await the thrashing, and yes, he who was the cause, did not see another carnival.

---

8. After Savonarola's execution, his ashes were collected and tossed into the Arno River.

Rome! Oh Rome! You will have such tribulation that you will wish you never acted against this movement!

Florence, I see what has been pronounced for you. Yet, it will not be for you, citizens, but for your children. Just as it was for the people of Israel.

Third of Lent

When all their interdictions are complete, and when they remove all the stops, then let them come. They will begin to make martyrs. I do not mean now, but I am preparing you bit by bit, because they will demand martyrs in due time.

Have no doubt, even if they want a tyrant, that the government of Christ will be victorious. Yet, take note, as I have told you on other occasions, that you could have a tyrant for a brief period, who will not reject what I have told up to now. I am not saying that this must be. Yet, if it does come to pass, then he will be the most wicked man in the world, and doubt not, he will not last for long. You say that they want to expel the friar. Have you not understood that it goes far beyond that and means relieving you of your possessions and your family, as was done before? However, if the interdiction comes it will be against you, not against the friar. Therefore, everyone must dedicate their lives to the honor of God and the common good.

Third Sunday of Lent

Yesterday, I thought, "Oh friar, you are in great danger!" I opened the Bible and found what happened to Jeremiah in chapter 20: *and he heard Phassur the son of Emor.*

Phassur may be interpreted as *pastor unidique,* the price of a priest. Pashhur was the son of Emor, which may be interpreted as an ass, for the ass is a libidinous animal, meaning that he was the son of every lascivity.

Pashhur placed Jeremiah in the stocks. Thus, we may say that we have been unjustly placed in the stocks of excommunication.

Jeremiah said, *Pashhur does not call you God, without fear,* meaning that the Lord will act according to his designs, that you will be the fear and terror of the world. One can say, watch for the Lord, for he may do to you as he did to others. Your friends will be cut to pieces by enemies and sheared by barbarians. A considerable number of your friends will die under the knife. Barbarians as cruel as lions will come, some coming here and others coming there. Italy, you will be in the hands of savage people, of strange people, who will do the worst they are able, and for Rome it will be worse than for all the other cities. Your possessions will be given into their hands. Yet, these barbarians will fight amongst themselves. I say to you, Pashhur, that you will go into captivity in Babylon, you and the inhabitants of your house as well as any friends you still have remaining, and you will die an eternal death in hell. I can tell you that places have already been prepared in hell for them, and there you will be in Babylon, in absolute confusion.

I tell you that those who persecute me will fall, by the sword or by pestilence.

After God had made use of Jeremiah according to his will, he then threw him there and he had him stoned. He will do thus also with this hammer, after having used it. He will throw it away.

Oh friar, you have said you will never remain silent, that as long as you have a head on your shoulders you will always speak. If I had told you the opposite of what I have told you, do not believe it, because these are matters of God, which must occur in any event. And if I were to die, you must hold for certain that it will proceed in any event. Now when I spoke about speaking as long as I have a head on my shoulder, I wanted to say that I was never here to repeat myself, oh, yet you have said to preach. This may be understood thus: if God had not already told me not to preach, then God would want me to preach. Therefore, I will preach without reticence.

I have been asked by those in power not to preach, and this is what will occur. God has granted and not granted. Be aware that God is mightily angered. Recall that in the time of Lorenzo de' Medici four of the most important citizens came to me. The four of them are still alive. They beseeched me not to say these things, claiming that they came on their own behalf. I responded that they had been sent and should tell Lorenzo to repent of his sins. That God wanted to punish him and his. To many others who told me that I would be exiled, I responded that I cared not, but be aware that I am a foreigner and he is the first citizen of the city. That he was the one who had to leave, that I was to remain, not him. Also, recall that year when the preaching was stopped, some had a fever, some pestilence, and some came under the knife. Of those who were behind the ban, many wanted to become powerful. You know who they are. From then until now, let me tell you that many people died, and many people went to hell. What will happen now? You will see what is to come. I do not want to say anymore now, for you will see. It is news that I do not want to have to tell. Remember those who came to the sermons last year when the great death toll began. None fell ill. One must note carefully those who procured these excommunications and these things, for then you will see what will happen. You say that you are afraid of the interdiction and of losing your possessions. Tell them that God will send an interdiction, and they could lose their lives and their possessions, and say once more to the wicked that they are the cause of these ills, and because of this they will not receive what they intend, but rather the contrary of what they schemed.

Oh Father! We were waiting for you to do something by now. You had told us to show this thing according to natural reasoning, by reason, and by supernatural signs. You have delayed what the sermon would have accelerated, but we will do by deed what I had to do by sermon.

From the exhortation, April 7th, 1528 [1498]

Last night we received an absolute, yet conditional prophecy. Absolute in that we will have victory in any event, conditional in that it is not clear to me if this experience will occur in any event, or not. God does not want to divulge everything. It is my steadfast opinion and belief that it will be sooner rather than later, because matters have gone too far. Yet, this is a secret of God, which I do not possess.

You know that yesterday I told you that our affairs and the excommunication do not require miracles, because they are clear. However, if we are provoked, then it will be necessary to go, so that faith does not become abject. Lord, you know that we do not go with presumption toward this event, but only after provocation. For we have been called, even though we did not issue the challenge.

Reiteration of the sermon "You Are Clear" on Saint Simon's day, October 28, 1496

I say a great scourge is approaching.

I hold a secret, which because of your sins I cannot pronounce, *for my secret is in me*. I will conclude with a word for you in the end, and let he who will do so, understand, understand, for it suffices that I have the truth.

The wicked are the cause of your ills, which are on the inside and outside, and rooted here. The apple has its disease rooted within. The Lord wants to place a knot inside this apple and pluck out the malady.

Is this clear to you? It is clear to me that God works beyond the thinking in Italy, for many will be deceived. Have you noticed that when you go to the market intending to do one thing, that you end up doing another? Have you ever seen a barber go somewhere to shave someone but end up shaving someone else? I tell you that is how it will be for those who do not understand these times.

You do not understand the things being predicted and are confused because you are thinking about how God usually proceeds, and yet he has not enlightened you because you are wicked.

I say to you, repent! Repent! I warn you that he who clings to the wall will have it fall on top of him.

My son, turn back. For I have become compassionate and now that I have entered this reading and seeing you here, I see you are on a crooked path, and will pray God for you. Yet, I fear that it will be difficult to hold back this flood.

In the psalm, the just state that the tribulations have arrived. You know what I predicted for you. Remember how many times I told you to take care of your business, your affairs. For it will be good when they are done, for the coming scarcity will be great. You may say, oh friar, you should have stated it more clearly and then we would have acted. I respond to you that the matters of God are not presented in any other manner. However, since you are a poor man, do what is right, run back to God, for he will not abandon you to starve to death.

Those of you who are among the just, have no fear, for great tribulations come *moving mountains into the heart of the sea*. The sea means the armies that will be turbulent like the sea, for there will be profound tribulations. God will take the mountains and cast them into the sea. Then for those chosen by God, the boats will approach the mountains, and the mountains shall defend them from the waves of the sea. The mountains shall be the angels and the saints, and the preachers, for against Sennacherib[9] will come the mountains. The angels will cast them asunder because they were defeated in war with the king of Ethiopia, taken by the nose and told, go back, have no fear, those of you among the just, because the mountains are there to help you. However, beware, those of you among the wicked, because God, the saints, the heavens, and all things are disturbed by you.

---

9. King of Assyria from 705 to 681 BC, mentioned in Kings 2:19. Sennacherib's Assyrian army was destroyed as it was about to attack Jerusalem.

Believe me, those of you among the wicked, your schemes will not succeed, because God is the one in charge of these works.

God has provided this government for the just to foster benefits that are spiritual, which the just will attain in any event. Yet there will also be temporal benefits, allotted mainly to maintain spiritual benefits. However, God will perform this bit by bit, as he has done with others. Thus, Florence must have faith in God, for he will deliver you. Remember what I have already told you. When the seed came in a corrupt and confused form, it approached the generation of man, and made man. Florence is among the just. The wicked shall have no part in it, and must be afraid.

There is no remedy for Italy. Some kingdoms are somewhat inclined, and others will be more inclined, but they will go their own way.

Note carefully what I tell you. If you return to God as one should, I have faith in Christ that we will receive great favor, and will not have to fear anyone.

Florence, do not put your faith in man, *accursed man*. The man who does not do what is good and does not help you is truly man, and has struggled enough to be able to recognize if they are doing good or not, and will have even greater tribulation by not doing as he should.

Go, all of you, and pray in the procession for God to deliver us from certain, great danger. Pray once more for these wicked so that God may convert them, because they bring great danger.

Now let us come to the words I want to speak to you. Let you create a true union. If we do not drive out all our enemies, then I want to lose the cowl. I say, if you act, I want to be the first to confront them, crucifix in hand. We will make them flee all the way to Pisa, and even further. For if no human remedies remain, then if you will, there remain the remedies of the divine.

Florence, you have been freed other times by God. Place hope in him this time yet again. The day in question, when the king of France was here, returning from Naples, I spoke once again with his majesty. He was in full retreat and I told him: if you do not do what I told you that God wills, then great tribulations will befall you. However, through prayer and running back to God, you may be delivered in every aspect. Now listen to some other words.

Florence, you have not wanted to make just laws. However, recall what I told you the other day. In any event, laws will be made to harm you. So be it. Here the damage is already prepared as well as its tribulation. You may want to turn me into a prophet. However, those of you among the wicked, note these words. For if you were to succeed and create a tyrant, and I am not saying that you must do so, yet, I say, that in the event you did, then I say to you *by the word of God* that you and he will end badly.

Florence, repent! People, repent! The good, pray for the wicked because they are in great danger! Florence, I see much blood.

Wednesday, after the Fourth

God has arranged his truth in such a way that there will always be someone to defend it.

If someone wants to debate with us reasonably, then we will respond reasonably. However, when force wants to overcome reason, we must then demonstrate the truth in ways greater than human force.

You have plotted to murder me. I do not have this from man. Yet, it is true and certain. Understand and take note. If you want to end your conspiracy, then observe how I speak and listen to my words. God has given me license to write down your sins and what will be seen but not known by human means. Thus, I will write about the plot and your plan to murder me, as well as everything you have done against your country. I have created sealed lists to be distributed to certain good and religious men. I am not sure how many, but I will find out, and these will be revealed. For when you commit wickedness, God demands punishment for you and all your followers. Let me tell you that I have already spoken about this with someone who I believe is here at the sermon. Thus, I have already begun to speak about it and will continue to do so. I have told you other times that the stones will become manifest to you. I am telling you once again, that if you do not desist, if you make no amends, woe unto you. God has decided that the works shall go forward, and when I am dead, seven greater than me will arise in one stroke.

June 12

Florence, I will never retract, even if such a crazy idea came into my head to say that I have told lies, or have deceived you. If I have uttered lies from my throat, then let me be damned.

Italy will be ruined. All the princes of Italy will be ruined. There is no remedy whatsoever, as you will see quite soon.

It will be a cruel, deadly, and turbulent time. Woe unto those who find themselves here, for so many will die that it will be stupefying!

Will his hammer return? I cannot tell you whether he will turn back or not owing to your infidelity. For your incredulity will deprive you of many things. If he does not come, God will send others.

You will come to a place where you will confess that the prayers of the just have delivered Florence.

Recall when there was the appeal of the six beans. I told you, look at those who contradict you, and see what happens to them. Let me repeat it once more. Note that those who oppose the reform for the women, and observe what will happen to them. The results will demonstrate how this is not idle talk.

A sword will come, killing many people. There will be famine and pestilence. So many people will die that it will be astonishing. Men will die in the streets. Corpses will remain uninterred in the streets.

To you, Florence, I say that a time will come soon when those who have harmed you will suffer. Yet, they will still have need of you and seek refuge here. I told you again that you had a good understanding of matters that did not involve you directly, and so be it. So, let these neighbors of yours commit some sins, so that it is right that you receive some of their possessions. I have always told you that you must be among the just for the tribulations to affect you less. If you are not, then God will place you between the mountains and the sea. I pray that he gives you enough of a thrashing for you to learn that if you do not act justly, then you cannot hope for anything. So, do as you will, but if you do not act justly, you will have nothing.

To Italy. I said that if she does not repent, there will be no remedy, that if she does not repent, there will be no remedy at all.

June 19

Florence, I fear that your sins have perpetuated so long through the generations that you will be like those who remained in the desert never to arrive at the Promised Land, from Joshua to Caleb, even though they were among the just. I am not saying that this must be, but I am afraid. Florence, you have but little faith in God. What would you do now if the enemy were at the gate?

Our proposals do not have to be proven by miracle, because they can be proven through reason and good works. However, when men lack in belief, and the wicked believe they can remove all reason from what I have said, keeping the simple-minded in hand, then by placing my faith in Christ, I say that we are prepared to prove things with miracles.

You citizens of the previous state, to whom God bestowed so much mercy, if you are ungrateful at this time, then woe unto you. Understand me well, if you do not go on the correct path, then woe unto you. God has noted you all down in a book, and has written all your sins. If you do not act well, then woe unto you this next time.

If it had not been for this advice, then you would now all be dead, dissipated, and driven away, each and every one of you. Your city would be destroyed if you had not held fast to this advice. Yet, a time could still come (and do not deny this, for this is what I must tell you) that this council could still be destroyed *at present*. Note carefully, how I speak to you. I am not saying that this must occur. I am saying not to deny the promise of favors. Believe, that those led astray are looking to have their houses burned and to be ruined, to have everything destroyed. Do not add meaning to my words by asking, "Oh and how is this going to happen?" Do not seek the ways of the Lord, which I hold close, for in less than fifteen days or a month everything shall be complete. For God will not lack a way, and I am not saying that this must be, but believe me, this is the advice that God has given you.

You presume to hinder ecclesiastical affairs, but you cannot really hinder them. Falling under excommunication means nothing less than being taken from God and given to the devil. However, the judge that falls under excommunication has the devil in him, and for the excommunicated, everything goes from bad to worse.

Believe me, Florence. God will give you a thrashing that you will feel for many days if you do not change.

Kill me when you want, for the smith does not lack a hammer. God can make ten rise out of one.

You may say, "Yet the king of France is going on his way, and does not come." I will respond that if he had not come, there would be no peace in Italy. For I say to you that the time is nigh. Let the king of France go where he desires. For I tell you that the time is pressing, and that Italy will be turned upside down and destroyed. If the king of France does not want to come, then God will not lack barbers. There will be, I say, so much war, pestilence, famine, and death, that only a few men will remain.

It is difficult for you to kick back against the facts.[10] Italy, you cannot fight this spirit. Florence, citizens, you cannot fight this spirit. I am replete with the spirit of the Lord.

Italy, Italy. Florence, Florence. *Thou that killest the prophets, and stonest them which are sent unto thee.*[11] You seek to kill prophets. Italy, Florence. You seek to kill those sent to you by God. You mock the prophets.

Punish the gossips slandering good men who have been wronged, who I know are on the right path. "Of Friar! they must be your friends." I have told you that I have no friends. I have no friendship with them other than to know that they are on the right path and they are your good citizens.

Pray, so that on this Saint John's day, we may have some grace.

July 1st

The sins of the wicked are the reason why God has not allowed everything to be manifest. Yet, for the wicked we have had the answer that there are some who seek to destroy the good God has done. Some want it to be known that they have done good for the city. I do not say all of them, but some of them and their seconds. God considers this to be quite wicked. Second, God considers other ingrates to be even worse. If this state had not been founded, then they would have neither life nor anything else, and yet now they want everything to be destroyed. God says that this ingratitude of theirs is drying the fountain of piety. Make amends, I say. Let he who can understand, understand. For God will not forgive a second time. Let there be nobody who judges on their own. I do not call out anyone, because it is not allowed for me to do so. Perhaps one of these stones will provide a sign, for it displeases God even more that many of the just are wrongly slandered. To slander he who does good, they have tried every avenue, even to the point of using the rope. It is even more displeasing that some are here who help your enemies and do them favors. This is the answer that we had had from God regarding the wicked. Pray, so that tomorrow, on the day of the Virgin, we may have the grace to open for you a bit of that key.

---

10. Savonarola seems to be quoting Acts 26:14, although the sentiment also appears in Aeschylus's *Agamemnon*.
11. The New Testament verse from Mathew 23 begins with "Jerusalem," for which Savonarola substituted "Florence."

I have seen the change once more, but in another manner, and I tell you *by the word of the Lord* that I have seen fire from the end here to there, lit in many places, coming from above and burning them so that the chickens will finally come to roost. For the chickens, I bear good tidings, have no fear, let come what will. God has placed his hands over the city and in one place, in particular, in the city where your favor will be granted. This is the answer obtained for the just. Florence, when you meet your enemies, run back to God and confide in him, and rest assured that nothing will harm you.

August 15th

Six years have passed since I began to shout that the good times were ending. You see now the change from six years to today. You will mark another six years for the changes from today until that time. I am not saying that we must wait another six years like these, but believe me and what I say in turn, that you will see changes in these next six years, like the last.

Florence's suffering did not have to come to this point. Yet, since you did not want to listen, you have brought it upon yourselves. However, you could shorten the tribulations by placing a hand on justice.

Italy, I want to warn you that the minister has not yet been relieved. Italy, you are reasoning without a keeper. I will say no more. I told you the other time that probation was conditional. Today I tell you what I heard, that the prayers of the chosen for the reformation of the church could be powerful enough for him not to proceed, although it would still cause harm.

RESPONSE ON BEHALF OF THE DUKE TO THE COMPLAINTS OF THE EXILES

If under the heading of the Florentine exiles are to be included those who, not owing to any need or just cause, have willfully undertaken to oppose His Excellency the duke,[1] then it is certainly surprising that they would adhere to complaints regarding the form of government and the penalties imposed upon those exiled. For as such, as is well known, some of them encouraged Clement[2] in revered memory to pursue and persevere in the war in Florence. Others were among the most determined to rearrange the government and to punish the exiles. However, perhaps they will understand if someone else explains matters.

If the complaints are from the rebels, then we cannot be sure that it is appropriate to hear them, as they are not recognized as holding citizenship in that country, having been justly and legitimately deprived because of their own demerits. They comprise only a part of the entire number and have not been exiled for any political reason but only joined the others after being banished for theft, murder, and other private crimes. In any event, to satisfy His Imperial Majesty[3] and to ensure justice for the duke and the present government, rebuttal will be offered briefly regarding the calumnies falsely proposed, in greatest accordance with the honor of His Majesty. For they have imprudently affirmed to have performed what they could not and should not have done against his knowledge.

1. Alessandro de' Medici (1510–1537).
2. Giulio di Giuliano de' Medici (1478–1534) was Pope Clement VII (1523–34).
3. Charles V (1500–1558).

FIG. 7 | Agnolo Bronzino, *Portrait of Duke Alessandro*, ca. 1555–65. Galleria degli Uffizi, Florence. Photo: Web Gallery of Art.

They claim mainly that the government introduced in Florence, which was done under agreement, cannot subsist by the will of the city because it was imposed through violent and unusual means, and not by order of His Majesty, and is therefore contrary to the terms of surrender, which held that the city of Florence would retain its liberty. Since the present government is not free, then in recognition of his supreme authority among Christian princes, His Majesty is obliged to heed the terms, to remove the government, and to replace it with one where Florentine liberty is conserved.

To this first point, one may respond that His Majesty had the authority to freely organize the city government, without any prescription or limit on introducing a Medici government. Since there is a difference between a Medici government and a popular government, it was left to the will of His Majesty to choose one or the other as he pleased. Since His Majesty acted with full authority as conferred by the entire city, and particularly by each faction, how can it be that they can recant what they agreed to and approved? Nor can the wording of the terms, with the

FIG. 8 | Juan Pantoja de la Cruz, portrait of Charles V, after Titian, ca. 1605. Charles V, grandson of Ferdinand II of Aragon and Isabel of Castile, ruled as Charles I of Spain (1516), as Holy Roman Emperor over Germany (1520), and king of Italy (1530) following the Sack of Rome and the Siege of Florence. Photo: Wikimedia Commons.

understanding that liberty will always be preserved, allow an interpretation whereby Caesar was prohibited from establishing a Medici government. It would be quite absurd for a side on the verge of victory to make an agreement obligating it not to choose in its favor, but to allow a choice favoring their adversaries who were already defeated and subjugated. However, the true sense of this section is that His Majesty was afforded the capacity to arrange for a Medici government or a free government, or one of his pleasing. Under this commutation, he could not deprive the city of its privileges, preeminent among which is freedom, as it had always been free, by putting it under foreign rule.

Secondarily, one may respond, although the first rebuttal should be more than sufficient, that for a greater understanding it is necessary to know that the city of Florence, in the memory of men, has had two forms of government. One began in the year 1434, in which the nobility, which before had been beaten by the plebeians, regrouped and legitimately established authority over the city. To better maintain themselves, they recognized Cosimo de' Medici, one of themselves, as leader, with an administration undertaking matters under the authority of magistrates and public deliberations.

This form of government continued under the authority of the descendants of Cosimo. The city preserved its freedom as a republic until the year 1494, when they were expelled, not owing to any fault of their own, but for having opposed Charles VIII of France, then in transit to conquer Naples. Under that form of government, the city was more tranquil, powerful, and prosperous than at any other time.

The other form of government was the popular government, which began in the year 1494 after the expulsion of the Medici. This lasted until 1512, while the French were in Italy, and was retained by them for having always adhered to that faction rather than any demonstration of their own abilities. Inasmuch as is the nature of the multitude, it was always replete with discord and civil strife. When the French were expelled, the government was immediately removed by His Majesty, the Catholic king,[4] with the agreement of Pope Julius and Maximilian Caesar,[5] to ensure that the city could participate with the others for the preservation of Italy. Thus, the Medici were restored under the terms like those before '94, and they continued thus until the events in Rome in 1527 afforded the opportunity for those who desired to satisfy their personal ambition more than public welfare. On this occasion, a popular government was introduced that endured until 1530, with great confusion, disorder, and iniquity. It is well known that the city never had a more pernicious and corrupt government than that one.

Let us therefore state that His Imperial Majesty, ever desirous of the health of the city and of the tranquility and security of Italy, declared that the form of government would be the same as ruled before the latest expulsion of the Medici, governed by the same magistrates and authorities who had ruled previously. This introduced an almost natural government adept for the long term, under the name and authority of which the republic had flourished greatly and which had been healthier for the city in comparison to the popular government. Nor can it be charged with not preserving liberty. To the contrary, it is necessary to confess that they organized it better than would have been the case if there were a return to the popular government. Freedom does not mean plebeians may oppress the nobility. Nor may the poor try to annihilate the authority of the rich out of envy. Nor in the administration of a republic should the ignorant and the unprepared have more sway than men of prudence and expertise. Nor, under the false pretense of liberty, should

---

4. Ferdinand II (1452–1516).
5. Pope Julius II (1443–1513), Holy Roman Emperor Maximilian I (1459–1519).

governmental affairs be conducted with dissolute license and dread as occurred every day in the people's state. Therefore, His Majesty took the foundations and fruits of liberty into consideration with great wisdom and respect for the peace in Italy, as evidently manifested by the decree. He declared for the traditional form of government, desiring rule based upon normal, well-ordered liberty, rather than the new and tumultuous manner that led to the latest slaughter of the nation, before the grace of God and the goodwill of His Majesty came to the rescue. Thus, it emerges that His Majesty made this declaration driven by the most just and excellent reasons and was quite well informed regarding the merits of the case, rather than acting from the suggestions of ambassadors, who were falsely reported to have been sent to His Majesty by followers of the Medici. In fact, no ambassadors were sent to thank him until after the declaration was made, as was proper following the bestowal of so many benefits upon the city. Thus, he made a well-informed declaration after having learned about everything upon many occasions about the popular faction from the ambassadors sent to Genoa by the popular government, and from ambassadors sent to Bologna. The declaration was made with a high level of understanding, as His Majesty was well informed about the condition of the city and the arguments of each faction. Nor is there any doubt that, by law (*de jure*), a well-prepared and well-informed judge would be required to reopen a case but may render a decision based upon previous news and information.

His Majesty's declaration was neither erroneous nor casual, as the plaintiffs would seem to infer. Rather, it was founded upon His Majesty's deliberative capacity and mature will, according to the terms of the Barcelona surrender treaty between His Majesty and His Holiness, Clement.[6] In the third section of the agreement, His Majesty was moved by the rule of law and allowed restoration for those who had suffered deprivation. He acted in memory of the restoration of the Medici by His Majesty's paternal and maternal forbearers,[7] out of respect for tranquility in Italy and in consideration of the matrimony celebrated between His Excellency the Duke and the most illustrious madam Margherita his daughter. For these and for other just reasons and promises, he obligated himself to

---

6. The Treaty of Barcelona, June 19, 1529, laid terms between Charles V and Clement VII with the de' Medici restored to power in Florence and Margaret, daughter of Charles V given in marriage to Alessandro de' Medici.

7. Ferdinand II and Isabel of Aragon and Castile.

the restoration of the house of the Medici in Florence. This regarded not only property during the occupation but also the welfare and breadth of government and administration prior to the year 1527, when the Medici did not hold any title of public authority as heads of the government and administration of the republic beyond the free will and reasoned deference of the citizens.

Nor may it be claimed that the arguments purported in the section are false, that the Medici had not been deprived, since His Magnificence Ippolito,[8] Cardinal Medici, and the Cardinal of Cortona had voluntarily left the government. Notwithstanding the falsity of this charge, there remain many other true ones based upon the obligations that would suffice to support it. One may respond that, in truth, the aforementioned did not act according to their free will but were coerced by enemies who had taken courage because of the events that had transpired in Rome. They departed fearing for their very lives, without any agreement with the city, as has been falsely insinuated, even though they had expected to receive many concessions under a law that was passed but never observed.[9]

Therefore, if His Majesty had promised and was obligated to restore the Medici family, then who could doubt that his declaration was made after mature and considered deliberation since His Majesty would be the one to observe the inviolable faith of his promises? From this, what the plaintiffs say emerges as manifestly false. Even had His Majesty so desired, he could not declare the form of government, for such a declaration would have been null and void. Therefore, the exact opposite has been demonstrated to be true. Even had he wanted to do so, he was not able because he could not violate the promises and obligations from Barcelona. It cannot truthfully be stated that the pope had compromised himself by ratifying the treaty because of Florence, because, as has been demonstrated, the treaty did not contradict His Majesty's decree. We do not know if His Holiness proceeded to ratification by way of a brief or another manner, because the negotiations were held so quickly, as explained below, that he was not given leave for ratification. There is also the obstinate persistence whereby the imperial decree was contrary to the terms of the agreement, which may be absolutely denied, despite the

---

8. Ippolito de' Medici (1511–1535).
9. Guicciardini was among those whose goods were confiscated following the restoration of the republic after the Sack of Rome.

retort that the agreement was not made as mandated by His Majesty. Nor does it contain a directive for surrender under the authority of captains and administrators general, because such an agreement would have been beyond the mind and will and in direct contradiction to His Majesty. His Majesty undertook the charge in observance of the obligation and promise to restore the Medici to their prior station. He refused many times during the siege to come to terms unless there would be a restoration. So how may it be believed that after such travail and expense, with victory in hand and the city reduced to its last resources, he would accept lesser terms than those offered prior to the outbreak of the war? Nor is it true that it appeared in His Majesty's act of ratification, even if his army accepted payment, for the fact the army could not be included in Caesar's terms of ratification. It has been claimed that the payment in question was not provided by the popular government but in part from monies from Clement and in part, as is well known, from those allied with the Medici, who by virtue of the terms had returned to the government. Does not the ratification also prove the authority bestowed upon His Majesty by terms that appear in the same decree, by which His Majesty assumed the authority to restore the Medici and based his declaration upon this supposition? If this supposition were to be false, then the ensuing ratification would be void, because everyone knows that ratification proceeds from consensus, for where there is an error there can be no consensus. Thus, it is not only superfluous but arrogant and risky to assign such an error to His Majesty, when the entire world is aware of the maturity, circumspection, and absolute knowledge from which his deliberations proceed.

Nor is it true that the parliament was held under threat of violence or in a manner unbefitting the city. For once the accord was reached, everyone realized that it would be impossible for the leaders of the popular faction, who were so reduced in their means and credit, to be able to provide the monies necessary to call off the army. There was also the understanding that if the army were removed, these leaders would once again incite the multitude to express contempt for His Majesty and His Holiness. Thus, it was ordered by the apostolic commissar, the most illustrious Don Ferrante, and Monsignor Balanson, His Majesty's representative, and by the request of those good and noble citizens who desired the tranquility of the city. There were assurances that the declaration that would be made by His Majesty would be observed. By means of the parliament, the traditional form of the republic could be restored with provision of funds for the army and other great needs in time to ensure acceptance and obedience to the declaration that His Majesty would make. Nor is it to be doubted that the form of the parliament, which is nothing less than a public council in a public square, is an ancient and legitimate practice that began some two hundred years ago, and by which in the past many governmental reforms have been enacted. In our time not only was this latest Medici restoration enacted by parliament but also in '94 when they were expelled and the city fell under popular government. This latest one was conducted with all the solemnity, order, and manner that occurred with all the others. If someone wanted to declare those void, then one can only imagine the confusion and chaos that would result.

Therefore, it is absolutely true that the government was legitimately organized by His Majesty according to the authority that each of the factions had given him in accordance with the wishes of the most qualified citizens. If there is opposition because the aforementioned government was altered with the removal of Signoria, the traditional and supreme magistrates, and the concession of greater rank and authority to the duke than he had prior, then one may respond that this was not contrary to the orders of His Majesty. Nor was it beyond the authority of Florence as a free city. As a free city, Florence has an ancient tradition of liberty, not only as conceded by past emperors but also as confirmed by Maximilian Caesar and subsequently by His Majesty and lately fully reintegrated as such. There is no doubt that in matters pertaining to its government, it may act freely in accordance with its wishes. Nor did orders from Caesar prohibit or place limits whereby the form of government could not be changed. In fact, once His Majesty had ordered that the government would have authority over the city, then consequently authority was conceded for that government to arrange for itself, as may be seen occurring in all free cities, which from time to time create new constitutions for their governments. This is in no way reproachable but quite praiseworthy when enacted for just reasons as occurred in this case, with the recall of the nobles, citizens, and magistrates who had cared for the republic and whose elimination had led to the ignorance and malice of the popular government. Consider that changes in Florence were commonly made by means of the arm of the magistrature known as the Signoria, which by continuously occupying the Palazzo had assumed more authority than allotted to it by ancient statute. They wanted to ensure the homeland and themselves in perpetuity from such pestiferous changes without transgression from anyone and in accordance among themselves, as in the case of the noted instigator and perpetrator, Filippo Strozzi.[10] This was not to alter and vary the form of government but to protect and stabilize for their own benefits and security. Thus, the office of the *gonfalonier* and the Signoria was replaced by His Excellence the duke and a magistrature of four counselors, who would change from time to time, with other magistrates and offices of the government remaining unchanged. There was also the consideration of honoring the duke himself, out of respect for His Majesty, who had deigned to choose him as a son-in-law. Thus, it seemed quite appropriate to designate him with a new rank and honor, with great deference for the stability and security of the government and the universal and particular welfare of those desiring prosperity. Since they are not present, let those who are present humbly convey to His Majesty how nothing could be more disturbing and pernicious for the city than to change, even minimally, any part of its current state. They had experienced the maliciousness of the popular government, which enacted every possible manner of injury against the nobility. The popular government's ambitions exposed the homeland to danger and calamity by inflicting intolerable monetary taxation, reducing the honor of the magistrature with the participation of base and incompetent persons, and expelling a considerable number without cause. Thus, should any event once again alter the situation, there would only be a small number of exiles as seen presently. However, they would not be insignificant in stature, as is the case with those currently in exile. Instead, it would be the near entirety of the nobility, the best and most qualified citizens who have the affairs of the city in their hands, with the result that the political life of the city would be disorganized and corrupted. Thus, it would be impossible to introduce another government with the form of a well-instituted and well-organized republic by altering the present government. This is just the plaintiffs' forced and impertinent argument, which is clouded by their unjust desires. In fact, it would require a return to the pernicious and licentious popularity that destroyed the homeland and directly contradicts His Majesty's authority and the peace and tranquility of Italy as that government demonstrated by experience of its duration.

---

10. Filippo Strozzi the Younger (1489–1538), leader of Florentine exiles who raised an army unsuccessful in deposing Cosimo I after the assassination of Alessandro de' Medici.

The second complaint is counteracted by two other sections of the agreement, by which the injuries done to our lord and his retinue would be redressed and by which each was promised to be able to go to Rome to live wherever they saw fit. Some were decapitated contrary to the terms of the agreement, whereas others were expelled or detained. To attribute this to His Excellency the duke is a calumny since he was in Flanders at the time and magistrates and citizens controlled affairs.

One may respond regarding the damages to our lord and his party, which even though they were numerous and very serious were never recognized or settled. By the terms of the agreement, the laws of the republic, and the authority of the magistrature, there is no exclusion under standards of justice for these infinite and atrocious crimes. Thus, many of these events and particularly the decapitations were the result of their base qualities and could not have occurred under a government that was properly instituted. They first plotted to await the sack and the final massacre of the homeland before coming to terms with our lord and His Majesty. Accompanied by a multitude of youths, they threatened with death the citizens who in council had favored making an agreement, and they forced them to remain silent in the future. They hid the letters sent by ambassadors in France and other places to give the people false hopes. In their stead, they published forged letters in their favor, suborning clerics who then claimed to be prophets revealing how God did not want the people to make an agreement. Those who returned from a diplomatic mission to Bologna pronounced falsities about the thinking of His Majesty upon their return. They led the people to think they would find no pardon from His Majesty and instigated youths to raze a building of the Medici and another belonging to Mr. Iacopo Salviati. For the same reason, they ruined numerous monasteries, buildings, and churches. They took by force the monies of widows and wards of the state deposited in public places. They sold the houses and the possessions of churches and holy places, despoiling them of ornaments and sacred silverware. Because of these atrocities, the city of Florence, which is usually among the richest, most populated, and beautiful in the world, was reduced to extreme poverty, devoid of inhabitants, with a large part of her beauty mangled and ruined. The city was quite reasonable and not contrary to surrender so that justice could be done with punishment not only for the injuries against our lord and his party, but for the nefarious and abominable crimes against the homeland by order from the government of false liberty, which they obstinately defended with patriotic partisanship and goodwill.

Opportunity and even necessity arose owing to the iniquitous nature of their ambitions. Once it had been discovered that the agreement had been made, many of them began to hold secret nocturnal meetings to prepare new conspiracies. After they were deposed, following the surrender, as the trials legitimately indicate, in order not to return to the previous danger, it was necessary to recognize the iniquity of what had been experienced and to set new limitations, which allowed for more clemency than severity. Many were punished more slightly than they deserved. The sins of many were relegated to silence. Nor have there been complaints that after the first exile there were orders to further restrict them with additional charges. Since they reacted poorly at the first decision, there were calls for them to be treated more restrictively. Since many of them were to be found in Lyon, Venice, or other places, they were not charged with any damages or suits, which may have easily occurred if one considers the level of wrath and insolence with which they proceed, hurting without regard those persons they should have held in utmost respect. However, many of these banishments were undertaken out of necessity and according to orders from the city, which on many occasions and circumstances had recurred to similar methods of banishment against malevolent citizens. This was done not so they would lose their possessions, as some falsely charge. Except for two or three of the exiles, the others are quite poor, and the possessions of those few are in large part covered in debt, from dowries or previous obligations.

Finally, they charge the present government with disobeying His Majesty, for instituting changes with regards to Francesco de' Pazzi, and with being violent, unjust, and wicked, as well as with arguments against the completion of the fortress and with many injustices and cruelties performed on citizens.[11]

As for the aforementioned charge, one could more readily impugn the mildness and clemency of His Excellency the duke and the magistrates than disobedience to His Majesty, to whom there has always been

---

11. Here Guicciardini seems to be referring to Francesco de' Pazzi (1444–1478) of the 1478 anti-Medici Pazzi conspiracy. The member of the Pazzi family involved in events during the siege of Florence was Alamanno de' Pazzi (1501–1573), who defended Florence against the Imperial/Papist siege but went into the military service of the Medici after the city fell.

the greatest obedience and devotion, as may be proven through trials and testimony. After His Majesty left Barcelona, Francesco and the others have never ceased to offend His Excellency and the city with words, acts, and procedures creating difficulty for Florence's dominion and occupation of the citadel of Pisa, Volterra, and other important places. It was thus legitimate to punish them all, for by the word of His Majesty, which may not be impugned, there was no intention to allow them immunity to commit new conspiracies. Therefore, if there have been proceedings against Francesco de' Pazzi and not against others, then he should not complain, since these acts were performed justly and not against His Majesty's authority. In fact, the rest should be thankful that something similar was not leveled against them.

The decision to build the fortress was enacted under proper and required consultation. There can be no argument demonstrating otherwise according to the testimony of those very same who now condemn it. They are related to the house of His Holiness and shared close ties and interests, as well as many great obligations. As soon as he died, they made a practice of bitterly disparaging his memory and relics according to the chicanery of those and others who share their mindset. If the complaints were not about the fortress, then it would suffice to discuss the safety of His Excellency and those citizens running similar risks. For their own good and the benefit of the city, discussions about this have been no less heated than His Excellency in persuading themselves that they are acting in service of His Majesty. As the government of the city becomes more secure and established, so there will be a reduction in the capacity of those who by means of revolution would seek to torment the rest of Italy, as His Majesty well understands from the wisdom gained regarding news of the appetites of those who think about nothing but disturbing the current peace and tranquility.

Let it be affirmed today that the city of Florence is governed with justice and impartial observance of the law in a manner that those who wish to live well have much to be content about, as is believed and noted in all of Italy. For one may not deny that it is not in the power of the enemies of His Excellency to purport various charges of homicide or harassment, which are generally alleged to have been performed by His Excellency or under his protection and are so evidently false that it is shameful to mention them. The injustices that were claimed to have been performed against particular individuals were not performed by the duke nor by his order but according to decisions from magistrates assigned to earlier criminal matters that proceeded according to civic order and are all things that can be easily justified. However, it is enough for persecutors and slanderers to criticize and accuse, as if they have already not done enough, when they are well aware that there will be no other consequence in Florence or abroad for citizens or merchants of the Florentine nation regarding the complaints heard and discussed before His Majesty. They may think that they are greatly diminishing the reputation of the duke by sowing seeds that in time may have pernicious effects, as would occur verily if they were to proceed further in these disputes. We believe that His Majesty's goodwill and prudence would not permit this; we believe this in absolute confirmation that they should not hope that these sinister motions will alter the authority of the duke and this government, which remains in complete obedience and devotion to His Majesty, who loves the present state of Italy upon which the preservation and health of the city of Florence depends.

INDEX

Aeschylus, 209
Afonso V of Portugal, 40
Alcibiades, 6, 23, 139, 146, 190
Alexander VI, Pope (Rodrigo de Borja), 19, 54, 114, 194, 199
Alfonso II of Naples, 44
Alighieri, Dante, 1, 2, 68, 157
Amos, 197
Aristotle, 174
Avalos, Francesco Ferdinando d', Marquis of Pescara, 187

Baglioni, Gian Paolo, 92
Balanson, Monsignor, 217
Barbadori, Donato, 23, 155
Betulia, biblical figure, 127
Borgia, Cesare (Valentino), 10, 54
Borja, Alfons de (Pope Callistus III), 53
Bozzolo, Federico da, 89, 91–94, 98, 99, 148
Bronzino (Agnolo di Cosimo), 212
Brutus, Lucius Iunius, 156
Brutus, Marcus Junius, 70, 71
Buonarroti, Michelangelo, 25, 127, 180
Buonavalle (Bonevale French captain), 93

Caccia, Alessandro del, 24, 25, 131–33, 181, 183–85
Caesar, Gaius Julius, 67, 139, 146
Caiazzo, Count (Roberto da Sanseverino), 26, 89, 183, 188, 189
Caleb (biblical figure), 207
Cambi, Lorenzo, 102

Carpi, Alberto III Pio da, 179
Carrara, Francesco da, 2
Castiglione, Baldassare, 2, 17
Castiglione, Giangiorgio da, 102
Cato, Marcus Porcius, 70, 71
Cellini, Benvenuto, 17
Cerberus, 23, 130
Ceri, Renzo da, 100
Cerrato, Giovan Francesco, 94
Charles III, of Bourbon, 100
Charles V, King of Spain, Holy Roman Emperor, 11, 14–19, 21, 25, 28–30, 113, 124, 162, 163, 211–23
Charles VIII of France, 2, 8, 9, 19, 27, 192–96, 205, 208, 214
Christ, Jesus, 205, 208
Cicero, Marcus Tullius, 67, 130, 171
Colonna, Marcantonio, 93–95, 97, 98
Colonna, Prospero, 91, 186

David, king of Israel, 22, 25, 127, 180, 196
De Sanctis, Francesco, 4, 5, 21
Decii (ancient Roman clan), 69
Demosthenes, 118, 130
Diocletian, 20, 120
Dolciati, Filippo, 193
Don Ferrante (Ferdinando Loffredo), 217
Donatello (Donato di Niccolò di Betto Bardi), 127
Donati, Corso, 23, 157

Emor (biblical figure), 201

Fabius Maximus (Quintus Fabius Maximus Verrucosus, the Cunctator), 24, 169
Faggiuola, Uguccione della, 157
Ferdinand II of Aragon, 7, 10, 11, 22, 31, 34, 35, 39–50, 141, 191, 213–15
Fermo, Ludovico da, 96, 98
Ferrara, Duke of (Alfonso I), 91, 92
Ferrero, Bonifacio (Count Ivrea), 90
Ferruccio, Francesco, 28, 31
Francis I of France, 14, 15, 52, 94, 113, 121, 162

Gennazzano, Mariano da, 198
Gonzaga, Federico II, Marquis of Mantua, 90, 91, 96, 187
Gonzalo Fernàndez de Córdoba, 36
Guiccciardini, Giovanni, 170
Guicciardini, Francesco, 2–33, 104, 124–29, 132, 133, 135, 137, 150, 154, 157–63, 172, 173
Guicciardini, Giovanni, 24, 170
Guicciardini, Girolamo, 182
Guicciardini, Iacopo, 90, 161
Guicciardini, Luigi di Piero, 27, 146, 147
Guicciardini, Piero, 27, 128, 140, 148, 159, 190, 191
Guicciardini, Rinieri, 6

Hadrian VI Pope (Adriaan Florensz Boeyens), 15, 25, 146, 178, 179
Hannibal Barca, 24, 120, 169
Henry II of Castile, 40, 41
Henry VII of Luxembourg, 1
Henry VIII of England, 113
Holofernes, 127
Hydra, 130

Innocent VIII Pope (Giovanni Battista Cybo), 50, 193, 194
Isabel of Castile, 35, 37, 40–45, 47, 48, 213, 215

Jeremiah (biblical figure), 201, 202
Joanna the Mad of Castile, 34, 43
John II of Aragon, 40, 44
John II of Castile, 40, 43
Joseph (biblical figure), 200
Joshua (biblical figure), 207
Judith, 22, 127

Julius II, Pope (Giuliano della Rovere), 8, 12, 214

Landsknechts, 16, 18, 137, 187, 188
Lazarus, 197
Lautrec, Odet de Foix, 187, 188
Livy (Titus Livius Patavinus), 18, 39
Louis XIII of France, 6
Louis XIV of France, 6
Lucan (Marcus Annaeus Lucanus), 39
Lucifer, 148
Lucius Tarquinius Superbus, 23
Luther, Martin, 4
Lycurgus, 13, 65

Machiavelli, Niccolò, 2, 8, 10, 17, 29, 142
Manuel I of Portugal, 35, 44
Marc Anthony (Marcus Antonius), 70
Marchetti, Marco, 35
Margaret of Parma, 30, 215
Maximilian I Holy Roman Emperor, 214, 218
Mazarin, Cardinal (Giulio Raimondo Mazzarino), 6
Medici, Alessandro de', 3, 28–32, 211, 212, 215, 218–20, 222, 223
Medici, Alfonsina de', 143, 144
Medici, Clarice de', 153
Medici, Cosimo de' (the Elder), 2, 29, 58, 170, 213
Medici, Cosimo I de', 3, 30, 31,32, 133, 152, 219
Medici, Giovanni di Lorenzo de' (Pope Leo X), 3–5, 7, 12–15, 25, 51–53, 61, 89, 92, 97, 108, 143, 146
Medici, Giuliano di Cosimo de', 58
Medici, Giuliano di Lorenzo de', 2, 12, 54, 143
Medici, Giulio di Giuliano de' (Pope Clement VII), 3–5, 7, 8, 15–19, 21, 28, 30, 32, 52, 89, 100, 101, 104–6, 108, 113, 114, 133, 135, 136, 143, 145, 146, 149, 150, 153, 161, 162, 179, 189, 211, 215–17, 222
Medici, Ippolito de', 3, 29, 216
Medici, Lorenzo di Cosimo de', 3, 4, 8, 27, 35, 56, 58, 59, 83, 133, 194, 202
Medici, Lorenzo di Piero de', 2, 3, 12, 52, 54, 142, 145, 146

Medici, Lorenzino (Lorenzaccio) de', 3, 30
Medici, Lorenzo (the Magnificent) de', 3, 4, 8, 27, 35, 54, 56, 58, 59, 83, 133, 193, 194, 202
Medici, Lorenzo di Piero de', 2, 3, 12, 52, 142, 145, 146
Medici, Lucrezia de', 133
Medici, Ludovico de' (Giovanni dalle Bande Nere), 16, 17, 26, 30, 133, 183, 187, 188
Medici, Piero di Cosimo de', 58
Medici, Piero di Lorenzo de', 8, 27, 35, 58, 83, 87, 153, 155, 159, 194
Monte, Francesco dal, 96, 97
Moses (biblical figure), 200

Nebuchadnezzar II of Babylon, 127
Neri di Gino Capponi, 148
Nero, Bernardo del, 23, 155

Octavian (Augustus), 70, 144
Orazio di Giampaolo Baglioni, 100

Pashhur (biblical figure), 201, 202
Paul III Pope (Alessandro Farnese), 30
Paul, the Apostle, 109
Pazzi, Alamanno de, 211, 221
Pazzi, Francesco de', 221, 222
Pericles, 20, 109, 170
Petrarca, Francesco, 2
Philip I of Castile, 43–45
Piccolomini, Enea Silvio Bartolomeo (Pope Pius II), 53
Pioppi, Count, 148, 149
Priscian (Priscianus Caesariensis), 174

Rangoni, Guido, 26, 90, 91, 100, 102, 179, 183, 187–89
Richelieu, Cardinal (Armand Jean du Plessis), 6
Ridolfi, Niccolò, 158
Rothbard, Murray N., 1

Rovere, Francesco Maria della, 16, 17, 21, 25, 91, 92, 100, 102, 147, 188
Rucellai, Bernardo, 23, 153, 154

Salamone, Francesco, 95–98
Saluzzo, Marquis of (Michele Antonio del Vasto), 147, 188
Salviati, Alamanno di Averardo, 7, 30, 140, 190
Salviati, Iacopo, 131, 140, 220
Salviati, Maria di Alamanno di Averardo, 7, 30, 140
Saul, king of Israel, 196
Savonarola, Girolamo, 8–10, 16, 19, 27, 28, 31, 62, 114, 158, 159, 192–210
Scipio Africanus, 120
Sennacherib of Assyria, 204
Sforza, Francesco, 54
Sisyphus, 110
Sixtus IV, Pope (Francesco della Rovere), 186
Soderini, Piero, 10, 57, 140, 150–54, 170
Solomon, 144
Solon, 82
Strozzi, Filippo, 23, 152, 153, 219
Sulla, Lucius Cornelius, 146

Tacitus, Publius Cornelius, 144
Tarquinius, Lucius, 156
Thucydides, 18, 24, 109
Tiberius, 144
Tintoretto (Jacopo Comin), 90
Titian (Tiziano Vecelli), 213
Torello, Cristoforo, 94, 98
Toricella, Francesco Maria Simonetta di, 93

Valori, Francesco, 158, 159
Vasari, Giorgio, 35
Virgin Mary, 194, 195, 210
Visconti, Bianca, 54
Visconti, Filippo Maria, 54

www.ingramcontent.com/pod-product-compliance
Lightning Source LLC
Chambersburg PA
CBHW021944290426
44108CB00012B/952